An EasyGuide to

APA
Style

3e

Dedicated to writers everywhere, fledgling or otherwise, gently bemused by the morass of stylistic red tape threatening to hinder their creative instinct and their quests for the holy grail of literary excellence

An EasyGuide to APA Style

3e

Beth M. Schwartz
Heidelberg University

R. Eric Landrum
Boise State University

Regan A. R. Gurung
University of Wisconsin-Green Bay

Los Angeles | London | New Delhi
Singapore | Washington DC | Melbourne

For information:

SAGE Publications, Inc.

2455 Teller Road

Thousand Oaks, California 91320

E-mail: order@sagepub.com

SAGE Publications Ltd.

1 Oliver's Yard

55 City Road

London EC1Y 1SP

United Kingdom

SAGE Publications India Pvt. Ltd.

B 1/I 1 Mohan Cooperative Industrial Area

Mathura Road, New Delhi 110 044

India

SAGE Publications Asia-Pacific Pte. Ltd.

3 Church Street

#10-04 Samsung Hub

Singapore 049483

Printed in the United States of America

Names: Schwartz, Beth M., author. | Landrum, R. Eric, author. Gurung, Regan A. R., author.

Title: An easy guide to APA style / Beth M. Schwartz, R. Eric Landrum, Regan A.R. Gurung.

Description: 3e [edition]. | Los Angeles : SAGE, [2016] | Includes bibliographical references and index.

Identifiers: LCCN 2015040055 | ISBN 978-1-4833-8323-1 (spiral : alk. paper)

Subjects: LCSH: Psychology—Authorship—Style manuals. | Social sciences—Authorship—Style manuals.

Classification: LCC BF76.7 .S39 2016 | DDC 808.06/615—dc23 LC record available at http://lccn.loc.gov/2015040055

This book is printed on acid-free paper.

Acquisitions Editor: Reid Hester

Editorial Assistant: Morgan Shannon

Production Editor: David C. Felts

Copy Editor: Kim Husband

Typesetter: C&M Digitals (P) Ltd.

Proofreader: Bonnie Moore

Indexer: Molly Hall

Cover Designer: Anupama Krishnan

Marketing Manager: Katherine Hepburn

Certified Chain of Custody
Promoting Sustainable Forestry
www.sfiprogram.org
SFI-01268

SFI label applies to text stock

16 17 18 19 20 10 9 8 7 6 5 4 3 2 1

Brief Contents

Detailed Contents

SAGE was founded in 1965 by Sara Miller McCune to support the dissemination of usable knowledge by publishing innovative and high-quality research and teaching content. Today, we publish over 900 journals, including those of more than 400 learned societies, more than 800 new books per year, and a growing range of library products including archives, data, case studies, reports, and video. SAGE remains majority-owned by our founder, and after Sara's lifetime will become owned by a charitable trust that secures our continued independence.

Los Angeles | London | New Delhi | Singapore | Washington DC

Preface

Traveling to a new place can be exciting, but going anywhere for the first time always has its challenges. Whether a new city, a new school, or a new job, it takes time to learn the ins and outs of the place, its rules and customs. It is a similar process learning to write in American Psychological Association (APA) style—that is, learning when to use italics, capitalization, and abbreviations; how to treat numbers; what citations and references should look like; how to set margins; and what headings, tables, and figures should look like as required by APA format. At first blush, APA style is almost like a foreign language with its own syntax and grammar, and the manual with all its rules can be as tricky as a labyrinth for any newcomer to navigate. With this *EasyGuide* in hand, you take a great step toward simplifying the process of learning how to write papers in APA style. We will help you through the maze of rules, and you may even have (some) fun along the way.

Over the years, we have witnessed the many problems our students have when confronting the numerous details involved in creating APA research papers, term papers, or lab reports. We see the frustration our students feel when trying to find the information they need in the APA *Publication Manual* (APA, 2010a) amid the voluminous details that primarily apply to faculty members or graduate students submitting manuscripts for publication. If your needs are similar to our students' needs (i.e., writing papers for class) or even if you are preparing a traditional manuscript for publication, this *EasyGuide* will serve you well. If you are in need of a way to cite and report an uncommon type of reference or statistic, then you may also need to consult the APA *Publication Manual*.

Our Reader-Friendly Approach

We decided to present the essentials of APA style using a more conversational tone in hopes of making this book and the task of learning how to write more enjoyable. We need to state up front that although we address the details of writing papers in APA style and format, *there are times in this book when we do not use APA style and format*. For example, because this book conforms to the publisher's design, you will not see double-spaced lines with 1-inch margins, and you will notice, for example, that the opening paragraph of each chapter and the first paragraph following a Level 1 heading are not indented. We also flex our funny bones (or muscles) when appropriate. We intend for this to make for easier reading, but note that it is *not* APA style.

We included some sample papers to illustrate where all the basic rules pertain to writing. We believe by using the sample papers, you will be less likely to overlook the different aspects of APA style commonly omitted when first learning this type of writing. We also believe that reviewing the most common errors (Chapter 20) that we have seen over the years, will help you focus on the content of your writing rather than the minutiae of APA style and format. The visual table of contents (Chapter 2) and the visual illustrations in the sample paper (Chapter 21) are unique, illustrating the details not to forget and where in the paper these details apply.

How to Use This Book

In this *EasyGuide,* we have eliminated the search for the basics that can be somewhat time consuming and confusing. We believe that using this book will save you a significant amount of time, allowing you to focus on writing your paper rather than searching for what you need to know about presenting it in APA style. Here, you will be able to easily find the information you need, with examples presented visually as well as in the text. We illustrate not only how to write using APA style but also what APA style really looks like when your paper is complete. The sample paper used in the visual table of contents (Chapter 2) lets you see within an actual paper the details you will need to consider when writing in APA style, and the sample indicates where in this book you can find the information needed to learn those details. In addition, that same sample paper is included in Chapter 21, where you'll see the research paper with the details accentuated, this time with the style and format details explained.

Although we organized the *EasyGuide* in a way that will help you learn the basics in an order we believe makes sense, it is important to remember that each chapter stands alone and you can choose to read the book in whatever order suits your needs best. This may not be the type of book you read cover to cover but, rather, one you keep next to you as a reference source while writing APA–style papers throughout your undergraduate career.

We end the book with a chapter that reviews the most common mistakes we see students encounter when first learning APA style. You can test your knowledge by trying to answer the multiple-choice questions on those common mistakes. We also include a sample paper (with APA errors purposely embedded) so you can test your knowledge. After you have read the book and when you want to make sure you are comfortable writing without constantly reaching for the guide, test yourself using the error-filled paper and see if you can find the errors. After all, it is hard to know what you *need* to know if you do not know *what* you know or if what you know is *right*—a little metacognitive self-test as it were. Up for the challenge? Go ahead. Also, to encourage you to use this book while writing and in hopes of making the writing process easier for you, a lay-flat spine was purposely used. It is what the *EasyGuide* is all about.

Acknowledgments

A number of individuals made valuable contributions during the development, writing, and editing of this book. We appreciate the learned expertise of our colleagues who helped us shape this book at all steps along the way. For their generous assistance, we are indebted to Stacie Christian (University of Wisconsin–Green Bay), Stephen F. Davis (Morningside College), Chriss Warren Foster (Merritt College), Chris Hakala (Quinnipiac University), Jane S. Halonen (University of West Florida), Andrew Johnson (Park University), Maureen A. McCarthy (Kennesaw State University), Cynthia Noyes (Olivet College), Pamela C. O'Brien (Bowie State University), Jean Raniseski (Alvin Community College), Angela M. Sikorski (Texas A&M University), James Truelove (Southwest Baptist University), and James Welch IV (University of Texas, Arlington). In addition, we are grateful to Randolph A. Smith for lending his special APA–editing expertise to improving our work. At SAGE, Christine Cardone was our guide throughout the journey, and without her support, this book would never have been completed. We also appreciate the additional guidance provided by Reid Hester throughout the work on this third edition and the attention to detail by Sarita Sarak, David Felts, Linda Gray, Astrid Virding, Laureen Gleason, and Meg Granger in helping our efforts come to fruition.

A number of our students were also instrumental in the development and review process, including Jerry Wells, Penny Trieu, and Christopher Hollingsworth from Randolph College, Tiffany Wilhelm from the University of Wisconsin–Green Bay, and Jessica Kesler from Boise State University. When working on any manuscript, family support is crucial, and we all thank our families for helping us maintain our sanity in the midst of deadlines, rewrites, e-mails, and other responsibilities in our lives. Finally, we thank all the students (past, present, and future) who learn to write in APA style and format. The idea for this book came about as we struggled to teach what some consider a foreign language without an appropriate student-friendly resource. Our colleagues in each of our home departments and in the Society for the Teaching of Psychology (www.teachpsych.org) supported us as we worked to create this resource; we are grateful for their support. We hope this *EasyGuide* minimizes or eliminates struggles for faculty and students.

Now, a message from the SAGE Legal Department. In a few chapters of this book, we include screenshots of Microsoft Word 2013 so we can show you what to do, in addition to telling you how to do it. Protecting intellectual property rights is important, and failure to do so is akin to plagiarism. So be sure to remember the following:

> This book includes screenshots of Microsoft Word 2013 to illustrate the methods and procedures described in this book. Microsoft Word 2013 is a product of the Microsoft Corporation.

We invite you to share the wisdom of your experience with us. We welcome your suggestions for how to make learning APA style even easier, and we welcome your comments as well as suggestions for the third edition of this book. Feel free to e-mail any of us: Beth (bschwart@heidelberg.edu), Eric (elandru@boisestate.edu), or Regan (gurungr@uwgb.edu).

About the Authors

Beth M. Schwartz is the Vice President for Academic Affairs and Provost and Professor of Psychology at Heidelberg University, in Tiffin, Ohio. She was on the faculty at Randolph College in Lynchburg, VA, for 24 years, where she was the William E. and Catherine Ehrman Thoresen '23 Professor of Psychology and Assistant Dean of the College. She received a BA at Colby College (Maine) and a PhD in cognitive psychology at the State University of New York at Buffalo. Her scholarship focuses on two areas of interest: (a) children's memory development and how this applies to children's eyewitness reports and (b) the scholarship of teaching and learning/pedagogical research. In addition to numerous professional presentations at conferences, she has published many book chapters and articles in a variety of scholarly journals, including the *Journal of Higher Education, Ethics and Behavior, Law and Human Behavior,* and *Applied Developmental Science.* She has also edited and coauthored books, including *Child Abuse: A Global View* (Schwartz, McCauley, & Epstein, 2001), *Optimizing Teaching and Learning* (Gurung & Schwartz, 2012), and *Evidence-Based Teaching for Higher Education* (Schwartz & Gurung, 2012). She is a member of the American Psychological Association (APA) and the American Psychological Society and is a Fellow of Division 2 of APA (Society for the Teaching of Psychology). She was an award-winning teacher at Randolph College, where she taught Introduction to Psychology, Research Methods, Cognitive Psychology, and the capstone course. She received the Award for Outstanding Teaching and Mentoring from the American Psych-Law Society, the Gillie A. Larew Award for Distinguished Teaching at Randolph College, the Katherine Graves Davidson Excellence in Scholarship Award from Randolph College, and the Distinguished Faculty Achievement Certificate from the State Council of Higher Education for Virginia.

R. Eric Landrum is a professor of psychology at Boise State University, receiving his PhD in cognitive psychology from Southern Illinois University-Carbondale. His research interests center on the educational conditions that best facilitate student success as well as the use of scholarship of teaching and learning strategies to advance the efforts of scientist-educators. He has more than 375 professional presentations at conferences, published over 45 books/book chapters, and has published more than 90 professional articles in scholarly, peer-reviewed journals. He has worked with more than 300 undergraduate research assistants and taught more than 14,000 students in 23 years at Boise State. During Summer 2008, he led an American Psychological Association working group at the National Conference for Undergraduate Education in Psychology studying the desired results of an undergraduate psychology education. During the October 2014 Educational Leadership Conference in Washington, DC, Eric was presented with a Presidential Citation from then APA President Nadine Kaslow for his outstanding contributions to the teaching of psychology. Eric is the lead author of *The Psychology Major: Career Options and Strategies for Success* (5th ed., 2013) and has authored *Undergraduate Writing in Psychology: Learning to Tell the Scientific Story* (2nd ed., 2012) and *Finding a Job With a Psychology Bachelor's Degree: Expert Advice for Launching Your Career* (2009). He coauthored *You've Received Your Doctorate in Psychology—Now What?* (2012), is the lead editor for *Teaching Ethically—Challenges and Opportunities* (2012), and coeditor of *Assessing Teaching and Learning in Psychology: Current and Future Perspectives* (2013). He and Regan Gurung are the inaugural coeditors of the APA journal *Scholarship of Teaching and Learning in Psychology*. He served as vice president for the Rocky Mountain region of Psi Chi (2009–2011). He is a member of the American Psychological Association, a fellow in APA's Division Two (Society for the Teaching of Psychology or STP), served as STP secretary (2009–2011), and served as the 2014 STP president. He will serve as the 2015–2016 president of the Rocky Mountain Psychological Association.

Regan A. R. Gurung is the Ben J. and Joyce Rosenberg Professor of Human Development and Psychology at the University of Wisconsin, Green Bay (UWGB). He received a BA at Carleton College (Minnesota) and a PhD at the University of Washington. He then spent 3 years at the University of California, Los Angeles. He has published articles in a variety of scholarly journals, including *Psychological Review* and *Teaching of Psychology*. He has a textbook, *Health Psychology: A Cultural Approach* (now in its third edition), and has coauthored/edited 12 other books, including *Doing the Scholarship of Teaching and Learning* (Gurung & Wilson, 2012); *Exploring Signature Pedagogies: Approaches to Teaching Disciplinary Habits of Mind* (Gurung, Chick, & Haynie, 2009); *Getting Culture* (Gurung & Prieto, 2009); and *Optimizing Teaching and Learning* (Gurung & Schwartz, 2012). He is a Fellow of the American Psychological Association, the American Psychological Society, and the Midwestern Psychological Association and a winner of the Founder's Award for Excellence in Teaching as well as of the Founder's Award for Scholarship at UWGB. He was also the Carnegie Foundation for the Advancement of Teaching's Wisconsin Professor of the Year (2009) and the UW System Regents' Teaching Excellence Award Winner. He is past president of the Society for the Teaching of Psychology. He is founding coeditor of the APA journal, *Scholarship of Teaching and Learning in Psychology*.

SECTION I

Overview

APA Style Versus Format 1

Why It Matters to Your Audience and Why It Should Matter to You

If you are in college, congratulations—we think you made a good choice! That means you have many papers to write in your future. This book is about helping you become a better writer and helping build your confidence in your writing ability. In particular, this book is about helping you learn how to write a scientific paper with precision and objectivity, one in which you are able to communicate accurately your ideas, findings, and interpretations using the type of writing style and format published by the American Psychological Association (APA). This is a writing style very different from what you likely learned in a high school English class, where you might have learned about narrative, expository, or descriptive styles of writing. Here, we are all about writing in APA style. To help you become APA–style compliant, we use plenty of examples, clever subtitles, and any trick we can think of to get your attention so you can learn from this book. In fact, the book is purposely spiral bound so it can lie flat on your desk next to your computer or in your lap as you work on your APA papers.

Regardless of whether you are writing a paper as a psychology, sociology, or nursing student, if a professor asks you to write in APA style, you are asked to do so to help communicate your ideas in writing in a way that will be more easily understood by others in your field. APA style reflects the scientific method in that its goals are precision and objectivity in writing, as well as standardization of style and format. Using APA style helps keep our personal style and eccentricities from affecting our writing and reporting of research. It helps maintain the goal of objectivity in science. Specific content is placed within specific sections and in a particular order, allowing the reader to know exactly where to find particular

1

pieces of information about your research. Following APA style and format, you will be able to provide the reader with a convincing argument that features clear and concise statements and logical development of your ideas. You will find a greater appreciation for the APA *Publication Manual* once you start reading articles for your assignments. Then you will start to notice how helpful it is to have a particular type of writing style and format from one paper to the next, expediting your reading and understanding of the material.

Let us introduce two of the more common terms applied when using the APA *Publication Manual* to write your papers: *APA style* and *APA format*. For some assignments, you might be told to "write in APA style"; others might say to "use APA format," or you might just hear, "Follow the *Publication Manual*." You may be confused by these different instructions. What does it all mean?

What Is the Difference Between APA Style and APA Format?

These terms can be confusing because they have no clear, set definitions. For instance, APA style has been characterized by these writing elements: clarity, literal writing, and brevity (Vipond, 1993). But other types of writing could share these characteristics; for example, would you not want an owner's manual to be clear, literal, and brief? Sure, but owners' manuals are not written in APA style (at least not the manuals we have read). For clarity *here* (and for our purposes), we define APA style as *a writing approach that embodies objectivity, credibility of sources, and an evidence-based approach.* For instance, objectivity implies a certain level of detachment and formality; APA style does not typically involve passionate stories written to resemble the dialogue between characters in a play or sitcom. Objectivity also implies distance and balance in approach. Scientists writing in APA style address variables, hypotheses, and theories (which could involve studying emotion and passion) and how they affect behavior generally. Scientists do not typically write about specific individuals (with the exception of descriptions of case studies). Objectivity in APA style also obligates the writer to avoid biased language and to respect the power of language and labels.

APA style necessitates an approach that respects and preserves the chain of evidence and how science builds on previous findings and refines theoretical explanations over time. An example is the citations an author uses to support claims made in scientific writing. When you see the flow of a sentence or paragraph interrupted by names and years in parentheses, this is the author giving credit for ideas—exemplified by someone writing about how to optimize teaching and learning (Gurung & Schwartz, 2009). Listing the last name of the author (or authors) and the year when the work was published provides evidence for the writer's claim and makes readers aware of the continued refinement of theories from one scientist's work to the next. Giving credit where credit is due also helps avoid plagiarism (see Chapter 5 for details on avoiding plagiarism). Taken as a whole, APA style is one important component of what helps the author of a journal article—and, correspondingly, the research presented in it—reflect scientific objectivity.

For our purposes, APA format is what makes a journal article "look" scientific. APA format refers to the precise method of generating your article, manuscript, or term paper by using the rules set forth in the *Publication Manual*. When we refer to "APA format," we mean the nitty-gritty details of how your written work will appear on paper: the margins, the font, when to use an ampersand (*&*) and when to use the word *and*, inserting the correct information in the top 1-inch margin of your paper, when to use numerals (*12*) and when to spell out numbers (*twelve*), how to format tables with only horizontal lines, and how citation styles in the text vary with the number of authors. These details address the appearance of an APA–formatted paper.

An EasyGuide to APA Style (3rd edition) is written for students who are learning to write in APA style using APA format. Why not just rely on the "official" book, the sixth edition of the *Publication Manual of the American Psychological Association* (hereafter known as the *PM*; APA, 2010a)? The *PM* is not evil. And if your instructor thinks you should purchase it, then you probably should. But you should know that the *PM* was not written primarily as a guide to help students learn to write better (that is the purpose of *this* book). The *PM* was originally written to provide guidance to researchers on how to submit journal article manuscripts for consideration to be published in the scientific literature. However, it is clear that the *PM* has evolved into much more than an instruction set and is now a prescriptive collection of rules (format) and writing advice (style) aimed at facilitating and fostering scientific research. Could you actually use our *EasyGuide* as a replacement for the *PM*? We think so, but be sure to follow the advice of your instructors. After all, they are the ones who are reading, grading, and providing feedback. That said, beware the itty-bitty style guides that are often required for English composition or first-year writing classes. It may be nice to have one book with all the major styles in it, but books such as these often do not provide all the key information needed and, therefore, are rarely ever a good substitute for the real thing—or better yet, for a resource such as the one you now hold in your hands.

Here is an analogy to consider when thinking about the *PM*: The 2015 rulebook for Major League Baseball is 282 pages long; knowing the rules to baseball may be important, but just knowing the rules will not make you a better baseball player. However, if you add tons of baseball practice with feedback from knowledgeable sources (such as coaches, older players, books, and videos), you can become a better ballplayer over time. We want this book to be one of those knowledgeable sources you consult on a regular basis to improve your scientific writing throughout your undergraduate career. Combined, the three of us have taught for a long time and have read and graded more than 10,001 pages of student papers. We take you behind the scenes of writing and point out major common errors so you can avoid them. We have organized this book to make it easy to find the information students typically need to know when learning APA style to write papers, which is sometimes not the case with the *PM*.

Why APA Style Anyway?
Wasn't MLA Good Enough?

Odds are you have already learned some of the rules of at least one other style guide, which may have been MLA (Modern Language Association). It might have been in high school or even in a college-level English composition class, but you may have used MLA style if you wrote your papers with footnotes, if you had a bibliography or works-cited page at the end of your paper, or if you used *op. cit.* or *ibid.* in your referencing. The typical MLA method of citing involves listing the author followed by the page number where the information came from (compared with APA style, which uses author followed by year published). So why APA format? Wasn't MLA good enough?

It is hard to know with certainty why MLA style was not adopted for psychological writing. The Modern Language Association was founded in 1883 (MLA, 2009); the American Psychological Association was founded in 1892. However, the first "Instructions" to APA authors were not published until 1929, and the *MLA Handbook* is now in its seventh edition—formally known as the *MLA Handbook for Writers of Research Papers* (MLA, 2009). So, for whatever reason, separate style guides emerged—and there are many more (e.g., Chicago style; American Sociological Association [ASA] style; Turabian style; Modern Humanities Research Association [MHRA] style; and for newspapers, Associated Press [AP] style).

So where did APA style and format come from? In the very first "Instructions in Regard to Preparation of Manuscript" (1929), a six-member panel recommended "a standard of procedure, to which exceptions would doubtless be necessary, but to which reference might be made in cases of doubt" (p. 57). On a less positive (but believable) note, the 1929 "Instructions" noted that "a badly prepared manuscript always suggests uncritical research and slovenly thinking" (p. 58). Whether fair or not, the quality of our writing reflects the quality of our thinking! Good science requires communication, and if we do not communicate well, even the best ideas in the world will not be understood by others (think about the professor who you know is brilliant but has a hard time communicating on a level any student can understand).

Even though APA format may seem cumbersome to learn, once you are familiar with it, you will feel more comfortable with its conventions. If you have started to read journal articles and papers, you may notice that most, if not all, follow the same organization. The more articles you read, the more thankful you will be that each article is written in the same format and style. It really does make reviewing the literature much easier. We cannot imagine reading a journal article in which the Results section appears before the Method section (and that is not because we lack imagination or are geeks). By following (and relying on) APA style and format, we provide readers scaffolding to process the complex ideas and information being presented. Ever watch a movie in which the sequence of events is shown out of order (e.g., multiple flashbacks)? Can you tell if something is foreshadowing or background information? Then the movie jumps again. Are we back to the present, or is this a peek into the future? Only once in a while does it work well (check out the movies *Memento* [Todd, Todd, & Nolan, 2000], *Inception* [Nolan, Thomas, & Nolan, 2010], and David Lynch's *Mulholland Drive* [Edelstein et al., 2001] for real mind-bending experiences). Following a sequence and order provides a framework for understanding what happened, what is happening, and what will happen.

1

In the Long Run, Attention to Detail Matters (Including APA Style and Format)

As you become familiar with the details of writing in APA style and format, either through using this book alone or with the *PM*, you should keep two important points in mind. First, there will be times when you are frustrated by having to learn a "new" format, when MLA, Chicago, or another style was working just fine before. Although it may be frustrating to learn something new, this is a task you will repeat hundreds if not thousands of times throughout your work career. This task is part of being an educated person. New procedures will be implemented, a new type of software will be installed, a new gadget will be invented—and your task will be to figure it all out. An inherent love of learning and taking on new challenges is an attitude that will serve you well with your future employers, whoever they may be. So the ability to learn how to write capably in APA style demonstrates a competence you have that others may not share; in fact, you might know fellow students who pick classes with the least amount of writing. If you develop a skill in an area others systematically avoid, you inevitably make yourself more marketable.

The ability to pay attention to detail, particularly in regard to APA format, can help separate the good from the great. In fact, in a study by Gardner (2007) on the reasons new collegiate hires get fired, failure to pay attention to details is one of the top reasons reported. If you can handle both the big picture and the minute details simultaneously, that is a gift. These gifts can be developed with practice. Practice may not make perfect, but practice allows one to get better and closer to perfect. You have to study, you have to learn from mistakes, and you have to be willing to make the mistakes to maximize your learning ability; obviously, you need to be willing to attempt the task numerous times to gain these experiences. Paying attention to the details can make the difference between earning an A or a B in a course. You may not like the details or how picky and arbitrary they seem, but knowing the rules (and knowing those occasions when you can break the rules) is invaluable. Plus, as you will read in this book, those seemingly "picky" rules can be very helpful to practicing robust science.

Keep in mind that these rules are not just in place for students learning to write. We have some evidence to support the fact that psychologists (including your professors) must also play by the same rules. Brewer, Scherzer, Van Raalte, Petitpas, and Andersen (2001) reported that in a survey of journal editors in psychology, 39% of the editors responding indicated that they had rejected an article submitted for publication solely because the writing did not adhere to APA style and format. These rules are the same rules scientists play by, and, clearly, the penalties for not following the rules can be harsh for faculty and students alike.

Write for Your Specific Audience: Term Papers Versus Formal Research Papers

1

Ultimately, we all have to play by the rules. Unfortunately, the rules are often a moving target. Have you heard the variation on the Golden Rule—those who have the gold make the rules? In this case, your audience makes the rules for your writing, and your audience (your instructor) may not always be clear about expectations, which means you have to be. Although there are many excellent, skilled, caring instructors out there (we know many of them and salute them all), not all pay as much attention to the assignment design as they could. For example, an instructor may give a writing assignment, like the one in the box below, thinking the instructions are perfectly clear. But see how many questions we have after reading the "assignment."

Before class next week, I want you to pick a topic in psychology and write a research paper about your topic. Be sure to use evidence to support your position. Make sure you complete the following:

1. Write in APA format.

2. Your paper must be 5 to 7 pages in length.

3. To save paper, use single-spacing.

4. Use reference citations in the text of your paper to support any claims you make.

The paper is due on Thursday, and here it is Wednesday night (though we do not recommend waiting until the night before); you sit down to write your paper—no problem? Take a closer look at this assignment; it is wide open and does not provide enough detail for you to be confident about what your audience (your instructor) wants. The instruction "write in APA format" is vague at best, especially because it is contradicted by the third point in the assignment; APA format uses double-spacing in the text. Does this instructor want a title page? An abstract (probably not)? A references page? Do the title page and the references page "count" toward the 5- to 7-page requirement? Are direct quotations OK? Are a minimum number of references required? Can you use all kinds of reference materials or just refereed journal articles?

First, an important point: We hope you know that it pays to start the writing process earlier. Not only would you have more time to get clarification on the assignment; you would have time to write more than one draft, something that contributes to higher quality papers (Landrum, 2012). Additionally, research shows that students who start assignments earlier do better in class (Gurung, 2009).

A basic tenet of any type of writing is this: Write for your audience. In most cases now, your audience is your instructor. So you need to know what your instructor wants, even if the instructor thinks he or she is being clear in the instructions. You need to know the questions to ask so you can get the answers you need to succeed. This book will help you identify which questions to ask, and when you get the answers, we will give you specific tips on how to do well on the major parts of your writing assignments, whether they are term papers or research papers.

So what would a research paper look like? A research paper, especially in psychology (as in an experimental paper), is typically scripted; you are likely to have specific subsections, such as a Method section and a Results section, and many other details to attend to. A research paper is likely to employ APA style and most, if not all, components of APA format. Even though APA style and format provide particulars about how to write your paper, what you will discover is that different instructors have different expectations about style and format; attention to detail will be of ultimate importance to some, and others may not care at all. You cannot use a "one-size-fits-all" approach and expect to be consistently successful in your coursework. You may need to change your writing approach to fit both the assignment and the instructor; in fact, your instructor's expectations during a semester may change as well (we know . . . that can be frustrating). Do not be shy. Ask questions. If you are brave, point out inconsistencies, pay attention to details, and work to meet the needs of your audience. If you can conquer these lessons as an undergraduate student, these skills and abilities will serve you well beyond graduation.

Your Visual Table of Contents QuickFinder 2

Have you ever had the challenge of looking up a word in the dictionary that you were not sure you knew how to spell? In a similar vein, you might not know you need help in formatting your running head if you do not know what a running head is. You cannot search for how to include a part of your paper or how to follow a certain rule if you do not even know that part of the paper or that rule exists. Consequently, we designed a "visual table of contents" for you in this chapter, where we show you a complete sample research paper. Rather than give you tips about it and suggestions for avoiding mistakes (which we will do in Chapter 19), in this chapter, we use the sample paper as a visual organizer. Not sure how to cite a reference in text? Find an example of what you are trying to do in the sample paper, and then follow the QuickFinder guide bubbles that will point you to the chapter and page in this book where you can find help.

By the way, this is a real student paper. Parts of it have been modified from the original, but this is meant to be a realistic example of student work. Is it a perfect paper? No (and Penny is OK with that). Will you be able to find errors or mistakes in the paper? Probably. ***We use this paper as a visual guide, not as an exemplar of perfection.*** The point is not to look for errors but to identify easily where in this guide we discuss the different parts of a paper. So do not use this paper as a model of exactly what to do (because, as we said, there are errors here); instead, use it as a way to find what you want to learn about. Some of our QuickFinder bubbles point at mistakes, but most are positioned just to draw your attention to different parts of a paper and what needs to be considered before you turn in a paper. If you want to use this sample paper to test your knowledge of APA style and format, feel free to mark up the errors and see if you can correct them once you have mastered this guide.

Most of the items included in the QuickFinder bubbles you will also find in the table of contents at the beginning of this book. We decided to include this visual table of contents in part for those of us who prefer and are more comfortable seeing content illustrated visually. We like the idea of helping you identify APA–style details using different mechanisms, including a sample paper with a visual table of contents. So if you are trying to find information that you think is or should be in this book, you can try the traditional table of contents at the front of the book, the index at the back of the book, and the visual table of contents here in this chapter, with the QuickFinder guides.

2

The Sample Paper With Content and Page Numbers

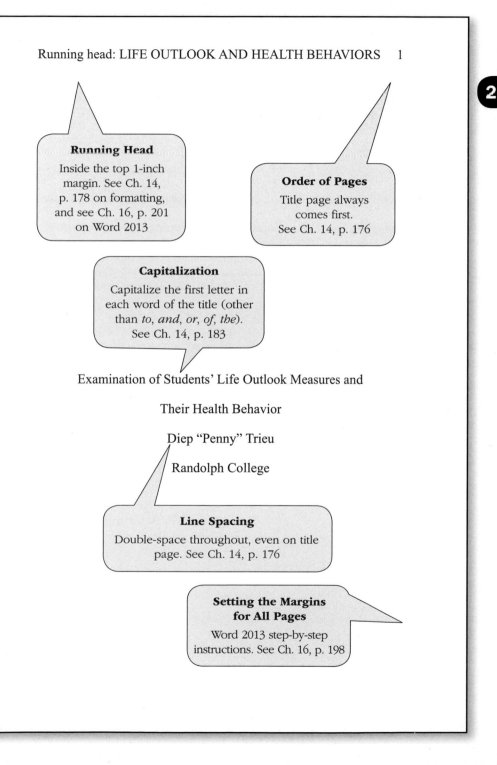

2

Abstract

The author exam_____ _e relationships of health locus of control,

dispos_____ _e risk and perceived risk of

skin c_____ ealth behaviors for skin cancer.

Twen_____ _ed questionnaires measuring

their internality of control, optimism, objective risk, perceived risk,

and healthy behaviors. There was a significant positive correlation

between internal locus of control and engagement in health

behaviors. Positive correlations also existed between health locus

of control and optimism and between perceived risks and objective

risk. Continued research on the influence of psychological states on

preventative health behaviors is warranted to und rstand specific

mechanisms that could help to reduce the likelih of disease such

as skin cancer.

Keywords: health locus of control, optimis cancer,

skin canc risk

Running Head Changes
Page 1 is different from all
subsequent pages.
See Ch. 14, p. 178

**Avoid
Anthropomorphism**
Attribute human
characteristics to only
humans. See Ch. 3, p. 40

**Include Keywords Below
the Abstract**
Format rules for keywords.
See Ch. 21, pp. 232, 256

LIFE OUTLOOK AND HEALTH BEHAVIORS   3

Examination of Students' Life Outlook Measures and Their

Health Behaviors

Within the ___ of health psychology, much attention

Center the Title
Instructions for Word 2013.
See Ch. 16, p. 204

is d ___ ___ which our mental state can affect

our ___ ___ t to the author are the i ___ actions

among sense of control, optimi

Common Mistakes to Avoid
Affect versus *effect*.
See Ch. 4, p. 49

behaviors. Understandably, ind ___

locus of control would find health behaviors of little

efficacy in affecting their health status and do not engage

in such preventions (Seeman & Seeman, 1983). Conversely,

individuals with internal senses of control have confidence

in their ability to influence their health with preventive

measures and take actions. The same logic applies to

optimism. Higher degrees of optimism encourage individuals

to believe in good outcomes from cancer-preventive actions

ar ___ ially for their health (Shazia, Hailey, &

Subject-Verb Agreement
Each . . . is
See Ch. 3, p. 37

Jo ___ diating factor is objective and perceived

risk, ___ ___ may override the low sense of control and

indu ___ individuals to engage in preventive cancer behaviors.

Each of these factors is analyzed in relation to existing

literature below.

2

LIFE OUTLOOK AND HEALTH BEHAVIORS   4

Optimism and Health-Positive Behaviors

Shazia, Hail[...]eir research on the link between [...]g behavior. One hundred twenty [...]ed the measures of optimism with the Life Orientation Test (LOT), health-behaviors with the Health-Promoting Lifestyle Profile, and participants' responses to hypothetical illnesses with the Strategies Used by People to Promote Health (SUPPH) questionnaire. The results indicated a positive correlation between optimism score LIFE and health behaviors. Similarly, a positive correlation emerged between optimism score and SUPPH score, suggesti[...] optimism planned more hea[...] faced with hypothetical illnesses. The findings o[...]y echo numerous other studies in the literature sugges[...] an encouraging relationship between optimism and health-enhancing behaviors.

> **Abbreviations**
> Good to define the entire term on first use.
> See Ch. 18, p. 223

> **Hyphenation and Spelling**
> See Webster's for questions about spelling and hyphenation.
> See Ch. 14, pp. 180, 182

The research of Luo and Isaacowitz (2007) went into more details and addressed the interaction between dispositional and health optimism, response to health information, health risk-assessment, and health-related behaviors. Sixty-four

LIFE OUTLOOK AND HEALTH BEHAVIORS   5

students self-reported on their dispositional optimism measured

by the LOT, health-related optimism, risk perception, and

objective risk measured by the Brief Skin Cancer Risk

Assessment Tool (BRAT). Afterward, they were tested on

attention to health information and recollection of

the information.

T most notable finding of the study was the significant

in -Related Optimism and

O ional Optimism and Objective

Use Your Tools

Use spell-checker and
grammar checker. See Ch. 16,
p. 213

R w in dispositional optimism

or high in health optimism pay more attention to health

information. Within these categories, individuals low in

dispositional optimism pay more attention especially when they

are high in objective risk. Individuals with high dispositional

optimism paid the same amount of attention whether they had

low or high risk of skin cancer. Among those low in objective

risk, low-optimism individuals paid less attention than those

high in optimism.

As for health optimism, participants high in health

optimism paid more attention when faced with high risks.

Participants with low health optimism paid the same levels of

attention regardless of their objective risk. If the participants

2

LIFE OUTLOOK AND HEALTH BEHAVIORS 6

possessed low risk, those high in optimism paid less attention

th_____ism. In case of high objective risk,

Common Grammar Mistakes to Avoid

There versus *their.*
See Ch. 4, p. 48

t_____ paid more attention than those low in

o_____ers speculated that people with high

levels of health optimism or low dispositional optimism would

be more aware of their risks and seek out information about skin

cancer accordingly (Luo & Issacowitz, 2007).

These two studies provided strong support for the

relationship between optimism and health-enhancing

behaviors. Drawing from the two studies' methodology, I

employed the LOT in our measure of optimism and the BRAT

scale in our measure of objective risk and health behaviors.

I also inquired participants of their perceived risk of skin

cancer. Due to the high degree of causality between health

behav_____sk, the current study evaluated the

Line and Paragraph Spacing

Double-space throughout.
See Ch. 16, p. 199

partic_____ancer and skin-cancer–preventive

behav

lth Locus of Control

In examination of the correlation between optimism

and health-enhancing behaviors, the researchers of the current

study posed that a helpful component of optimism lies in the

LIFE OUTLOOK AND HEALTH BEHAVIORS   7

sense of control: optimistic individuals believe in the efficacy

of their actions to improve their health. This sense of control

is much relevant to the discu   of the relation between

the Health Locus o   r, as

Avoid Gender-Biased Language
Use *their* when grammatically
appropriate to avoid *he/she*.
See Ch. 6, p. 67

LIFE examined in   1983).

Seeman and Seeman examined the relationships between sense

of control and indi   ventive care, health

Avoid Plagiarism
Paraphrase in your own
words. See Ch. 5, p. 59

knowledge, and p   dinal study. One

thousand two hund   ults were interviewed

every 6 weeks from Fall 1976 to Fall 1977 to track their illnesses

and responses to those illnesses. The experimenters gathered

participants' health beliefs (first interview), knowledge or

perspective of cancer (last interview), and sense of health control

(in between). In analyzing the results, the experimenters also

control for possibly confounding variables such as health state

and socioeconomic resources. The dependent variables were

preventive health behavior, health knowledge and perspectives,

and physical health status. There was an overall positive

relationship between higher sense of control and various

health factors, including frequency of preventive health

actions, optimism of early medical treatment for cancer, higher

LIFE OUTLOOK AND HEALTH BEHAVIORS   8

self-ratings of health, fewer episodes of illnesses, and proactive

responses to illnesses. Considering this study's strong suggestion

of a relationship between locus of control and health status, the

authors incorporated this measure into our study.

The Current Study

In regard of the literature reviewed, the current study

surveyed the interrelationships among health sense of control as

measured by t[...]OC) scale, optimism

measured by t[...]ctive risk and health

behaviors measured [...] by the skin cancer assessment tool.

In this article, I ref[...]d to the score of objective risk as the

BRAT score and [...]e score of health behaviors as the BEH score.

I tested the hypothesis that higher scores on the HLOC (more

internal sense of control), self-reported risk, the BRAT, and the

LOT would correspond to higher score on the BEH with a linear

regression.

Avoid Passive Voice
Active voice preferred over
"It was hypothesized that . . ."
See Ch. 3, p. 37

Method

Participants

P[...]re all[...]cipant[...]al
at Ran[...]
age, approximately 20 years old. The gender ratio reflected

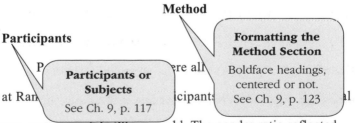

Participants or Subjects
See Ch. 9, p. 117

Formatting the Method Section
Boldface headings, centered or not.
See Ch. 9, p. 123

LIFE OUTLOOK AND HEALTH BEHAVIORS   9

the gender ratio at Randolph College (65% females). The

participants were recruited fr〔   a

mandatory part of class activi

> **Expressing Numbers**
> General rules and exceptions.
> See Ch. 13, p. 165

Instruments

Life Orientation Test

> **Materials or Apparatus**
> What to include.
> See Ch. 9, p. 119

The Life Orientation Test (

1994) consisted of 10 items, including 3 items pertaining to

optimism, 3 items to pessim

> **In-Text Citations, Multiple Authors**
> Learn the rules for using et al.
> See Ch. 8, p. 106

ranged from 0 = *strongly d*

scores on the pessimism ite

score indicating more optimistic outlook.

The Brief Skin Cancer Assessment Tool

The brief skin cancer assessment tool (Glanz et al., 2003)

was used to measure objective risk (BRAT) and health behaviors

(BEH). The BRAT scale consisted of the first nine items of the

assessment tool inquiring about characteristics such as skin

color, sun sensitivity, and personal history. A high score on the

BRAT suggested a high objective risk of skin cancer. The BEH

scale, composed of seven questions, evaluated participants'

tanning frequency and protective measures such as wearing

sunscreen, with higher score demonstrating healthier behaviors.

2

LIFE OUTLOOK AND HEALTH BEHAVIORS   10

Health Locus of Control

> **Multiple Citations Within Parentheses**
> Separate with semicolon.
> See Ch. 8, p. 107

I used a shortened versi... ...ston, Stein, & Smith, 1994; Wallston, Wallston, & DeVellis, 1978) with six items, with a higher score indicating a more internal

> **Follow In-Text Citation Rules**
> In parentheses, use &, not *and*.
> See Ch. 8, p. 106

s... ...from 1 = s*trongly disagree* to 6...

Subjective Risk

Subjective risk was measured with a single question asking the participants' own assessment of their chances of skin cancer. The scale ran from 1 to 6, with a higher score indicating higher perceived risks.

Procedure

All the participants completed the scales during class time. After completing the scales, they were debriefed on the meanings of the scale and the purpose of the study.

Results

A simultaneous multiple regression analysis, with the HLOC, BRAT, LOT, and Perceived Risk scores as the predictors and BEH score as the criterion, was computed. The regression analysis was not significant ($F(4, 16) = 1.410$, $p = .275$). When controlled for other variables, none of the

LIFE OUTLOOK AND HEALTH BEHAVIORS   11

predictors produced significant correlation with BEH in this

analysis. A summary of the results of the multiple regression

a[n]   Th[e]

s[u]

produced a significa[nt] [c]orrelation with BEH ($r(19)$= .50, p = .010).

Among other variables, H[LO]C and LOT produced a significant

positive correlation ($r(19)$ = .62, p = .002). Another significant positive

[...] ($r(19)$ = .46, p = .018). A summary

of the results of the linear regression equation is p[ro]vided in Table 2.

Properly Present Statistical Symbols
Know what the symbols mean.
See Ch. 10, p. 128

Formatting Numbers
When to include a leading zero.
See Ch.13, p. 171

Number of Decimal Places
When the rules change.
See Ch. 13, p. 171

Treat Each Number as a Separate Word
Spaces around the equals sign. See Ch. 10, p. 130

Discussion

Even though the results were[...]

show support for the hypothesis, s[...]

study were worth examination. Fi[rst,]

the findings in literature of a positive relationship between

a more internal health locus of control and more preventive

health behaviors. In consideration of the literature, this finding

is congruent with the finding of Luo and Issacowitz (2007),

where health optimism, not dispositional optimism, correlated

with health behaviors. A possible explanation is that health

2

LIFE OUTLOOK AND HEALTH BEHAVIORS   12

measures, including health optimism and health locus of control, capture more intimately the participants' feelings of control and optimism towards their health. A dispositional optimism scale or a general locus of control scale measure people's general life outlooks, and other factors of their lives may override the health factor. However, when health is salient, as in health scales, the scores will be more reflective of the participants' evaluations of their health status and thus correlate better with their health behaviors.

Another noteworthy finding is the significant positive correlation between participants' perceived risk and objective risk, suggesting participants' accurate awareness of their own health status, which is a reassuring finding.

Finally, the strongest correlation in this study was between the HLOC score and the LOT score. The relationship between optimism and sense of control is intricate, as one subtly influences the other. Optimism, a confidence in good outcomes of one's encouragement for people to be proactive and preserve their health. Future research can attempt to analyze this relationship further by presenting four scales: (1) health optimism scale, (2) dispositional optimism scale, (3) health locus of control

Present Lists With Proper Format

Seriation and enumeration. See Ch. 17, p. 221

LIFE OUTLOOK AND HEALTH BEHAVIORS   13

scale, and (4) general locus of control scale. The results of such

study can provide a direct comparison of the efficacy of each

measure to predict health behaviors and address the distinction

between health-specific scale and general scale.

The present study was also affected by several

limitations. First, I had a small sample size of 21, which might

have subdued possible gene   cs.

Second, these participants   from a

health psychology class, an   ealth

psychology discussions regarding optimism and locus of control

might have reduced the objectivity of participants' completion

of the questionnaires. Last, I did not control for participants'

actual health status pertaining to skin cancer, which likely

influenced to some extent their optimism and health locus of

control.

**Use Commonly Confused
Words Properly**
Affect versus *effect*.
See Ch. 3, p. 35

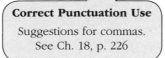

Correct Punctuation Use
Suggestions for commas.
See Ch. 18, p. 226

Insert a Page Break
Learn how and when
you need to.
See Ch. 16, p.211

LIFE OUTLOOK AND HEALTH BEHAVIORS   14

References

Chang, E. C., & Sanna, L. J. (2003). Experience of life hassles and psychological adjustment among adolescents: Does it make a difference is one is optimistic or pessimistic? *Personality and Individual Differences, 34*, 867–879. doi: 10.1016/s0191-8869(0) 00077-6

Glanz, K., S penfeld, E., Weinstock, M. A., Lavi, G. Kidd, J. & Shigak M. (2003). Deve brief skin risk assessmen P

Luo, 7). How optimists face skin cancer in attention, memory, and behavior. *Psychology and Health, 22*, 963–984.

Mulkana, S., S., & Hailey, B. J. (2001). The role of optimism in health-enhancing behaviors. *American Journal of Health Behavior*, *25, 388–395*.

Scheier, M., Carver, C., & Bridges, M. (1994). Distinguishing optimism from neuroticism (and trait anxiety, self-mastery, and self-esteem): A re-evaluation of the Life Orientation Test. *Journal of Personality and Social Psychology, 67*, 1063–1078.

Seeman, M., & Seeman, T. (1983). Health behavior and personal autonomy: A longitudinal study of the sense of control in illness. *Journal of Health and Social Behavior*, *24*, 144–160.

Including DOIs for Online Journal Articles

Learn when a doi is needed. See Ch. 12, p. 157

Detailed Punctuation and Spacing Rules

Tend to the details. See Ch. 18, p. 225

LIFE OUTLOOK AND HEALTH BEHAVIORS   15

W[...]., & Smith, K. A. (1994). Form C of the

[...]on-specific measure of locus of control.

[...]*ssessment, 63,* 534–553.

Wa[...], B. S., & DeVellis, R. (1978).

Development of the multidimensional health locus of control

(MHLC) scales. *Health Education Monographs, 6,* 160–170.

> **Many Details in a Journal Article Reference**
> Tend to the details.
> See Ch. 12, p. 155

> **Format References With a Hanging Indent**
> Use a Word shortcut.
> See Ch. 12, p. 161
> Step-by-step instructions.
> See Ch. 16, p. 207

> **Capitalization Rules**
> May not be what you are used to.
> See Ch. 14, p. 183

> **What About the Paper's Content**
> This same paper, with content feedback.
> See Ch. 21, pp. 255–270

LIFE OUTLOOK AND HEALTH BEHAVIORS   16

Table 1

Multiple Regression to Predict Risky Health Behaviors (N = 21)

Predictors	*r*	B	β
BRAT	-.05	.00	.01
HLOC	.50*	.41	.52
LOT	.26	-.04	-.06
Perceived Risk	-.24	-.13	-.06

Note: R = .51, R^2 = .26

p = .010

Creating Tables in Word 2013

Use the tables function for greater flexibility. See Ch. 16, p. 208

Why All These APA–Formatting Rules?

What is the point? Why not MLA? See Ch. 1, p. 6

The Most Common Mistakes to Avoid

Your presubmission quiz. See Ch. 22, p. 271

LIFE OUTLOOK AND HEALTH BEHA[**Abbreviations**] 17

Tend to the details.
See Ch. 18, p. 223

Table 2

Linear Regression Equation Pearson Correlation

	BRAT	HLOC	LOT	Perceived Risk
BEH	-.05	.50*	.26	-.24
BRAT		-.04	.16	.46*
HLOC			.62**	-.34
LOT				.17

*Note: *p < .05. **p < .01*

The Table Note

Specific rules for
table notes.
See Ch. 15, p. 192

SECTION II

Writing With (APA) Style

Big-Picture Items

General Writing Tips Specific to APA Style 3

General Bare-Bones
Fundamentals

It would be difficult to teach (or reteach) the complexities of how to write within one book such as this one. However, informed by our experience in teaching students how to write (specifically, how to write using APA style and format), we offer some targeted advice about the most common mistakes we see in our students' writing and the actions to take to help prevent those mistakes in the future. This way, you benefit from the past mistakes of others. It is almost no pain, but with gain. Or in the words of the Dread Pirate Roberts (watch *The Princess Bride*), "Life is pain, . . . and if anyone says otherwise they are trying to sell you something." Below we provide the basics of how best to approach an APA–style paper, including details on using a scholarly voice.

Clear and Succinct Writing: Using Your Scholarly Voice

As with any type or genre of writing, it takes both time and practice to get good at it and build your confidence. Scientific writing has its own voice, with the appropriate levels of formality, detachment, and objectivity, and this scholarly writing is written with a different style than is typically used in creative or

33

technical writing. Be sure to avoid slang words, excessive use of first person, quotations, contractions, and passive voice. You should also avoid wordiness, especially just for the sake of reaching a mandatory page length. Even with these style rules, scientific writing does not have to be boring. In fact, the better journal articles in psychology are written to tell a good story. Even though the language may not use a conversational tone, this decision is a purposeful one to be clear and concise. Clear communication is the primary objective—to present ideas precisely, with logic and a smooth flow from idea to idea (Knight & Ingersoll, 1996).

In some college student writing assignments, such as composing a term paper or answering an essay question on an exam, you might tend to go on and on, hoping the instructor "finds" the right answer buried somewhere in your prose—this could be called the "kitchen sink" approach. Scientific writing does not share that same strategy. You should always strive to be succinct—concise and to the point. As readers, we appreciate the courtesy of authors who write in this manner; the author does not waste our time with unnecessary words or ideas that clutter the central message. However, as writers, it takes time and practice to acquire this skill; we have designed this book to help you improve as a succinct writer. Knight and Ingersoll (1996) captured the essence of this approach:

> Vigorous writing is concise and direct. A sentence should contain no unnecessary words and a paragraph no unnecessary sentences. This does not mean that all sentences and paragraphs should be short or lacking in detail, but that every word is purposeful. (p. 210)

Here's one more idea to share about writing clearly and succinctly—what about quotations and contractions? If you are going to use direct quotations in your writing, be sure you have noted the exact page or paragraph number from where the quote appeared—the citation might look like (Smith, 2014, p. 712) or (Jones, 2015, para. 7). Prior to completing the assignment, we strongly recommend that you consult with the person grading the assignment to determine her/his preferences about direct quotations. Some instructors might welcome the use of an occasional quote, whereas others might discourage it completely. Since your results may vary, why not inquire first?

Now, about contractions—we don't recommend them for formal APA–style writing (in this sentence, the word "don't" is a contraction—the shortened form of "do not"). Contractions connote a more informal style of writing (as your authors have aspired to in this user-friendly *EasyGuide*), but if we were writing for a more formal outlet (such as a journal article manuscript or a book chapter), we would not use contractions. It's about formality. In addition to using words properly, you'll want to use the right words in the right places—that is, avoiding those commonly confused words.

Commonly Confused Words
in Psychology and Beyond

Like other disciplines, psychology has its own terminology and jargon. Your topic-specific textbooks (such as your introductory psychology textbook, cognitive psychology textbook, etc.) introduce you to the specific, technical terms. But even in your own writing about psychology, common words are frequently confused; sometimes this is due to a psychological "spin" placed on those words. Honestly, many of these words are commonly confused in disciplines beyond psychology, so keep this list in mind when writing any paper. Following is a brief listing of commonly confused words, with definitions designed to clear up the confusion (with some assistance from www.dictionary.com).

3

advice/advise
 advice: *noun,* an opinion given, such as a recommended action
 advise: *verb,* to give counsel to, information, or notice

affect/effect
 affect: *verb,* to act on or produce a change in; *noun,* feeling or
  emotion
 effect: *noun,* a result or consequence; *verb,* to bring about

allusion/illusion
 allusion: *noun,* the incidental mentioning or casual referral
 illusion: *noun,* a type of deception or false impression of reality

cite/site/sight
 cite: *verb,* to quote (typically) an authority, to mention as proof
 site: *noun,* the position or location of an item to be located; *verb,*
  to put into position or locate
 sight: *noun,* vision, the perception of objects with your eyes; *verb,*
  to see or notice or observe

conscience/conscious
 conscience: *noun,* one's inner sense of right and wrong; ethical,
  moral principles
 conscious: *adjective,* one's own awareness of thoughts, sensations,
  existence

council/counsel
 council: *noun,* an assembly of individuals selected to provide con-
  sultation or advice
 counsel: *noun,* advice given to direct the conduct of someone else;
  verb, to advise or give advice

data/datum
> data: *noun, plural form,* individual facts, statistics, or items of infor-
> mation
>
> datum: *noun,* singular form of data for one number or a single case

elicit/illicit
> elicit: *verb,* to extract, bring out, or evoke
>
> illicit: *adjective,* unlawful, not legally permitted or authorized

3

lay/lie
> lay: *verb,* to place or to put an object at rest, or set down
>
> lie: *verb,* to be in a horizontal position, recline, to rest, remain,
> to be situated; to spread a falsehood; *noun,* a false statement
> made with intention to deceive, a falsehood

personal/personnel
> personal: *adjective,* pertaining to one individual, private
>
> personnel: *noun,* the collection of individuals employed in an
> organization

precede/proceed
> precede: *verb,* to go before, to introduce something preliminary
>
> proceed: *verb,* to move or go forward, to carry on or continue an
> action; *noun,* the total amount derived from a sale or
> transaction

principal/principle
> principal: *adjective,* highest rank of importance or value; *noun,* a
> chief or head or director
>
> principle: *noun,* fundamental or general law or truth from which
> other truths are derived

respectfully/respectively
> respectfully: *adverb,* showing politeness or deference
>
> respectively: *adverb,* in the precise order given, sequentially

then/than
> then: *adverb,* at that time, next in order of time, in that case;
> *noun,* that time; *adjective,* existing or acting (e.g., "the then
> president")
>
> than: *conjunction,* used to show unequal comparison (e.g., "colder
> than yesterday"), used to show difference or diversity; *prepo-
> sition,* to connect two nouns (e.g., "this is better than that")

Subject–Verb Agreement

The idea of subject–verb agreement may seem simple at first, but the rules get complicated quickly. The subject of a sentence is typically the source of action in a sentence, and often, the subject appears before the verb. The subject of a sentence can be singular or plural, and thus the verb used has to "agree" with the singularity or plurality of the subject (EzineArticles.com, 2009a). Consider the sentence, "I love you." *I* is the subject, which is to the left of the verb *love*. The object of the sentence (i.e., the one who receives love) is *you* (EzineArticles.com, 2009b).

The most common subject–verb error we come across in our students' papers involves a sentence about the data collected for an experiment. *Data* is a plural noun and therefore should always be followed by the verb *are* rather than *is* (or *were* rather than *was* for the past tense).

> The data were collected after all 20 participants were seated in the laboratory.

Here are some general tips to help you figure out the *basic* rules of subject–verb agreement (About.com, n.d.; EzineArticles.com, 2009a), followed by some practice sentences to see if you can identify errors (not every sample sentence has an error, however).

1. Add an *s* to the verb if the subject is a singular noun (a word that names one person, place, or thing).

   A good research idea **takes** time to develop.

2. Add an *s* to the verb if the subject is any one of the third-person singular pronouns: *he, she, it, this, that.*

   She **writes** well and should have her work published.

3. Do not add an *s* to the verb if the subject is the pronoun *I, you, we,* or *they.*

   You **create** a new data file for each online survey.

4. Do not add an *s* to the verb if two subjects are joined by *and.*

   Utah and Idaho **compete** for similar grant projects.

5. *Everybody* is singular and uses a singular verb (as do *anybody, no one, somebody, nobody, each, either,* and *neither*).

   Everybody **is** invited to the colloquium on Thursday afternoon.

Active Voice Versus Passive Voice in APA Style

For many native English speakers, subject–verb agreement is only an occasional problem, and if we practice and attend to the rules, these types of errors can be minimized or eliminated. However, depending on your prior writing experience, slipping into passive voice can be natural. Additionally, some students think that passive voice is more "scientific sounding" and makes the text seem more detached and objective, as scientific writing often strives to be. Unfortunately, passive voice makes writing more muddled, often placing the subject of the sentence after the verb. We generally prefer—and understand better—when we follow the subject–verb–object pattern in a sentence. Clarity is key, and writing in active voice typically provides the best shot at clear communications.

3

So what is the difference between "active voice" and "passive voice"? The structure of an active-voice sentence tends to follow the pattern, performer (subject) → verb → receiver (object). The active voice indicates stronger writing because the sentence gives credit to who is performing the action; in other words, the active voice focuses on the performer of the action. Active voice is an indicator of clear and vigorous writing and is preferred in most academic writing (BioMedical Editor, 2009; DailyWritingTips.com, n.d.; Knight & Ingersoll, 1996; PlainLanguage.gov, n.d.). Active voice is typically clearer because the person performing the action is made clear.

Using passive voice (in which the pattern is receiver → verb → performer, with the performer often not named) is sometimes a difficult habit to break for some educators, because the tradition at one time preferred a passive-voice–third-person approach because it implied a sense of detachment and objectivity (BioMedical Editor, 2009; Knight & Ingersoll, 1996). A sentence written in passive voice emphasizes the receiver of the action and not the subject performing the action. Unfortunately, passive voice often adds confusion to the sentence, particularly the subject of the sentence. This is not to say that the use of passive voice is evil but that the use of passive voice is not preferred in APA–style writing.

Here are some examples of **active**-voice sentences:

My students completed the survey before time elapsed.

I analyzed possible sex differences using an independent means t-test.

We recruited students from introductory psychology to participate in this research project.

I prefer using Word on a PC rather than on a Mac.

As you can see, all these sentences are straightforward and relatively easy to understand. Consider these passive sentences and their active counterparts (PlainLanguage.gov, n.d.):

Passive: My car was driven to work. **Active**: I drove my car to work.

Passive: Breakfast was eaten by me this morning. **Active**: I ate breakfast this morning.

And here's another:

Passive: The survey was conducted by me. **Active**: I conducted the survey.

It may seem absurd that anyone would purposely use passive voice, but writers (often new to scientific writing) slip into passive voice by accident (and there are times when passive voice is preferred; see the following examples). Knight and Ingersoll (1996) expressed slightly stronger opinions about using passive voice, calling it "dry, dull, rigid, pompous, ambiguous, weak, evasive, convoluting, tentative, timid, sluggish, amateurish" (p. 212)—you get the picture. Notice how easily you can slip into passive voice by accident:

The data were analyzed using SPSS. (The subject is not named: Who used SPSS to analyze the data?) Better to say, "I analyzed the data using SPSS."

This conclusion was reached by the researchers in the study. (Notice the pattern: The object—*conclusion*—precedes the verb, and the subject—*researchers*—follows the verb.) Better to say, "We reached the following conclusions . . ."

Although manic depression was identified in some of the participants, the drug treatment was beneficial for all participants in the study. (The first part of the sentence—"manic depression was identified"—is passive; the second part—"drug treatment was beneficial"—is not passive, because the subject precedes the verb.) Better to start the sentence with "Although we identified manic depression symptoms in some of the participants, . . ."

You can imagine reading each of these three sentences in a journal article, yet all three are written in passive voice. So when would you use passive voice? Passive voice is useful when you want to emphasize the receiver (or object) of the action (BioMedical Editor, 2009). That is, passive voice is appropriate when you are writing a sentence and you do not know the performer of the action or when the performer of the action is unimportant (PlainLanguage.gov, n.d.). For instance, passive voice may be more appropriate when writing the Method section of a manuscript, because the Method section is likely to focus on objects such as materials and procedures (APA, 2010a).

An excellent tip to help you find possible instances of your inadvertent use of passive voice is to check your file for some form of the verb "to be"—including *is, are, was,* or *were* (DailyWritingTips.com, n.d.; Knight & Ingersoll, 1996). Notice in the examples, the "to be" verb is included with an additional verb in each passive-voice sentence but not in the active-voice sentences. Before you hand in a paper, you might use your *Find* feature in Word 2013 found to the far right under the *Home* tab. You can also use just press Ctrl+F to get the *Navigation box* that allows you to type in a word to find throughout your document. You can then find all occurrences of *is, are, was,* and *were* to check for passive-voice sentences, keeping in mind that passive voice includes these "to be" verbs with another verb that follows (e.g., "Surveys *were collected* by the research assistants").

Some (But Not Too Much) First-Person Usage

Our students often ask if they should use first person when writing APA–style papers. In the previous section, we went into detail about how to avoid the passive voice. The problem is that so often students think they need to avoid first person completely and they slip into passive voice. For example:

First person: We assessed accuracy of responses using nonleading questions.

Passive voice: Accuracy was assessed using nonleading questions.

Which is the better choice? When writing in a scholarly voice, you need to minimize the use of first person and at the same time attempt to avoid passive voice. However, the *PM* (Section 3.09) also states that you should avoid ambiguity and use of the third person (e.g., "the author," "the experimenters") and simply use first person. I know what you are probably thinking at this point. "OK, so what should I do?" This is a situation that requires you to determine the word choice that will provide the most precise sentence.

The section of your paper in which you will most likely want to use first person is the one in which you state your hypothesis. Typically, your hypothesis is included at the end of your Introduction. Here you will want to write, "I hypothesized that . . ." rather than "It was hypothesized . . ." Given that a hypothesis is essential in a scientific paper, you need to hypothesize. What you should watch out for is sentences that start with "I think . . ." Thinking is essential too of course and the phrase "I think" is first person, but scientific papers rely less on opinion than peer-reviewed facts. Focus on interpreting findings and tying them together. Also, when writing your Method section or Discussion section, you will sometimes find it necessary to use first person to indicate what steps you followed to carry out your research. When writing your Discussion section, you often include your own interpretation of your findings. It certainly makes sense to use first person in that section when stating your own opinion. So the rule to keep in mind is to limit the use of first person but to use it when you believe it enhances the clarity of your writing.

Avoiding Anthropomorphism

Another common error to avoid in your writing is attributing human characteristics to nonhuman entities. This is known as anthropomorphism, sometimes called pathetic fallacy (which seems a bit harsh). The *PM* states (Section 3.09) that when writing in your scholarly voice, you achieve greater clarity when you avoid anthropomorphism. Notice in the example that follows, the experiment (nonhuman) is doing something that only humans can do.

> **Incorrect:** The experiment will demonstrate the early development of children's vocabulary.

> **Better:** The purpose of the experiment is to demonstrate the early development of children's vocabulary.

So keep in mind that "things," such as experiments, figures, and tables, can illustrate or include but cannot discuss or explore. You want to make sure the subject of your sentence can indeed do what you state it can do.

This notion of proofreading your work before you turn it in brings up another vital practice you need to use if you want to improve your writing skills: You must learn to write for your audience, and in college, that will typically mean writing for your professors. They may ask for deviations from APA style and APA format, and that is OK. Remember, they are the folks who are grading your work. So if they prefer more passive voice than first person in scientific writing, follow that advice over the course of the class; just know that the *PM* indicates a preference for the active voice (Section 3.18). In Chapter 20, we provide details on how best to proofread your papers.

As with everything else regarding writing, we get better with practice. So we close this chapter with some sentences you might encounter in scientific writing; your task is to rewrite them in the active voice. Your rewrites do not need to match perfectly, but take note of the different methods you can use to rewrite into the active voice by putting the "do-er" of the action first, followed by the verb, and ending with the object or receiver of the action. Also, take a stab at rewriting the sentences below that include the errors described above. This practice will help you communicate clearly and concisely with your desired audience.

Start with these (you saw some of them on the previous page):

The data were analyzed using SPSS.

This conclusion was reached by the researchers in the study.

Although manic depression was found in some of the participants, the drug treatment was beneficial for all participants in the study.

The questions were developed by the interviewer.

It was determined by the researcher that the results were inconclusive.

Participants were asked by the experimenter to read the instructions carefully before proceeding.

The proposed methodology will likely be passed by the Institutional Review Board.

As I observed the interaction patterns between participants, I noticed that body language played an important role in communication.

As I was reading this study of mental illness during the 20th century, I noticed that classification of disorders was not very clearly defined.

The speech laboratory wanted to explore the underlying causes of stammering.

The *EasyGuide* improved the understanding of APA style.

Remember, as with any other complex skill, practice makes perfect!

A Quick Grammar Summary for APA–Style Writing

4

Do you play cards? Nowadays, you can watch competition card games on TV; one of the most popular is Texas No Limit Hold 'Em tournaments. If you have watched any of these shows, you have probably heard the announcers say something like, "Texas Hold 'Em takes a minute to learn but a lifetime to master." We wish that the rules of English grammar (and APA style and format) took a minute to learn and then a lifetime to master; alas, it is more complicated (in our opinion). If only it took a minute to learn the rules! When we say a lifetime to master, we do not mean that you have to memorize the rules, but you need to practice the rules and become familiar enough with them that you can avoid embarrassing mistakes (and some memorization is good for the brain, too). In this chapter, we provide plenty of tips on how to avoid those embarrassing (and not-so-embarrassing) writing mistakes.

Of course, entire textbooks and college courses are devoted to grammar and style. Four of our favorite books include *Woe Is I: The Grammarphobe's Guide to Better English in Plain English* (O'Conner, 1996), *Words Fail Me: What Everyone Who Writes Should Know About Writing* (O'Conner, 1999), *Eats, Shoots & Leaves* (Truss, 2003), and the ever-classic *The Elements of Style* (Strunk & White, 1979). This chapter is just a brief summary of the key components you need to know and practice to be a better writer of APA style and format. We organize our brief presentation here around parts of a sentence and parts of speech, and we end with common grammatical mistakes to avoid.

Parts of a Sentence

Texas No Limit Hold 'Em is a card game with its own terminology that must be learned to play—terms such as *the flop, the turn, the button, big slick,* and *trips.* If you did not understand those No Limit Hold 'Em terms, you would have a hard time just following the game (much less playing it). The same is true for grammar terminology. If you do not know what the terms mean, then it will be difficult to apply any rules. So we start here with parts of a sentence. By the way, many of these explanations come from Maddox and Scocco (2009), who provide a wonderful resource on basic English grammar, available online as a PDF. Next up will be parts of speech, followed by grammatical errors you want to avoid.

4

Subject: The part of a sentence that is being written about.

The researchers studied the effects of Alzheimer's disease. (The subject is *researchers.*)

Predicate: What we say about the subject of the sentence (the main word in the predicate is the verb).

I hypothesize that younger adults spend more time on Facebook than do older adults. (The predicate is *hypothesize.*)

Phrase: Grammatically related words of a sentence that do not contain the main verb (a sentence fragment that would not exist as a sentence on its own).

I attended the session at the conference on applying to graduate school. (Both "at the conference" and "on applying to graduate school" are phrases—written alone, they would not stand as sentences.)

Clause: Grammatically related words that do contain a main verb. An independent clause is part of a larger sentence that could stand on its own as a complete sentence. A subordinate clause cannot stand on its own as a sentence because the clause begins with a qualifier, such as *because* or *when.*

I want to take more statistics, unless the class time conflicts with my work schedule. ("I want to take more statistics" is an independent clause because it can stand on its own as a complete sentence. The second clause, "unless the class time conflicts with my work schedule," is a subordinate clause because of the qualifier *unless.*)

Object: The part of the sentence that receives the action of the action verb.

I completed an application to graduate school. (The object of the sentence is application, which is the receiver of the action of the verb *completed.*)

Parts of Speech

Next, we provide definitions for each of the parts of speech. This compilation of information comes from multiple sources, including Maddox and Scocco (2009), EzineArticles.com (2009b), and Knight and Ingersoll (1996).

Noun

Words used to indicate people, places, things, events, or ideas, nouns are typically the subjects or objects of a sentence. A noun can be singular or plural, which has implications for the verb used with the noun. There are many different types of nouns, but one important distinction for APA format is the proper noun, used to describe a unique person or thing. Proper nouns start with a capital letter (which also applies to APA–format citations).

4

> **Example:** "The role of the Rorschach in the clinical intake exam: Impact on psychotherapy effectiveness."
>
> In this journal article title from a reference section, Rorschach is capitalized because it is a proper noun, referring to a specific projective test.

Pronoun

A pronoun is a word used to replace a noun, typically used to avoid repetition. There are also singular and plural pronouns, and the pronoun rules differ depending on whether the pronoun is used as the subject (e.g., *she, he, they, who*) or the object of the sentence (e.g., *her, him, them, whom*).

> **Example:** "I hypothesize that students reading online textbook pages will score lower on a multiple-choice test than will students reading a traditional textbook."
>
> The pronoun *I* takes the place of the author's name.

Adjective

An adjective is a word that describes or qualifies a noun or pronoun. Adjectives can be found before a noun being described (attributive adjective) or after a verb that follows a noun being described (predicative adjective).

> **Example 1:** "The **first-year** student signed up for the research study."
>
> *First-year* is the attributive adjective describing the student.
>
> **Example 2:** "This study is **incomplete**."
>
> *Incomplete* is the predicative adjective describing the study.

Article

Articles (*a, and, the*) are actually a special form of adjective called demonstrative adjectives. A definite article (*the*) points out something specific or already introduced. An indefinite article (*a, an*) introduces something unspecific or something mentioned for the first time.

> **Example:** "**The** Method section follows immediately after **the** Introduction section of **a** research paper."
>
> *The* in both cases refers to specific parts of a research paper (definite article), and *a* refers to any (unspecific) research paper (indefinite article).

4

Verb

Verbs typically describe the action within the sentence. Verbs are the most important words in a sentence; they describe the action the subject takes or the subject's state of being.

> **Example 1:** "The student **wrote** a fine paper."
>
> *Student* is the subject; *wrote* tells us what the student did.
>
> **Example 2:** "The student **was happy** with the paper."
>
> *Student* is the subject; *was*, with the adjective *happy*, tells us the student's state of being.

There are many different kinds of verbs, and verb forms change depending on, for example, the subject (singular or plural), the tense, the voice (active or passive), and the verb form (regular or irregular).

> **Examples:** First-person verbs are formed using the subject pronouns **I** and **we**. It is appropriate to write in APA style using first-person pronouns and their accompanying verbs, because writing in the first person helps avoid passive voice (see Chapter 3). Second-person verbs are used with **you**. Third-person verbs are used with the pronouns **he, she, it**, and **they**.

Adverb

Adverbs are words used to modify or qualify a verb, an adjective, another adverb, or clauses.

> **Example 1:** "Participants completed the survey **quickly.**"
>
> *Quickly* is the adverb that describes how the survey was completed.
>
> **Example 2:** "Study 1 **successfully** demonstrated the phi phenomenon; **moreover**, Study 1 replicated previous research."

Both *successfully* and *moreover* are adverbs; *moreover* is an example of a conjunctive adverb (within a sentence, if a clause begins with a conjunctive adverb, it is preceded by a semicolon).

Preposition

Prepositions are words that combine with nouns or pronouns to provide the connections between two words or clauses. Some prepositions are *about, above, after, among, around, along, at, before, behind, beneath, beside, between, by, down, from, in, into, like, near, of, off, on, out, over, through, to, up, upon, under, until, with,* and *without.*

4

Example: "My manuscript is **under** review **at** the journal."

Conjunction

Conjunctions are used to join words, phrases, or clauses. There are coordinate conjunctions (*and, but, for, or, nor, so, yet*) and subordinate conjunctions (*that, as, after, before, if, since, when, where, unless*).

Example: "Beth, Eric, **and** Regan enjoyed writing this book. **Because** writing in APA style can be difficult, we thought this book would be helpful to students."

And is a coordinate conjunction, and *because* is a subordinate conjunction.

Interjection

Interjections are words, phrases, or sentences that express emotion; often, interjections end with an exclamation point or a question mark.

Examples: "Take care!" "Are you kidding me?"

Interjections are used infrequently in APA–style writing.

Common Grammar Mistakes to Avoid

Many rules and much advice are available to students who want to improve their writing. We certainly applaud you for reading this book and wanting to improve your writing skills. Table 4.1 at the end of this chapter presents some common writing errors to avoid, with a brief label for each error. These are some common mistakes to avoid that deserve your special attention, and different authors have suggested that if you make any of the grammar mistakes listed next, these types of mistakes make you look "dumb" (Clark, n.d.) or "stupid" (Gilbert, 2006). Those labels may be taking conclusions a bit far, but you clearly want to avoid making these errors. They make you look as though you wrote your paper at the last minute and/or suggest you did not have the time or inclination to proofread. Following is a summary of the combined lists (Clark, n.d.; Gilbert, 2006), with examples relevant to APA style and format.

Your—You're

You're is a contraction for the words "you are." Contractions are typically not used in APA–style writing, so this one is easy: *You're* should never appear in your formal research paper. *Your* is a possessive pronoun, and the following example indicates proper use.

> **Example:** We asked participants to answer the open-ended survey question, "What is **your** preferred time of day to study?"

It's—Its

The apostrophe plus *s* ('s) is a typical indicator of a contraction, and as with *you're* above, contractions are not used in formal APA style. When you use *it's*, you mean "it is"; *its* is a possessive pronoun. Notice there is **no** apostrophe in the word *its*, used properly in the following example.

> **Example:** After the rat traversed the open-field exploration box, the experimenter returned the rat to **its** cage for 24-hr. rest.

There—Their—They're

First, you should recognize the pattern by now; you will not be using *they're* in APA–style writing, because it is a contraction meaning "they are." Use *there* as a reference to a place ("Put it over there"). *Their* is a plural possessive pronoun, so it needs to refer to more than one object or person and indicate possession.

> **Example 1:** After the debriefing was complete, **there** were no other tasks for the participants to perform, so the participants were dismissed.

> **Example 2:** In the driving simulator, I instructed participants to put **their** belongings someplace that would not cause any distractions during the driving tasks.

To—Too—Two

Although the difference between *to* and *two* is clear given the first is a preposition and the second is a number, quick typing can often make *to* a *too*. *To* can be used as a verb in its infinite form—"I want to run around the stadium"—or as a preposition "I handed the report to Provost Schwartz." *Too* is used to represent excess or "as well."

> **Example 1:** I asked **two** students **to** serve as confederates in my study.

> **Example 2:** Although most people procrastinate, some people go **too** far.

Loose—Lose

Lose is a verb meaning to misplace something, whereas *loose* can be an adjective, adverb, or verb depending on usage.

Example 1: If participants did not arrive to the experiment on time, they would **lose** the opportunity to participate.

Example 2: In the two-string problem, the knot was too **loose** to allow any other solution.

Example 3: The teachers let the children **loose** from the classroom for recess.

Affect—Effect

This distinction is a bit tricky, because psychology adds a different twist to the meanings of *affect* and *effect*. Typically, *affect* is used as a verb, such as to act on something; *effect* is used as a noun, such as the bystander effect. But in psychology, *affect* can also be used as a noun to describe an observable feeling or emotion. Although less common, *effect* can be used as a verb to mean accomplishing something or bringing about a result. So all the following are appropriate uses of the words *affect* and *effect*.

Example 1: Prior research **affected** our approach to forming our hypotheses. (*affect* as verb)

Example 2: The newly admitted patient to the hospital ward showed signs of blunt **affect**. (*affect* as noun)

Example 3: The **effect** of the new intervention was moderated by other intervening variables. (*effect* as noun)

Example 4: The researcher was interested in evaluating how each type of study strategy would **effect** a change in student performance. (*effect* as verb)

i.e.—e.g.

These are two Latin abbreviations that should be used only in a parenthetical phrase (in parentheses) in APA format and should always be followed by a comma. The Latin abbreviation *i.e.* stands for *id est*, meaning "that is." The Latin abbreviation *e.g.* stands for *exempli gratia*, meaning "for example" or "such as."

Example 1: The appropriate analyses were completed post hoc (**i.e.**, after the fact).

Example 2: Survey responses to the career-path question were coded based on eventual outcome (**e.g.**, bachelor's degree leading to a good job, bachelor's degree leading to a graduate school application).

Lay—Lie

Mentioned already in Chapter 3, *lay* is a verb that means "to place" or "put down," as in placing an object on the table. *Lie* can be used as a verb, as in "taking a horizontal position" or lying down, or *lie* can be used as a noun, as in "I told a lie."

> **Example 1:** After the students recorded their reaction times, we asked students to **lay** the stopwatches on their desks.

> **Example 2:** The key to lowering one's heart rate is to recline and **lie** still while practicing the indicated breathing exercises.

Then—Than

Then can be used as an adverb, adjective, or noun, which often applies to a description of time. *Than* can be used as a conjunction or preposition. Typically, *than* is used as part of a comparison.

> **Example 1:** After the experiment was completed, participants **then** were allowed to ask questions during the debriefing.

> **Example 2:** It took longer to complete Study 1 **than** to complete Study 2.

That—Which

Although the rules are actually more complicated than the summary provided here, typically, *that* is used to begin a restrictive clause; a restrictive clause introduces essential information. Also, in the typical sentence form, the word *that* is not preceded by a comma. *Which* is typically used to begin a nonrestrictive clause; a nonrestrictive clause introduces extra information. A comma precedes *which* in this instance (Gaertner-Johnston, 2006). Be careful to avoid using *that* as a filler word; will the sentence still make sense if the word *that* is removed?

> **Example 1:** A well-written literature review is one **that** summarizes and organizes the diverse research on a topic of interest.

> **Example 2:** Some students struggle with knowing what level of detail to write about in the Introduction section, **which** is to say that not all students struggle with this task.

Could of, Would of—Could have, Would have

According to Blue (2000), there is no such phrase as "could of" in English. What happens is that when we are speaking, many times we do not articulate well; so when we say "could have," it actually sounds like "could of." In fact, if you were to use the contraction form, "could've," it sounds very similar to "could of." However, the proper phrases are *could have, would have, must have,* and so on; our writing should reflect the proper usage.

> **Example 1:** I **could have** used a between-groups or within-groups design.

> **Example 2:** If I had known, I **would have** attended that conference last spring.

Avoid these 11 common errors, and you will show your audience that you are conscientious about your writing and that you pay attention to details. For more types of errors (with examples), see Tables 4.1 and 4.2. We have bolded the changes in the corrected sentences so you can find exactly what was changed. You may also want to pay attention to grammar checkers available in most word-processing programs. In Microsoft Word, grammatical errors show up underlined with little squiggly green lines (spelling errors have red squiggly lines). Right clicking on the underlined green words provides suggestions for change.

As you continue to practice your writing, these rules should eventually become second nature. Although it may be handy to know the name of the rule and what parts of speech are involved, we believe it is much more important to infuse these rules into your writing to avoid making the mistakes. You may not know that the first draft of a sentence you have just written in a research paper includes a dangling participle or a misplaced modifier, but we want you to practice enough so that you can "hear" or "see" the error and correct it while revising your draft. Writing is a "use it or lose it" skill. Practicing your writing with helpful feedback is essential if you want to be able to think and write clearly. Rest assured, to this day, we write and rewrite our papers. We go back and check our work before we pass it on. We try to get another set of eyes to proofread for grammatical errors (or we hire good editors). Very few folks naturally have the magical gift of grammatical writing.

4

Table 4.1 Common Writing Errors to Avoid

Type of Grammatical Error	Erroneous Sentence	Corrected Sentence
1. No comma after an introductory element	Well it was not really true.	Well**,** it was not really true.
2. Vague pronoun reference	John told his father that his car had been stolen.	John told his father that **his father's** car had been stolen.
3. No comma in compound sentence	I like to eat but I hate to gain weight.	I like to eat**,** but I hate to gain weight.
4. Wrong word	His F in math enhanced his alarm about his D in chemistry.	His F in math **amplified** his alarm about his D in chemistry.
5. Missing comma(s) with a nonrestrictive element	The students who had unsuccessfully concealed their participation in the prank were expelled.	The students**,** who had unsuccessfully concealed their participation in the prank**,** were expelled.

(Continued)

Table 4.1 (Continued)

Type of Grammatical Error	Erroneous Sentence	Corrected Sentence
6. Wrong or missing verb ending	I often use to go to town.	I often **used** to go to town.
7. Wrong or missing preposition	Cottonwood Grille is located at Boise.	Cottonwood Grille is located **in** Boise.
8. Comma splice	Chloe liked the cat, however, she was allergic to it.	Chloe liked the cat**;** however, she was allergic to it.
9. Missing or misplaced possessive apostrophe	Student's backpacks weigh far too much.	Student**s'** backpacks weigh far too much.
10. Unnecessary shift in tense	I was happily watching TV when suddenly my sister attacks me.	I was happily watching TV when suddenly my sister **attacked** me.
11. Unnecessary shift in pronoun	When one is tired, you should sleep.	When **you** are tired, you should sleep.
12. Sentence fragment (second part)	He went shopping in the local sports store. An outing he usually enjoyed.	He went shopping in the local sports store**,** **an** outing he usually enjoyed.
13. Wrong tense or verb form	I would not have said that if I thought it would have shocked her.	I would not have said that if I thought it **would shock** her.
14. Lack of subject–verb agreement	Having many close friends, especially if you have known them for a long time, are a great help in times of trouble.	Having many close friends, especially if you have known them for a long time, **is** a great help in times of trouble.
15. Missing comma in a series	Students eat, sleep and do homework.	Students eat, sleep**,** and do homework.
16. Lack of agreement between pronoun and antecedent	When someone plagiarizes from material on a website, they are likely to be caught.	When **you** plagiarize from material on a website, **you** are likely to be caught.

Type of Grammatical Error	Erroneous Sentence	Corrected Sentence
17. Unnecessary comma(s) with a restrictive element	The novel, that my teacher assigned, was very boring.	The novel that my teacher assigned was very boring.
18. Run-on or fused sentence	He loved the seminar he even loved the readings.	He loved the seminar; he even loved the readings.
19. Dangling or misplaced modifier	After being put to sleep, a small incision is made below the navel by the surgeon.	The surgeon made a small incision below the navel **after the patient was anesthetized.**
20. Its/it's confusion	Its a splendid day for everyone.	**It's** a splendid day for everyone.

Note: The examples in the table are adapted from Gottschalk and Hjortshoj (2004) and Landrum (2012).

Table 4.2 Common Grammatical Mistakes		
Type of Grammatical Error	Erroneous Sentence	Corrected Sentence
1. *Your—You're*	Your taking the wrong turn.	**You're** taking the wrong turn.
2. *It's—Its*	Its always 5 o'clock somewhere in the world.	**It's** always 5 o'clock somewhere in the world.
3. *There—Their— They're*	Their are many great sights to see in New Zealand.	**There** are many great sights to see in New Zealand.
4. *To—Too—Two*	Gizmo worked to hard too build to snowmen and needed a nap.	Gizmo worked **too** hard **to** build **two** snowmen and needed a nap.
5. *Loose—Lose*	I do not want to loose all my hard work so I backup my computer often.	I do not want to **lose** all my hard work so I backup my computer often.

(Continued)

Table 4.2 (Continued)

Type of Grammatical Error	Erroneous Sentence	Corrected Sentence
6. *Affect—Effect*	My life experiences effected my view of school.	My life experiences **affected** my view of school.
	The affect of caffeine is debatable.	The **effect** of caffeine is debatable.
	She was very sad but showed no signs of effect.	She was very sad but showed no signs of **affect**.
7. *i.e.—e.g.*	We used four flavors in our study (i.e., grape).	We used four flavors in our study (**e.g.**, grape).
8. *Lay—Lie*	After a hard day in the field, I just want to lay down and take a nap.	After a hard day in the field, I just want to **lie** down and take a nap.
9. *Then—Than*	I wake up, eat breakfast, and only than check my e-mail.	I wake up, eat breakfast, and only **then** check my e-mail.
10. *That—Which*	A great student paper is one which follows all the instructions well.	A great student paper is one **that** follows all the instructions well.
11. *Could of, Would of— Could have, Would have*	I could of worked in the business world and earned a lot more money than working in academia.	I **could have** worked in the business world and earned a lot more money than working in academia.

Plagiarism and How to Avoid It 5

Thou Shalt Not Steal
(or Be Lazy)

S omeone once said every good idea worth thinking has already been thought. Or at least it went something like that. If there is even a hint of truth to this statement, it is clear that whenever we write a paper, we are probably writing something that someone has said or thought about before. Now, if we just left it at that and moved on—note that there is no citation in the first sentence of this paragraph—it would be plagiarism. If we were not trying to make a point, we would have ended the first sentence with a citation in parentheses (e.g., Lorde, 1984). More on this paraphrase in a moment. When assigned to explicitly review research on a certain topic or when writing the introduction to a research paper, a large part of which is a literature review, you have to refer to other published work. If you use someone's ideas, you have to give them credit. If you do not, you are plagiarizing their work and committing intellectual theft. Plagiarizing is wrong, unethical, and just not a good idea. Worse, plagiarism can result in a failing grade or sometimes even more severe consequences, such as expulsion from school or termination from a job.

But I Didn't Know . . .

First, the tough love: Not knowing how to cite your information correctly, or that you were supposed to, is not an acceptable excuse. It is the same thing as telling a police officer you did not know the speed limit was only 55 mph. Ignorance does not work in that case, and it will not work when it comes to not appropriately citing the information you use in your papers. If you use information or data from someone else's work, you have to cite it (or else it is stealing). Not being able to locate the source of your information and so not citing it is not an acceptable excuse for not citing your source either (it is being lazy). Unfortunately, with most documents available in digital format and in turn the ability to copy and paste from those documents, the effortlessness to plagiarize (either intentionally or unintentionally) is even more likely than in the days of typewriters when we actually had to type every word manually and even retype entire papers if an error was found even on a single page (ask your parents or grandparents about using Wite-Out and the erase cartridge on a typewriter!).

Not knowing that someone else had the same idea or thought is somewhat more understandable. Sometimes we read something and forget we did. Then we remember the gist of what we once read but forget we read it somewhere, thinking instead that it is our own wonderful idea. If you ever feel as though you are using information from somewhere else, take the trouble to find it. It may not be too difficult. In fact, the source of the statement paraphrased in the first sentence of this section eluded us until a Google search (0.13 secs), and a little digging (0.45 secs) led us to conclude that Audre Lorde is the source. Lorde (1984) said, "There are no new ideas. There are only new ways of making them felt" (p. 39). The Bible provides a similar sentiment: "What has been will be again, what has been done will be done again; there is nothing new under the sun" (Ecclesiastes 1:9, New International Version). (Can you paraphrase this biblical saying to avoid using a direct quotation? The answer in a few pages . . .) What is the long and short of the story? Make sure you cite your sources. In this chapter, we spell out some of the key ways to avoid being a plagiarizer.

It Sounds Like a Bad Word

Plagiarism is despicable. Although what we said in the opening paragraph seems simple, this is exactly what plagiarism is: using someone else's ideas without giving them credit. Many students do not realize how dishonest this act really is. At some institutions, issues of academic dishonesty are clearly presented in honor system policies or in some cases in honor codes. We strongly recommend that you become aware of your institution's academic honor policies. However, although most colleges and universities have institutional statements indicating that cheating is not tolerated, many institutions do not have detailed honor codes that state what constitutes academic dishonesty (e.g., clear definitions of plagiarism), nor do they have honor systems that provide an infrastructure of rules on how to handle violations of the honor code. As a result, students are not aware of the complexities surrounding academic integrity and how it applies to their own work or for particular class assignments (Schwartz, Tatum, & Hageman, 2013). Even more disturbing, many students know it is wrong and still try to pull it off. Yes, we know the draw of writing an A paper is appealing, and using someone else's A paper may seem like an easy way to get an A on your paper, but it is really no laughing matter. Remember, it is also getting exceedingly easy for faculty to track down plagiarism. Sometimes we notice suspicious-looking sentences—say, sentences that seem overly technical or different from the bulk of a student paper—and just put the sentence into a search engine (either a specialized search engine, such as turnitin.com, or even plain ol' Google). This simple move has resulted in the location (often within the first few search results) of online sources of the sentences that have not been cited properly—or at all. Many universities subscribe to web services that will check whether papers have been plagiarized. So again, it may be easy to plagiarize, but it is also getting easier to identify who plagiarized. Faculty who use the Desire2Learn course-management system can even get a report on each paper stating what percentage of the paper may be plagiarized.

Make sure you do not forget to cite the sources of the information you use in your papers. In fact, avoiding plagiarizing is pretty simple. Cite your sources, use direct quotations if need be, and even better, paraphrase (and cite). Each of these methods is somewhat easy to master, as you shall soon see. The best way to avoid this problem is to write down the source information but to put aside the actual source when you are writing your paper. That way, you have to write in your own words. Putting away the original book or article will help you avoid the mistake of writing something directly from the source and forgetting to include the citation. It will also help you avoid the common problem of just reorganizing the same words or deleting a few words and assuming that the thoughts are now yours and no longer those of the original author.

Quoting: More Than Just a Copy and Paste

It is tempting to play it completely safe and directly quote—that is, copy verbatim (exactly what is written in the original source). You then cite the source in the text (see guides for this in Chapter 8), using the correct punctuation, and you are home free. Or so it seems. First, let us look at how you would do this seemingly simple task in APA format, and then we will talk a little more about why you should limit your use of quotations.

When you are quoting, you need to have handy the author, year, and page number or numbers to make up the in-text citations. If your source is a website, you will need the paragraph number. Now comes the fine-tuning. Short quotations (up to 40 words) can be cordoned off with double quotation marks (" ") and appear within the text. Here's an example:

> Some psychologists have used colorful phrases to describe how the mind works, such as its being "as one great blooming, buzzing confusion" (James, 1890/1950, p. 462).

Note that the second set of double quotation marks is followed by the standard in-text citation (author, year) but also includes the page number. Also notice in the example that there is not a period at the end of the quoted phrase.

The period comes *after* the citation is completed. If the quotation comes from a single page, use a single p followed by a period and a space before the page number (e.g., p. 462); if the quotation spans two pages, use a double p followed by a period, a space, and the range of pages (e.g., pp. 144–145). The quotation marks are important, as they make it clear that you have used someone else's words. We sometimes see students copy and paste a sentence from a journal article, cite the author and year at the end (without quotations), and believe they now have an academic paper because they have a citation. That is not enough. If you take exact words, use quotation marks. For online sources without page numbers, use the abbreviation "para." for *paragraph* instead of "p." for *page*, or you can use the paragraph symbol (¶). You will need to count down to the paragraph on the website you took the quotation from and use that to indicate where the original text can be found (e.g., para. 7). Sometimes the quotation may be within the sentence and not at the end, as shown in the preceding example. In that case, the sentence will look like this:

> William James (1890/1950) provides us with colorful phrases to describe how the mind works, such as its being "as one great blooming, buzzing confusion" (p. 462), and wrote at length about how consciousness may work.

As you can see, there is no real way to paraphrase "blooming, buzzing confusion" without losing the essence of what James said. Keeping some of the author's distinctive voice is one of the most important reasons to quote and not paraphrase—but again, keep it short. If you really need to directly quote more than 40 words (not something you should aim to do), you do not need the double quotation marks. Instead, you give the quotation its own place of honor in your paper by starting it on a new line and indenting the block of text of the quotation by half an inch from both the left margin and the right margin (i.e., an additional half an inch from the APA style required one-inch margin), however, the first line is not indented (APA, 2010a). Your citation now comes at the end of the block. This time, the parentheses in which the text is cited follow the period at the end of the block quotation. There is no additional period after the parentheses, and the entire quotation is double-spaced (like the rest of your paper). It looks like this:

> It is difficult to examine how students study. Some of the problems inherent in such research are demonstrated by the results of a recent study on the topic.

> Studying with a friend was negatively correlated to exam scores in our study. Perhaps students need to be trained in the best way to study with a friend. Instructors can model how students should make up examples with the material and quiz each other. For some students "studying with a friend" may mean sitting on a couch reading notes and chatting with the

television on. Whereas you can control and monitor what a student is doing in a laboratory experiment on studying, a simple questionnaire measure may not accurately tap into what students do as they study in college. (Gurung, Weidert, & Jeske, 2010, p. 33)

This is a good time for an example. Instead of the whole paragraph, how would you paraphrase the quotation? The answer is at the end of the next section in this chapter on paraphrasing.

One of the reasons we caution against the use of long quotations is that for publications (journal articles or books), one often needs written permission from the author of the source material or, more accurately, from the owner of the copyright for the work. Obtaining permission can be expensive and time-consuming. Now, to be fair, the long arm of copyright law is probably not going to track down a student paper and fine you for not paying for the quotation or asking permission, but the time and expense involved in obtaining permission are still good reasons not to use long quotations. Another reason is that you do not want your paper to be a string of someone else's words. Including someone else's words within your text usually creates a choppy flow to your writing, because your style of writing is usually different from those of the other authors you quote. Sometimes students think that if they string together a sequence of direct quotations, writing the paper is simplified because less of the paper actually needs to be written. Avoid this strategy; stringing together a bunch of direct quotations with in-text citations is not scholarly writing, in our collective opinion.

There are some instances when a direct word-for-word quotation is critical. When you are using a previously published scale or questionnaire, you should use the exact wording of the original. Especially colorful or well-worded sentences or ideas are also often better directly quoted. One of the founders of American psychology, William James, was a particularly colorful writer. His pre-20th-century English and word choices make for fun reading (and the psychology is pretty good, too), as shown in the earlier example. Sometimes an idea may be exceedingly complex or composed of unique or newly generated terms or phrases, which is another good reason to quote directly. In all cases, be sure you have a clear understanding of the quotation so that it fits well within the surrounding paragraph. These exceptions notwithstanding, it is preferable to convey the gist of the idea or thoughts by paraphrasing.

Paraphrasing: In Your Own Words

When you paraphrase, you are essentially discussing someone else's ideas or results in your own words. You still have to cite your source, but given you are not copying (right?) the other material word for word, you do not need to use double quotation marks around the paraphrased material. You do not *need* to cite the page or paragraph number (in text) either, *but* it is a good idea to do so

(APA, 2010a). One of our friends provided a useful tip on how to paraphrase. Our friend (remembering what a teacher told him) said that paraphrasing is something like reading a journal article, thinking about it, and then turning to your neighbor and describing in your own words the main gist of what you read (W. Fulton, personal communication, June 24, 1995). Yes, we paraphrased that.

As we mentioned earlier, the easiest way to paraphrase and avoid using the original author's words is to close the book (or the webpage) and not have the original source in front of you when you are attempting to get across the main points. But keep this in mind: This technique will also help you determine if you really understand the gist. If you have trouble putting it in your own words, you might need to reread the original source for a better understanding. Dunn (2011) suggested drafting a summary of the material you want to use by thinking about the main idea in the material, determining if there is a position taken, assertion made, or hypothesis stated (p. 46). If you have thought hard about the material you want to use and drafted a summary of it, you are less likely to commit plagiarism. Another easy way to paraphrase includes using catchphrases that refer to the original author. Let us say you want to write about material from an article by Jesuphat (2013). You could say, "According to Jesuphat (2013)," "Jesuphat (2013) states," or "Jesuphat (2013) argues," "declares," "finds," or "demonstrates."

Speaking of paraphrasing, our paraphrase of the block quote in the previous section is as follows:

> Gurung, Weidert, and Jeske (2010) reported that students who studied with a friend did worse on exams and suggested training students on how best to study with others, as this advice could mean different things to different students. The authors suggested the negative correlation between studying with a friend and exam scores could be because the survey question in the lab did not tap into the richness of real student study behavior. The authors also suggested that instructors should demonstrate effective studying with others by making up examples of course content and questions that students can ask each other.

Our paraphrase of the biblical saying that started this chapter goes like this: There is nothing new, as everything that is done has been done before and what exists now will exist again (Ecclesiastes 1:9, New International Version).

That's Really Sic [and Not a Typo]

Sometimes you may want or need to directly quote someone or some text that contains misspellings, poor grammar, or poor punctuation. How do you do it without making it look as though you could not copy correctly or perhaps made a mistake? Easy. Latin to the rescue! You insert the word *sic* in italics and brackets (e.g., [*sic*]) right in the quotation where the troublesome language resides. *Sic* means "thus" or "so" and implies the word was "intentionally so written" ("Sic," 2003, p. 1156). The brackets show that the word is not part of the quotation.

An Author's License (Yours): Modifying Source Material

For the most part, when you paraphrase, you are modifying the words used in the original material, but you are not modifying the actual message, idea, or finding. But there are times when you use a direct quotation and want to make minor changes to what you are using. For example, sometimes you may not want to use an entire sentence. Some authors can write very long sentences, and the key element may be in the first part. This is where you can use three spaced periods (. . .), called ellipsis points. Interestingly, if the omitted information is at the end of the sentence, then you place the ellipses after the period before continuing with the rest of the quotation. If the omitted information comes at the end of the quotation, there's no need for ellipses. Likewise, if the omitted information comes before the text you want to quote, there's no need for ellipses.

There is one other modification to consider, although you should probably not use it too often. It looks like a handy tool, and it is—but it can also be easily overused. If you want to stress a word or phrase in a quotation, italicize the word or phrase and then follow it with the phrase "emphasis added," placed in brackets.

> Intuitively useful study strategies may not be as useful as they may seem. Gurung, Weidert, and Jeske (2010) found that "some often recommended strategies turned out to correlate *negatively* [emphasis added] with exam scores" (p. 32).

If the emphasized word or phrase was like that in the original source (e.g., a word was originally italicized), you might add the phrase "emphasis in original" just as we did with "emphasis added" in the example above, using brackets.

But I Can Freely Use My Own Work, Right?

So you have written a great paper on the history of the Roman Empire for one class. Now you need to write a shorter paper on how Roman society went into decline. You already tackled this topic in your big Roman society paper. Should you just cut the relevant section of your big paper and turn it in as your short paper? Believe it or not, there is something known as *self-plagiarism*. Self-plagiarism explicitly refers to work that has already been published. "The new document must constitute an original contribution to knowledge, and only the amount of previously published material necessary to understand that contribution should be included" (APA, 2010a, p. 16). In other words, do not present your own previous work as if it is brand new. Does this apply to you presenting what you wrote for one class to an instructor of another class? Honestly, this is a judgment call for you to make. The best solution is to check with your instructor to see if your modification of another paper would be acceptable. Often, if your institution has an honor system, you will know or can easily find out whether using a paper for two classes is acceptable or not.

How About This for a
Plagiarism Awareness Exercise?

As we write this guide about APA style, we are of course providing the details of the information from the APA *PM* by covering the many rules of writing in APA style without plagiarizing. This in itself is an exercise in using appropriate citations and paraphrasing. Want models of how to avoid plagiarism? You can map chapters of our book against the corresponding material in the APA *PM* (APA, 2010a). Just for the (somewhat geeky) fun of it, place this *EasyGuide* and the *PM* side by side and open up to a similar topic. Given that we have paid exquisite attention to ensuring our material is adequately cited while giving you the most accurate information about APA style and format, you are in the good position of being able to see a book-length example about how one (or three, in our case) can write explicitly about source material without committing the sin of plagiarism. You will find lots of good examples of paraphrasing, too. Enjoy.

5

Avoiding Biased Language 6

Psychologists are interested in the behavior of individuals, either as a means of forming generalizations about human behavior or for the sake of understanding the unique behavior of one person. This focus on the individual, regardless of the research approach taken, necessitates both common sense and sensibility to the uniqueness of individuals. When we are not careful, we take mental shortcuts that allow us to describe a group of individuals quickly, but that description could be far from accurate (which can lead to prejudice, discrimination, and stereotyping). APA guidelines are clear about the preference for accuracy in description, even if sentence structures become more complicated and an economy of words is lost (APA, 2010a). When describing humans involved in psychological research, it is better to be accurate and complete than to be overly concise or vague. Taking mental shortcuts with our descriptions of research participants can lead to biased language and misunderstandings about both the participants and the intent of the research.

The Fundamental Lesson:
View People as Individuals First

One of the basic lessons that physicians learn in medical school is, "First, do no harm." With regard to the potential for biased language when describing human participants in psychology, the fundamental lesson is, "View people as individuals first." That is, individuals are much more than the labels attached by others. With a nod to Gestalt psychology, people are more than the sum of their labels. Avoiding labels applies to all participants in research, not just to participants from a clinical setting. So the preference would be to refer to someone as "a person with schizophrenia" rather than "a schizophrenic" (literally, putting the *person first* in the phrase). Rather than describing the correlation between GPA and high–self-esteem students, it would be better to present the correlation between GPA and students who report high self-esteem levels. Ulrich (2005) shared the example that it is preferable to describe "people with diabetes" rather than "diabetics." Diabetics have a universe of characteristics much more complex than the singular description of diabetes. Not all diabetics share the same characteristics at one time over the course of the disorder; therefore, it is actually more accurate to use "people with diabetes," because that connotes different individuals who happen to share one characteristic—in some cases, their only common characteristic.

Specific Recommendations for Reducing Bias: Nonsexist Language and Other Areas

6

It is important to provide concrete examples of possible bias, because we may not even be aware of this bias during our writing. There are typically no "absolutes," but we do make specific suggestions about what to avoid ("biased") and the preferred approach ("unbiased"). Of course, *preferred* could be seen in the eye of the beholder, but we base these recommendations not only on our teaching experience but also on various sources (APA, 2010a, 2010b; Driscoll, 2009b; Kessler & McDonald, 2008). Because gender bias in writing remains a difficult problem to solve, we address this topic separately at the close of this chapter.

Sexual Orientation

Perhaps there is no other characteristic so essential to each of us yet at times so complicated to describe as our sexual orientation (an indicator of the gender we are attracted to). Note, this is different from one's "gender identity," a person's subjective sense of his or her gender. Writing in APA style necessitates accuracy and precision but, at the same time, sensitivity to individual difference and honoring the preferences for the naming of groups of individuals who may be dramatically different yet share similar sexual-orientation characteristics. Specificity is preferred. For instance, the broad term *homosexual* is too vague; even the singular term *gay* is not precise enough. The preferred terminology is *lesbian, gay man, bisexual man,* and *bisexual woman* (APA, 2010a). This level of precision helps prevent misunderstandings about the precise nature of the individuals in a study.

It is also important not to mix descriptions of sexual orientation with presumptions about sexual behavior. Once again, specificity is key. In a Results section, for example, rather than writing, "Forty-two percent of gays reported at least one instance of homosexual fantasies," it would be better to add more precision to the description: "Forty-two percent of gay men reported at least one instance of male–male sexual fantasies." The first sentence is much too vague to convey the accurate information needed in a Results section. Descriptions of sexual behavior should be precise as well. So instead of asking the survey question, "At what age did you first have sexual intercourse?" it would be better to reword that question as (a) "At what age did you first have penile–vaginal intercourse?" or (b) "At what age did you first have sexual intercourse or sex with another person?" Although the sentence structure is more complex, the information gleaned from the survey responses should be better, because participants will understand precisely what you mean (with the benefits of avoiding bias and improving clarity).

Racial and Ethnic Identity

As a general rule, the more precise you can be in describing the participants of your research, the better; this added precision comes with an important bonus— a reduced likelihood of using terms with racial or ethnic bias. First, let us address the difference between those two terms—*race* versus *ethnicity*. Of course people's definitions of these topics can differ, but here goes ours. Ethnicity tends to refer to groups of people who self-identify with one another, typically on the basis of common ancestry. Examples of ethnic groups in America include American Indians, African Americans, Latinos, and Chinese; you might also include Irish Americans and German Americans here. Race tends to refer to a biological variety of species with similar anatomical traits; the term may also be used by some external entity to divide or categorize people based on certain physical characteristics (O'Neil, 2006).

For example, the U.S. Census Bureau asks separate questions about race and ethnicity. When asking about race, the Census Bureau uses the following categories:

- White
- Black or African American
- American Indian or Alaska Native
- Asian
- Native Hawaiian and Other Pacific Islander

In the census format, a person can also select more than one of these categories, and there are write-in areas as well. Note the capitalization of "White" and "Black." Ethnicity is captured by just two categories in census questions:

- Hispanic or Latino
- Not Hispanic or Latino

In this case, the idea underlying this sequence of questions about race and ethnicity is that a person of Hispanic or Latino heritage can be of any race; that is, race and ethnicity are treated as different concepts (U.S. Census Bureau, 2008).

These ideas are important for our communication of race and ethnic data when writing in APA style, but our preference is to be even more precise than Census Bureau categories when possible. So when referring to American Indians, naming specific tribes involved would be preferable, or using the First Nations designation in some situations. Avoid using the term *minority*, because without additional context, it is difficult to determine the minority of what. Similarly, rather than a White versus non-White distinction, specify the individual subgroups that compose the non-White participants in a study (African Americans, American Indians, or Alaska Natives). In some cases, the label "European American" may be preferable to "White." Even when using proper terminology, such as *Hispanic* or *Latino*, if you have more detailed information about the nations or regions of the participants, be more specific—Cuban, Guatemalan, Salvadoran, and so on (APA, 2010a). In fact, you can be more specific than *Mexican American*. For example, Mexican Americans in Texas often prefer the term *Tejano*.

6

Disabilities

Following the advice of this chapter's opening mantra—put people first—will serve you well when discussing individuals with disabilities (notice the wording in this sentence: "individuals with disabilities," not "disabled people"). The disability a person possesses does not completely define that person; it is but one aspect of someone's situation or behavior (i.e., a person's physical health or mental health). So rather than discuss an ADHD child, it would be better to discuss a child with ADHD or a child who exhibits ADHD symptoms. It is preferable to be more precise in describing the potential disabilities rather than applying a large categorical label that masks the complexities and individual differences of the persons with a particular disorder or condition. Rather than saying, "Schizophrenics were divided into the treatment and control groups," it would be better to describe the individuals with schizophrenia in greater detail: "those individuals with paranoid schizophrenic symptoms" or "those individuals with catatonic schizophrenic symptoms," and so on.

One last note about writing about disabilities: Avoid emotionally charged words or words that are inaccurate in describing the totality of a person. So avoid using words such as *crippled, handicapped, retarded, physically challenged*, and *stroke victim*; these descriptors are often inaccurate and offensive to people with a particular disability. In fact, "differently abled" is sometimes preferred to "disabled." Being sensitive to these perceptions will help you avoid using biased language in your writing.

Occupations

Related to issues of gender bias, a number of occupations over time used the embedded *man* as part of the description of the career or occupation. In Table

6.1, we present a listing of original or biased terms and then substitute unbiased terms for use. In some cases, you will have to rewrite the structure of the sentence to make the sentence grammatically correct. This is a small price to pay to avoid gender bias as it relates to occupations.

Table 6.1 Biased Versus Unbiased Occupational Titles	
Biased Occupational Title	Unbiased Occupational Title
Businessman, businesswoman	Businessperson, business executive, entrepreneur
Chairman	Chair, chairperson, head, presiding officer
Congressman	Senator, Representative
Fireman	Firefighter
Foreman	Supervisor
Mailman	Mail carrier
Male nurse	Nurse
Newsman	Reporter
Policeman, policewoman	Police officer
Salesman	Sales clerk, sales representative
Spokesman	Representative, leader, spokesperson
Steward, stewardess	Flight attendant
Woman doctor	Doctor

6

Gender and Pronouns:
With an Indefinite Recommendation

The generic *he* is well embedded in our writing (Kessler & McDonald, 2008), and when writing scientifically with precision, we must work to avoid this assumption. This is no easy task, because the presumption is pervasive in our culture. In addition to the occupational examples in Table 6.1, see Table 6.2 for more examples of the lack of inclusivity we often exhibit in our writing (Driscoll, 2009b; Kessler & McDonald, 2008).

APA style strongly recommends that you avoid the use of *he* or *she* whenever possible. Avoiding such gendered pronouns helps minimize

Table 6.2 Gender References: Less Versus More Inclusive Terms

Less Inclusive	More Inclusive
Man, men	Person, people
Mankind	People, humanity, human beings
Founding fathers	Founders, forebears
Gentlemen's agreement	Informal agreement
Manpower	Workforce
Man (as a verb, *to man*)	Staff, operate
Man's achievements	Human achievements
Manmade	Synthetic, manufactured, machine-made
Common man	Average person, ordinary person
Man-hours	Staff hours

confusion on the reader's part. However, this does not mean that the awkward phrase "he/she" should be substituted. A better alternative is to rewrite the sentence so that the gendered pronoun is avoided altogether. Wagner and colleagues (2009) made some specific recommendations on how to do that and conform to APA style. See the following examples for suggestions to avoid biased language:

- Rephrase the sentence to avoid the necessity of using *he* or *she*.

  Biased: After the study, he determined that the main effect of age was statistically significant.

  Unbiased: The author found age to be statistically significant at the conclusion of the study.

- Use a plural noun or plural pronoun, meaning that you can then use *they* or *their*—but try to do this sparingly.

  Biased: Men and women were tested individually; either he or she flipped a coin to see who would go first.

  Unbiased: Men and women were tested individually; they flipped a coin to see who would go first.

- When possible, replace the pronoun with an article; instead of *her* or *him*, use *the*.

  Biased: The confederate then asked her research participant to complete the survey.

  Unbiased: The confederate then asked the research participant to complete the survey.

- Drop the pronoun and see if the sentence still makes sense; often, it will.

  Biased: The experimenter checked to see if his class points were recorded.

  Unbiased: The experimenter checked to see if class points were recorded.

- Replace the pronoun with a noun such as *person, individual, researcher,* or *participant*.

  Biased: We wanted to determine if his or her prior experiences influenced current attitudes.

  Unbiased: We wanted to determine if the person's prior experiences influenced current attitudes.

One other method of avoiding gender bias in your scientific writing is to use indefinite pronouns rather than gendered pronouns (Driscoll, 2009a). Use indefinite pronouns such as *everybody, everyone, anybody,* and *anyone* to avoid gender bias. However, strive to avoid overuse of the indefinite pronoun *one*. Check out the following examples.

  Biased: When signing up for the experiment, each participant needs to use his or her student identification number.

  Unbiased: When signing up for the experiment, each participant needs to use one's student identification number.

Or just rewrite the sentence to avoid the gender reference altogether.

  Biased: When signing up for the experiment, each participant needs to use his or her student identification number.

  Unbiased: Student identification numbers are necessary to sign up for the experiment.

As it turns out, even with all the available resources to help us avoid gender bias, we still tend to be sexist in our writing. A study published in the *British*

Journal of Social Psychology (Hegarty, Watson, Fletcher, & McQueen, 2010) reported research illustrating that some of the 16th-century naming conventions still strongly exist today. For example, we say "Mr. and Mrs." and not the reverse, and "his and hers towels" but typically not "hers and his towels." If you really think about it, why should the "Mr." be said (and written) first; why not list "Mrs." first? When we think about the names of couples who are heterosexual (especially individuals we do not know), the researchers reported that we tend to say the man's name before the woman's—David and Sarah, Brad and Angelina, Romeo and Juliet. The one exception that the researchers noted was when we know the couple and know one person better than the other. So if you are sending a holiday card to your sister and her husband, you are more likely to address it to your sister first (Janet and Dan) rather than the reverse. So you see, we still need to be vigilant about possible occurrences of gender bias.

With attention to detail, with practice, and by following the advice provided in this chapter, you can improve the accuracy and precision of your scientific writing as well as avoid bias and be respectful of the individual differences (on so many different levels—gender, sexual orientation, race, ethnicity, disabilities, occupation) that make humans unique and fascinating to study.

6

SECTION III

Writing With (APA) Style

Getting Down to Business

Writing Your Introduction 7

Tying the Story All Together

When reading any journal article, we want to understand what led the authors to propose a particular hypothesis. What led to that prediction? How does that hypothesis connect to past research findings? What is the untold story that needs to be satisfied by the study in question? In an APA–style paper, answers to those questions can be found in the introduction section, the first major section of this type of research paper (technically, the Introduction section is preceded by the title page and the abstract page). In your Introduction, we want to be sure you capture the reader's attention and then provide a clear review of the literature that logically supports your hypothesis. You state what you did, why you did it, and why it matters. In this chapter, we explain what to include in your Introduction, how to format this section, how to get started writing, and how to organize your Introduction. We close the chapter with a checklist of common errors to avoid!

What to Include in Your Introduction

When asked to write a formal research paper in any of your psychology courses, your paper will start with an introductory section. But what exactly is included in this first part of your paper? The easiest way we find to explain this section to our students is by starting with a set of questions that you could ask yourself and answer when writing your Introduction. Someone reading your paper should be able to answer all, if not most of these questions, after reading this section of your paper. These questions include:

- What is the topic of my research?
- What is the purpose of my research?
- Why is this research important?
- What question(s) will my research answer?
- What theoretical implications does my research address?
- What gap in the literature is my study filling?
- How am I defining the variables discussed?
- How does my research connect to related studies already published?
- What does the past research conclude or predict in relation to my research?
- How will the study proceed (provide a brief preview of what happens next)?
- What hypothesis am I testing?
- What is the rationale for my hypothesis given past research findings?

7

Formatting Your Introduction Section

Now that you know what information to include in the Introduction, here are the APA rules for formatting this section. You start the Introduction on a new page following the title page or abstract, depending upon the stage of your research. Though in some journals you see the heading "introduction" used, as you see in our sample papers included in Chapter 2 and Chapter 21, the title of your paper is centered and serves as the heading for this section of your paper. According to APA style, you do not write the word "Introduction" above this section of your paper. This error is made by many of our own students. And, we understand why that error occurs. All other sections of the paper use the name of the section as headings (e.g., Method). But just remember, the Introduction is different. Here the heading is the title of your paper. As stated in other chapters of this book, remember to stick to the notion "when in doubt, double-space throughout." This is true for your Introduction as well. No additional spacing is needed between your title and the first paragraph in this section of your paper. Just stick to the double-spacing rule. Also remember to use past tense when writing about past research findings. Only when you are writing a research proposal, before the data are collected, before you have run your experiment, do you write about your own research in future tense and discuss what you "will" do when introducing your experiment at the end of your Introduction section. So when writing the Introduction before the study is conducted you would write, "In this study, participants will complete a questionnaire that . . ." That's the future tense. But after the study is completed, when revising your Introduction, the tense should change to past tense because the study already happened ("In this study, participants completed a questionnaire that . . .".). Remember for completed research, both your own and any you are citing, stick to past tense.

To summarize, we have listed the formatting rules for the Introduction section below:

- Start the Introduction section on a new page after your Abstract.
- Use the title of your research for the Introduction heading.
- The title of your paper is centered but NOT boldfaced.
- Double-space the entire Introduction section.
- Write the Introduction section using future tense before collecting data and past tense for completed research.

Getting Your Introduction Started

Essentially, in the introductory section of your research proposal or final research paper, you need to set the stage for your research idea. We often tell our students that when starting this type of paper, you should make sure you explain not only what topic you are studying but also why your topic of choice is an interesting one; that is, make the case that your idea is so important that it is worthy of additional research efforts. Why should the reader want to continue reading your paper or be interested in the results of your research? Perhaps it impacts a large number of people, or it is an essential component of daily life. For example, if you are conducting a study to examine the influence of suggestive questioning on young children's accuracy about a witnessed event, you could start the introduction by explaining the involvement of young children in the legal system and the importance of developing interview techniques that can lead to the most accurate reports. Or, if you decide to test the influence of academic honor systems on academic dishonesty, you could start your introduction by citing the statistics of the number of cases of cheating in education and, in turn, the importance of understanding what policies can be put in place to increase academic integrity. Capture the reader's attention. Write the start of your introduction so that they want to read on! One way to hook the reader is to include sentences that would pique the reader's interest. For example, "Can children accurately report an event from their past? Can they do so even when leading questions are asked?" Or, "Have you witnessed cheating on your campus or in your classrooms? Are there policies or strategies that could reduce the amount of cheating?"

Once you have described your incredibly interesting research topic, it is time to review the literature. We find that this can be the most challenging part of an APA–style paper for many students. You need to know what past studies you should include and, importantly, how to organize that past research into a coherent review of the literature that naturally leads to your own research. Other books on the research process provide details on how to go about finding the relevant research (e.g., Harris, 2011; Pyrczak, 2008). When starting the search process, many students often ask "how many articles should we include?" The answer to that question often requires you to figure out the number of articles needed to provide a strong foundation for your project but not so many that you are overwhelmed by the number of sources. An Introduction should be complete and include the most relevant articles on your topic. For example, you would never write a research proposal about obedience and not mention Milgram's study. That said, you need to be sure you include not only the classic studies on the topic but also the most up-to-date articles from the literature. Including only research from 1965 will not do. In contrast, some students only look for recent articles (e.g., published after 2000 or 2010). Recent does not always mean best. Some very relevant work may have been published many years ago. Of course you cannot include every article on the topic of obedience. We are certain there are thousands on "obedience" alone (2,049 when searching "obedience" in APA's PsychNet in May, 2015). Your task is to include any study that is considered a "classic" on the topic and then those additional sources that help to provide evidence for the hypothesis you are interested in testing.

7

As we discuss in a number of other chapters in this book, be sure you include primary sources and not secondary sources. Again, this means that you should include only those articles that you have read yourself and not any additional studies cited in the articles you actually read. Those cited articles from articles you read are considered secondary sources because you did not read the original article. Most faculty will tell you to avoid secondary sources simply because you are including an article in your literature review that is based on the interpretation of another researcher and not on your own reading.

Back to the question of how many articles—we do not have a number to share with you. As is true for a number of writing questions raised throughout this book, we recommend you check with the faculty member teaching the class to address the question of how many articles to include. He or she could have a particular number required, and he or she is a great resource to discuss the plan you have for your Introduction. Our focus here is not to tell you how many articles to include but to explain how to organize and write about that past research. We often use an hourglass analogy when describing the "shape" of a research paper—this is a classic analogy from Bem (1987). Think of the overall paper as an hourglass, with a shape that is large at the top and bottom and narrow in the middle (where the sand slips from one side to the other). The wider top is where you introduce the overarching topic. Then in your Introduction you review past research that narrows down the question at hand, eventually leading to the narrow section of the hourglass where you present your hypothesis. So it goes from general to specific. The bottom half of the hourglass represents starting with your methodology and results and eventually interpreting your findings and connecting your research to the larger relevant topics in the field. Once again, the second part of your paper starts off with a narrow focus and then ends with a more general discussion of the topic (see Chapter 11 for more details on the Discussion section).

Using an Outline:
Organizing Your Literature Review

Let's get back to writing the Introduction section or, really, how to get started. For our students, we suggest starting with an outline that helps determine the topics and different areas of focus that are related to your research. Throughout our years of teaching, we have found that without the outline, many students end up with an Introduction section that includes a paragraph for each separate journal article with little connection between paragraphs. That type of organization often lacks the cohesion needed to provide the logic leading to your prediction. We find that when students use an outline, they can more easily connect articles to a specific topic area or theoretical models. With permission from Christopher Hollingsworth, the Introduction section from his senior research paper (based on research conducted in collaboration with Reynolds Martin) is included at the end of this chapter. Throughout this part of the chapter, we will refer to sections of his paper, titled *Effects of Chronotype and Time of Day on Ethical Decision Making in College Students*. We also include an outline that illustrates the organization of the paper, that when developed upfront, can help to create a logical order to the topics and in turn the related articles. We encourage you to use this sample outline and paper to help you understand how to best organize and write your Introduction section.

As a result of developing an outline, the paper is organized by topic or a particular theory you want to focus on in each section, which allows you to then connect each topic to the question(s) addressed by your own research. Outlines start with the overall topic and major constructs, as suggested by the hourglass analogy above. For example, if you are studying the influence of the use of different types of social media sites on narcissism, you can start with citations and statements concerning the prevalence of the use of social network sites and the increase in levels of narcissism as indicated by the literature. Or, if you are studying the effects of individual differences in academic dishonesty decision making based on chronotypes or sleeping patterns over a 24-hour period (the topic for the sample paper included at the end of this chapter), you can start by discussing the prevalence of cheating and in turn the need to address how to address this problem in higher education. Then the sections that follow will focus on a particular aspect of the area of research you are addressing—your own research. In the latter example, after introducing the problem, the paragraphs that follow could address different factors known to influence academic dishonesty. One section could focus on situational factors, another on institutional factors, and another on individual differences that could influence academic integrity. Given that the research focuses on chronotypes, a section should be included that reviews the literature on what we know about the influence of differences in sleeping patterns on behavior in general. As you see, each section focuses on a related topic. Once you decide on the topic, you can then review the articles you found and place them in the appropriate section of your outline. You might be thinking, "sounds easier said than done." And, indeed you are correct. Like other complex skills, it takes practice to acquire proficiency. But we can help make it easier.

The writing challenge does often come in after introducing the general topic, when the decisions are made as to how to organize the articles within each paragraph or each section of your paper. It is easy to become overwhelmed by a stack of articles that you need to coherently organize in your paper; here's some guidance for what can often be considered an overwhelming stack. We have found great success with creating brief summaries for each article, noting the part of the article that is most relevant to the research addressed in the paper, and including the parts of the article that need to be included in your paper. Remember, not all the details for each article are included in your Introduction. You need to carefully choose what information is most relevant to your research and in turn what should be included in your paper. The summaries can be written on index cards or printed out using a separate page for each article. That index card or page should include enough details so you do not need to search out the original article each time and reread the article to find the information needed. We recommend you include the following in these summaries:

- APA–style reference
- Hypothesis
- Concise description of the methods used (e.g., participants, materials, task)
- Results of statistical analyses
- Conclusions noted by the author in the Discussion section
- Connection to your research project

Then, using a large table, we spread out the summaries that represent each article we would like to include in the Introduction. You can also take your outline, cut the different sections out, and order those sections across the table. Using your outline sections, start to rearrange the summaries around the table, and try to fit each article within the outline structure that provides the logical progression needed to support the hypothesis. Take a look at the topic or focus for each part of your outline and determine the point you want to make for each section. This process allows you to work on your paper like a puzzle, putting together the pieces in a way that fits the logic of your "story" or, in this case, your Introduction. After you have completed this puzzle-like task, you can gather up the summaries, keeping the order intact, and then head to your computer and start to fill in your outline with information about the articles as they relate to each section and in the order you created.

As you start to write using this organization tool, we also recommend that you develop transitions that connect one section to the next. The transitions are essential to create a flow to your paper that allows the reader to understand the relationship of the articles you are writing about and the overall focus of your research. If you take a look at the sample Introduction included in this chapter, you will see the types of transitions to consider. These include the following direct excerpts from this paper:

- To answer these questions . . .
- In addition to self-efficacy and school identification . . .
- Another situational factor that may influence levels of cheating . . .
- Individual differences may also cause certain people to cheat more . . .
- Other researchers have turned to one's level of self-control to explain . . .
- Several studies have supported the idea that . . .

In all cases, these statements connect the material covered in the previous paragraph with the material about to be covered so the reader understands the logic of the presentation of past research as it relates to the topic at hand. Finally, keep those summaries handy, just in case you find that additional reorganizing is needed. We can tell you, having written many papers of this sort, reorganizing the paper and writing multiple drafts will lead to a stronger paper in the end. Often, although the review of the literature includes numerous articles, your study might stem from one or two key studies. Those are the studies you should include in greater detail in your literature review.

In the end, your Introduction section should illustrate the development of your research idea and that you have done your scholarly homework; it should support your hypothesis, stated at the end of your Introduction. We should note that typically your professor will ask that you develop a directional hypothesis. This means that you are not just predicting any difference between the groups in your study but also the direction in which those groups will differ. For example, in a study on young children's deception, you might predict that those children who feel a greater connection with another individual are less likely to deceive compared to those children who lack that connection. Here is also where you would clearly define the variables. What do you mean by "a greater connection"? How is that defined in your research? That detail is often found at the end of your Introduction section. As you write this section of your paper, always keep in mind that by the time one is reading your hypothesis at the end of your introduction, the reader should be thinking "of course, that makes perfect sense! That question needs to be answered!" Remember to keep in mind that your Introduction is the section of your paper in which you review the literature and introduce your research. This is not where you get to write about your opinions; that should take place in the Discussion section, the last part of your paper.

Common Mistakes to Avoid in Your Introduction

Use the following as a mini-checklist to **avoid** these **common errors:**

- Starting the Introduction on the same page as your Abstract
- Using the heading "Introduction" instead of your title

- Forgetting to use citations when reviewing the literature
- Including too many direct quotations
- Plagiarizing: Not giving credit, where credit is due
- Using colloquial (informal) writing such as using contractions and abbreviations
- Not explaining why your research addresses an interesting topic
- Not organizing your introduction in a manner that leads logically to your hypothesis
- Not including your hypothesis in the last paragraph
- Forgetting to connect your hypothesis to past research findings
- Including personal opinions
- Stating that findings from past research "prove"...
- Using anthropomorphism (e.g., data indicate, research found)
- Writing about past research in future tense

7

Outline for the Sample Introduction Section

I. Academic dishonesty prevalence (Jones, 2011)

II. Situational factors related to academic dishonesty
   a. Self-efficacy (Finn & Frone, 2004)
   b. School identification
   c. Surveillance (Covey, Saladin, & Killen, 2011)
   d. Self-monitoring
   e. Incentives
   f. Honor codes and academic dishonesty (Schwartz, Tatum, & Hageman, 2013)
      i. Institutional policies (Jordan, 2001)

III. Individual difference factors related to academic dishonesty
   a. Moral identity (Detert, Treviño, & Sweitzer, 2008)
   b. Impulsivity (Anderman, Cupp, & Lane, 2010)
   c. Self-control (Mead, Baumeister, Gino, Schweitzer, & Ariely, 2009)

IV. Biological factors related to unethical decision making/academic dishonesty (Wittman & Paulus, 2009)
   a. Circadian rhythms (Tempesta, Couyoumdjian, Moroni, Marzano, Gennaro, & Ferrara, 2012)
   b. Sleep deprivation (Wagner, Barnes, Lim, & Ferris, 2012)
   c. Circadian rhythms
      i. Morning morality effect (Kouchaki & Smith, 2014)
      ii. Chronotypes (Gunia, Barnes, & Sah, in press)
      iii. Chronotypes and college students (Digdon & Howell, 2008)
      iv. Academic performance (Taylor, Clay, Bramoweth, Sethi, & Roane, 2011)

V. Causative model of cheating-situational, individual differences, and biological factors
   a. Chronotypes and perception of academic dishonesty
      i. Hypothesis and how it was tested: In-sync chronotypes → increased perception of academic dishonesty

7

Sample Paper

Running head: EFFECTS OF CHRONOTYPE 1

Effects of Chronotype and Time of Day on Ethical Decision Making

in College Students

Christopher A. Hollingsworth and Reynolds Martin

Randolph College

EFFECTS OF CHRONOTYPE   2

Abstract

Chronotype is a set of processes that determines an individual's circadian rhythm. Gunia, Barnes, and Sah (in press) found evidence for a "chronotype morality effect" by which people act more ethically when in sync with their chronotypes than when not in sync. To replicate their findings and investigate this effect in a college setting, we sorted Randolph College students ($n = 55$) into morning, neutral, and evening chronotype groups and randomly assigned them to morning and evening testing groups. Participants then rated their perceptions of, and likelihood to report, scenarios of academically questionable behavior defined by Schwartz, Tatum, and Hageman (2013). Contrary to our hypothesis, chronotype and time of day did not interact to affect perception. However, our study revealed an interaction on likelihood to report. Uneven chronotype group sizes and social desirability may have contributed to the absence of an interaction on perception and affected responses to the scenarios.

Keywords: chronotype, ethical decision making, college students

Effects of Chronotype and Time of Day on

Ethical Decision Making in College Students

Academic dishonesty has become a very significant

issue in higher education. In her survey of students registered

in an online business communications class, Jones (2011)

found that a vast majority of students either knew someone

who had cheated on an assignment or had cheated themselves.

In addition, when asked specifically if they would cheat, a

majority of students reported that they would. The researcher

also found similar results concerning online plagiarism. Half

of the students reported that they knew of someone who

had plagiarized or had plagiarized themselves, and two-

thirds reported that they would intentionally plagiarize. The

prevalence of academic dishonesty, at both the high school and

university levels, has caused many educators and researchers to

question what causes these behaviors and what can be done to

combat them.

To answer these questions, researchers have identified

several situational factors that may play roles in students'

academic dishonesty; these factors include self-efficacy and

school identification (Finn & Frone, 2004). Self-efficacy

is the extent to which individuals feel they can complete a

EFFECTS OF CHRONOTYPE   4

desired task on their own. School identification is the degree
to which students identify with and feel like they belong in
a school setting. In their study investigating the moderating
effect of these variables on the relationship between academic
performance and cheating, Finn and Frone found that students
with low levels of self-efficacy were more likely to cheat,
irrespective of their performance. Additionally, cheating was
even more likely among students who displayed both low
levels of self-efficacy and high performance. The researchers
believe that when students are performing well, but feel they
cannot continue doing so on their own, they will be more
likely to cheat in order to maintain their performance.
Moreover, Finn and Frone found that students who exhibit both
low levels of school identification and poor performance are
more likely to cheat. Hence, when students do not feel as
though they belong in the classroom, they begin to detach
from the school's standards and engage in academic
dishonesty.

In addition to self-efficacy and school identification,
situational factors such as surveillance, self-monitoring, and
incentives may facilitate cheating behavior in students. For their
study, Covey, Saladin, and Killen (2011) defined self-monitoring

EFFECTS OF CHRONOTYPE   5

as the degree to which individuals change their public image to fit a given situation. In theory, low self-monitors should be less concerned about their appearance and, therefore, less affected by social pressures than high self-monitors. The researchers found that participants exhibited lower levels of cheating behavior while under surveillance similar to what they would experience from a proctor during a test. An interaction between self-monitoring and incentives emerged, with higher performance on a maze-solving task than they actually scored. This interaction was such that incentives increased cheating behavior for participants who displayed low levels of self-monitoring. This interaction effect was not found for high self-monitors, however. These findings led Covey and colleagues to conclude that for high self-monitors, the benefits associated with the incentives did not overcome the costs of being caught cheating and sacrificing their public image. However, for low self-monitors the benefits did overcome the costs and, hence, these individuals cheated more often than high self-monitors when offered an incentive.

Another situational factor that may influence levels of cheating by students is the type of honor code implemented at their institution (Schwartz, Tatum, & Hageman, 2013).

EFFECTS OF CHRONOTYPE   6

For their study, Schwartz and colleagues defined traditional

honor system institutions as those with an honor code and

honor pledge, a dual responsibility requirement, and a student-

majority-run adjudication system. Modified honor system

institutions were defined as those with an honor pledge but no

dual responsibility requirement. Additionally, modified honor

system institutions do not have a student-majority in their

adjudication processes. Finally, non-honor system institutions

have procedures concerning cheating and plagiarism, but do

not have an official honor pledge. Schwartz et al. created a set

of scenarios of academically questionable behavior based on

common honor code violations at their institution and a review

of previous literature. They then presented these scenarios to

undergraduate students at traditional honor system, modified

honor system, and non-honor system colleges. For each

scenario, participants were asked to rate their perceptions of,

and likelihood to report, the behavior. Students at traditional

honor system institutions perceive the scenarios to be more

dishonest and are more likely to report them than are students

at modified honor or non-honor system institutions. The

researchers argued that these differences may be due to social

desirability effects that occur for students at traditional honor

EFFECTS OF CHRONOTYPE   7

system institutions. Students at traditional honor system colleges are also more involved in the judicial process and, consequently, may have a better understanding of institutional policies regarding cheating than those at modified honor and non-honor system colleges. They may, in turn, be less likely to rationalize academically dishonest behaviors and, thus, less willing to cheat.

The conclusion that knowledge regarding institutional policies may affect cheating is supported by Jordan (2001). To investigate the relationships between rates of cheating and knowledge of institutional policy, attitudes about cheating, and perceived social acceptability of cheating, Jordan had college students indicate how many times they had cheated for each of their classes during the previous semester. He also had participants estimate the frequency of cheating by their friends, hall mates, and the overall student body. Additionally, participants were asked to rate their own beliefs concerning the acceptability of cheating occasionally, when it is used to pass a course, and when a close friend asks for help. Finally, participants indicated the extent to which they had received, read, and understood the college's policies regarding cheating. Therefore, Jordan found that students who cheated more often

EFFECTS OF CHRONOTYPE   8

also believed that their peers cheated more often than those who did not cheat. Moreover, those who reported being exposed more often to actual occurrences of cheating also cheated more often themselves. Regarding knowledge of cheating policies, students with lesser understanding of honor code policies tended to cheat more than those with greater understanding. However, that difference did not appear to be due to lesser exposure to the honor code. Finally, most participants did not agree that cheating is acceptable in any situation. However, significant differences in attitudes between cheaters and non-cheaters did emerge. Cheaters were significantly more likely to justify cheating than non-cheaters. Jordan concluded that perceived social acceptability of cheating, understanding of institutional policies regarding cheating, and attitudes toward cheating may all predict levels of academic dishonesty by students.

Individual differences may also cause certain people to cheat more often than others. With business and education undergraduate students, Detert, Treviño, and Sweitzer (2008) examined the relationships between moral disengagement, unethical decision making, and six individual differences: empathy; moral identity; trait cynicism; and chance, internal, and power loci of control. Several of these traits may be related to academic dishonesty. Only four of the factors (empathy, moral identity, trait cynicism, and chance locus of control) were found to be related to moral disengagement and unethical decision making. Empathy is defined as the ability to recognize and understand another's thoughts and feelings. Moral identity is the salience of ethics/morals in the self-identity. Trait cynicism is a general distrust of other persons, groups, ideologies, social conventions, and institutions. Finally, a chance locus of control is a belief that one's decisions and life are controlled by chance. The researchers defined moral disengagement as a mechanism that deactivates self-monitoring behavior, thereby allowing individuals to behave unethically without feeling uncomfortable.

They found that empathy and moral identity are negatively correlated with moral disengagement, while trait cynicism and chance loci of control are positively correlated with moral disengagement. However, internal and power loci of control do not correlate significantly with moral disengagement. The researchers also found that moral disengagement is positively correlated with unethical decision making. Moreover, moral disengagement acts as a mediator between

EFFECTS OF CHRONOTYPE   10

the individual differences and unethical decision making.
Therefore, people who are less empathetic or less concerned
about their moral identity, and those with higher levels of
trait cynicism or chance loci of control, are more likely
to act unethically because they are more likely to
morally disengage.

High levels of impulsivity, perceived classroom goal
structure, and perceived teacher credibility may also relate
to higher levels of cheating in some students. In their study,
Anderman, Cupp, and Lane (2010) investigated the relationships
between these variables and cheating among high school students
in a health class. They found that when comparing students
who engaged in high levels of cheating with those who reported
no cheating, high perceptions of teacher credibility negatively
correlated with cheating. However, for those students, mastery
goal structures and impulsivity did not correlate significantly
with cheating. When comparing students who engaged in only
moderate levels of cheating and students who reported no
cheating, the researchers again found a negative correlation
between teacher credibility and cheating. In addition, they found a
negative correlation between mastery goal structure and cheating,
and a positive correlation between impulsivity and cheating.

EFFECTS OF CHRONOTYPE   11

Based on these findings, the researchers concluded that students'

individual levels of impulsivity can increase their likelihood of

behaving in an academically dishonest manner. However, when

the students perceive that their teacher is credible and emphasizes

mastery rather than performance, their chances of dishonesty

actually decrease.

Other researchers have turned to one's levels of self-

control to explain cheating behavior. Self-control is defined

as the propensity to change one's reactions or behavior to

meet societal standards (Mead, Baumeister, Gino, Schweitzer,

& Ariely, 2009). Muraven and Baumeister (2000) conducted

a literature review of the existing research concerning self-

control to examine the theory that all acts of self-control stem

from a single limited resource which is regularly depleted. The

researchers concluded that this self-control resource is indeed

depleted after even a single act of self-control and, as a result,

subsequent attempts at self-control are often unsuccessful.

Acts that may deplete this self-control resource include

dealing with stress, regulating emotional states, and fighting

temptations. Thus, we conclude that when their self-control

resources have been depleted, students may be more likely to

cheat. Despite these findings, the researchers also concluded

EFFECTS OF CHRONOTYPE   12

that the strength of this self-control resource can be increased

through repeated use, assuming one rests sufficiently to allow

it to replenish. In other words, Mead and colleagues explain that

self-control is comparable to a muscle and can even be called

the moral muscle.

Several additional researchers supported this self-

control depletion theory. In their study, Mead et al. (2009)

conducted two experiments to test the effects of self-control

depletion on unethical behavior. They found that depleted

participants were more likely than non-depleted participants

to act dishonestly during a matrix-solving task, in which they

were asked to find two 3-digit numbers within the matrix that

summed to 10. Their second experiment verified the external

validity of their previous findings by testing the effects of

depletion on whether the participants subjected themselves to

temptations to act dishonestly. Mead and colleagues found that

depleted participants were both more likely to cheat and to put

themselves in situations in which cheating was possible. Despite

these findings, however, it did not appear that the participants

were aware of the effect of depletion on their behavior.

Therefore, they did not recognize the potential danger of the

situations in which they chose to involve themselves.

EFFECTS OF CHRONOTYPE   13

In addition to the situational and individual factors presented above, some researchers, including Wittman and Paulus (2009), have suggested that biological processes may contribute to unethical decision making and cheating. Specifically, circadian rhythms and duration of sleep may contribute significantly to these behaviors. Lack of sleep can lead to impulsivity because it does not allow depleted self-control resources to regenerate, since the regenerative process would normally occur during sleep. Therefore, people who suffer from sleep deprivation may be more likely to make unethical decisions.

Several researchers supported the idea that circadian rhythms and lack of sleep may influence decision making. Tempesta et al. (2012) investigated the effects of one night of sleep deprivation on moral decision making in university students. They found that students who were sleep deprived responded to impersonal moral dilemmas more quickly than well-rested students. A typical impersonal moral dilemma is one that involves making a choice between a runaway trolley killing one person or five people (i.e., the trolley dilemma). Sleep-deprived students also responded more quickly to impersonal moral dilemmas than to personal moral and non-moral dilemmas, which require less emotional investment. Personal moral dilemmas involve deciding whether or not to push

EFFECTS OF CHRONOTYPE   14

one person in front of a trolley to save five other people (i.e., the

footbridge dilemma). A non-moral dilemma involves a predicament

that cannot be classified as either a personal moral or impersonal

moral dilemma. These researchers therefore suggest that even a

single night of sleep deprivation can affect moral decision making

(and, hence, the propensity to cheat), although only for decisions

that do not require a significant emotional investment.

　　Additional evidence in support of the idea that circadian

rhythms and lack of sleep can affect moral decision making derives

from a study designed to measure the effects of lost and low-quality

sleep on cyberloafing behavior. Using a quasi-experimental design,

Wagner, Barnes, Lim, and Ferris (2012) tested for the effects of

Daylight Saving Time (DST) on cyberloafing behavior, which

they defined as the amount of non-work related internet searches

initiated by workers during a workday. They reported that on the

Monday immediately following the shift to DST, workers engaged

in significantly more cyberloafing than on comparison Mondays.

To test the effects of lost and low quality sleep in a controlled

setting, Wagner and colleagues conducted another experiment in

a laboratory and found that the amount of cyberloafing behavior

was significantly affected by both the quantity and quality of sleep

experienced by the participants the previous night.

EFFECTS OF CHRONOTYPE   15

Based on the self-control depletion theory and the previous literature concerning effects of moral disengagement, sleep loss, and circadian rhythms on moral decision making, Kouchaki and Smith (2014) proposed what they coined as the morning morality effect, in which they purport self-control resources are gradually depleted throughout the day. The researchers proposed that this effect causes individuals to behave more ethically in the morning when their self-control resource has not yet been depleted, and less so in the evening once that resource has been used. To investigate this morning morality effect, Kouchaki and Smith randomly assigned their participants to morning (8–11 a.m.) and afternoon (3–6 p.m.) testing groups. They then presented their participants 20 matrices, each with twelve 3-digit numbers (e.g., 4.27), and instructed participants to indicate whether they identified a pair of numbers that summed to 10. Ten of the matrices had these matching pairs and, thus, were considered solvable; 10 did not and were considered unsolvable. Participants were paid based on how many matrices they reportedly solved. This gave participants an incentive to report that they solved more matrices than they actually had (and that were actually solvable), and gave the researchers a method of measuring unethical behavior. As predicted by Kouchaki and Smith, participants were more likely to act unethically in the afternoon than

EFFECTS OF CHRONOTYPE   16

in the morning. In addition, this effect was stronger in participants who displayed lower levels of moral disengagement than those who displayed higher levels. This suggests that people who disengage more often are less affected by self-control depletion than those who disengage less often.

To account for the fact that approximately two-thirds of the population has more energy in the evening than in the morning, Gunia, Barnes, and Sah (in press) proposed a "chronotype morality effect." Chronotype is defined as a set of processes that determines an individual's circadian rhythm. Similar to Kouchaki and Smith (2014), Gunia and colleagues proposed that people with a morning chronotype (identified as "larks") would exhibit more ethical behavior in the morning and less at night. However, unlike Kouchaki and Smith, Gunia and colleagues also proposed that people with an evening chronotype (identified as "owls") would exhibit more ethical behavior in the evening and less in the morning. Gunia and colleagues conducted two experiments, using the same matrix task as Kouchaki and Smith, to test for their proposed effect. They first determined participants' chronotypes using the Horne-Östberg Morningness-Eveningness Questionnaire (MEQ), a measure of morning-eveningness preferences described in detail later in this paper. They then tested the effect of morning testing

EFFECTS OF CHRONOTYPE   17

on moral decision making in owls. As expected, the participants

were less ethical in the morning than in the evening. Their second

experiment randomly assigned larks and owls to morning and

evening testing groups and an expected interaction between

chronotype and testing session on moral decision making emerged,

such that both larks and owls displayed less moral decision making

when they were tested out of sync with their respective chronotypes.

There is evidence that chronotype may also be related to

procrastination in college students (Digdon & Howell, 2008).

These researchers investigated the relationship between chronotype

and various measures of self-control (including procrastination).

Participants were first sorted into chronotype groups using the

MEQ. They then were asked to complete the Self-Control Scale,

a 36-item questionnaire consisting of statements rated on a five-

point Likert scale. This scale yields a global self-control score, as

well as self-discipline, deliberate/non-impulsive action, healthy

habits, work ethic, and reliability subscale scores. Participants

also completed the Procrastination Scale, a self-report measure

of procrastination consisting of 16 statements answered using a

4-point Likert scale. Digdon and Howell found that participants

with evening chronotypes were more likely to have lower levels of

self-control and procrastinate more often than those with morning

EFFECTS OF CHRONOTYPE   18

chronotypes. Although, having an evening chronotype does not

necessarily cause students to procrastinate, these researchers did

illustrate a positive correlation between MEQ scores and various

measures of self-control, including procrastination.

There is also evidence of a relationship between eveningness

and low academic performance (Taylor, Clay, Bramoweth, Sethi,

& Roane, 2011). These researchers conducted a correlational study

to investigate the relationship between circadian rhythms and

academic performance among college students. The researchers

first administered the Horne-Östberg MEQ in order to measure

participants' chronotypes. Then, upon completion of the semester, the

researchers requested access to participants' academic records and

used grade point average as their measure of academic performance.

Students with an evening chronotype performed significantly worse

academically than those with a morning chronotype, suggesting that

circadian rhythm may influence academic performance.

Given the self-control depletion theory, as well as the findings

of Gunia and colleagues (in press), Digdon and Howell (2008), and

Taylor and colleagues (2011), one might begin to form a causative

model of cheating. Students with evening chronotypes may be more

prone to procrastination than other students. This procrastination, in

conjunction with individual differences such as perceived classroom

EFFECTS OF CHRONOTYPE   19

goal structure and perceived teacher credibility, may cause these
students to begin performing poorly academically. The stress
caused by this low performance may then deplete even more of the
students' self-control resource, making them particularly susceptible
to performing academically dishonest acts. This effect may be
amplified by certain situational factors, such as low self-efficacy
and school identification or attending a modified-honor or non-
honor institution. Even at colleges with traditional honor systems,
this effect may be exacerbated by unfamiliarity with honor code
policies, perceived social acceptability of cheating, and personal
attitudes towards cheating.

Based on the research conducted by Kouchaki and Smith
(2014) and Gunia and colleagues (in press), we investigated
the effects of chronotype and time of day on college students'
perceptions of academic dishonesty. To our knowledge, the current
study is the first investigation of the chronotype morality effect
in relation to academic dishonesty in college students. As a result
of the self-control depletion theory, we predicted an interaction
between time of day and chronotype, such that when presented
with scenarios judging academic honesty, those participants in
sync with their chronotypes (i.e., larks tested in the morning and
owls tested in the evening) would perceive the scenarios to be

EFFECTS OF CHRONOTYPE   20

more dishonest and be more likely to report the behavior than

those tested out of sync (i.e., larks tested in the evening and owls

tested in the morning). The focus on the relationship between

chronotype and time of day, rather than their individual effects,

was derived from the findings of Gunia and colleagues who

refuted the original findings of Kouchaki and Smith regarding the

effect of time of day alone ("morning morality effect").

7

Citing Sources in Text 8

Whodunit (or Said It)?

When it comes to citing works you have read—essentially, giving credit to the authors of information you are using in your paper—we have good news and bad news. The good news is that doing it right is not too difficult at all with even a little practice. The bad news is that it is one of the most common things for students to get wrong when first learning to write in APA style. It is also one of *the* easiest mistakes for your instructor to pick up on. Just a quick look at your paper, even with eyes squinted partially shut, and one can tell if you have cited your sources correctly. This of course assumes you have cited your sources in the first place. Not mentioning where you got your information, ideas, or findings is called plagiarism, an even bigger problem that we discussed in Chapter 5. The bottom line is that science involves building on past findings, and even a paper breaking new ground has to connect new ideas to related information from the past. This information has to be properly acknowledged and cited, which is what this chapter is all about.

A Good Rule of Thumb

If you are writing something that is not 100% your own original idea, whether your opinion, your observations, or your findings from a study you conducted, you should cite your source. A citation can range from a statistic you use to start your paper (e.g., "There are more bars than grocery stores in the state of Wisconsin") to a result or conclusion of a research study that is pertinent to your paper (e.g., "Underage drinking is associated with cognitive processing impairments"). In both cases, you need to cite your source in the main part of your paper (any part up to the References section) using an in-text citation. You then write out the complete information for the source of the data in APA style in the aptly named References section. We describe the basics of the References section in Chapter 12.

Ready, Cite, GO

So allow us to set the stage for citing. You are writing a paper for class. Any search for answers or exploration of an issue—research in general—often begins with a thorough examination of what others already investigated on the topic. After you received the assignment and figured out your topic, you conducted a search for what is written on the topic. You used online databases through your school library website or a similar source and generated a number of journal articles, book chapters, and books that you want to read for information to possibly include in your paper. You now must use the online databases to get either the full text or complete articles. You can save PDF files to your computer or mobile device (go green), or you can print them out. You might be interested in going beyond the electronic resources and checking out a book, or perhaps you need to copy a journal article not available in full text online, in which case you will be heading to the library. Regardless of how you do it, the key is to have the complete article(s) in front of you (including all the references in the article you are retrieving). Now you can read it and see if you want to refer to it in your paper. If you want to include it, then you are ready to cite it in the text. Whenever you are writing on a topic, citing relevant articles that relate to your points is critical to credible papers. In papers for a class, citing outside sources is often an explicit part of the assignment.

An important side note: Your initial searches (perhaps you used Google or another online search engine) may have dug up some online webpages with relevant information (e.g., Wikipedia). A word of advice: Do not use or cite Wikipedia or personal webpages in your paper (even if they are personal pages of famous researchers). Wikipedia can be a great place to get ideas, but it should not be the last place you look, and it is a lousy source to cite in a formal research paper. By this, we mean the best sources of information for your papers are peer-reviewed publications, whether journal articles or book chapters or books. Note, we are not saying you should use the information from Wikipedia without citing it so no one knows where you got it; that would be plagiarism (see Chapter 5). There are many useful, credible websites you may use as well. For example, more and more government information (e.g., National Institute of Mental Health) is available on the web. The difference is that we cannot change what is posted on the National Institute of Mental Health website, but we can change what is posted on

Wikipedia, which alerts us to a potential concern about the credibility of that source.

Want the most impressive source of information? A journal article is the best option according to many academics. In the nonacademic world, *journal* may conjure up images of something in which you jot down daily reflections. That is not what we mean. We do not mean *magazine* either. *Cosmopolitan* and *People* magazine may have surveys and tips, but they are not academic sources of information. Here we mean "scholarly publications" of either write-ups of research or theoretical discussions. Most areas of psychology have journals dedicated to publishing research from their respective fields (e.g., *Journal of Experimental Psychology, Journal of Abnormal Psychology*). Mind you, not all journals have the word *journal* in the title (e.g., *Developmental Psychology, Psychology and Aging*). Researchers write journal articles that are then edited and reviewed by the authors' peers (i.e., "peer reviewed") and, in many cases, have to follow stringent criteria. Although magazines sometimes feature contributions by researchers, there is no peer review of the work written by either researchers or paid journalists. Such sources include *Psychology Today* (hint: not a good citation for a research paper)—although *Psychology Today* might be good for ideas about a research paper. Most books are reviewed before publication, but the process of review is very different (e.g., publishers hire experts to review the manuscript before publication). Conclusions and data from a journal article carry more weight.

In-Text Citation Basics

Once you want to cite an article and you have it ready (online or on paper next to you), there is important information to look for. An in-text citation has two main parts, the author and the date of publication (note how this differs from an MLA citation; in MLA, you would cite the author, then the page number from which the information came). (Note: You need the page number or numbers only if you are directly quoting/copying and pasting. See Chapter 5 for a discussion of when page numbers are needed.) In the majority of cases, the author will be an individual or individuals. In some cases, the source will be an organization or its website (e.g., American Psychological Association, 2016). When your source is not an organization, use only the author's (or authors') last name, a comma, and the year of publication (e.g., Gurung & Schwartz, 2009). Notice, we *did not* include in the example any information about the authors' first names. One common error students make when first learning APA style is including an author's first name or initial(s). A basic citation of one author will look like this:

> Starting studying early and reading material prior to and after class were not related to exam scores (Gurung, 2005).

If there are two authors, separate their names with the ampersand symbol (&). A basic citation of two authors will look like this:

> There are a variety of ways to measure how students study and which methods work better than others (Gurung & Schwartz, 2009).

When you want to cite articles written by three or more authors (up to five), separate the last two authors by the ampersand symbol (&), and separate the preceding ones with a comma or commas. Make a note to yourself that you even need to include a comma after the second-to-last author, before the ampersand symbol. Not adding this comma (called a serial comma or Oxford comma) is another common error students make. The basic citation of three to five authors looks like this:

> A truly fun and readable book on APA style can successfully do away with excessive and unneeded jargon (Schwartz, Landrum, & Gurung, 2016).

Multiple-Author Bonus

Every time you cite the work of one or two authors, you have to cite the author or authors, which for two authors means including both last names each time you cite the work. However, if you cite the work of three or more authors (up to five) more than once, you cite all the names only the first time (as illustrated in the previous example). The next time you cite the source, you use only the first author's last name and then the Latin abbreviation *et al.*, which means "and others" (note, there is no period after *et* but a period after *al*—this is an abbreviation of the Latin *et alia*); then another comma; and, finally, the publication year. You leave out all the other authors' last names. So let us say you want to cite this APA style guide more than once; the second and all other citations would look something like this:

> This is your sentence that refers again to that great APA style guide (Schwartz et al., 2016).

When you are thinking about these sentences grammatically, remember that *et al.* stands for "and others" and that your verb needs to agree with a plural noun (*others*).

If the source you are citing has more than five authors (i.e., six and upward), you have to cite only the last name of the first author, followed by the Latin abbreviation *et al.* (again, with a period after *al*), even the first time you cite that work. Although this seems like a raw deal for the other authors, whose names do not see the light of day in any in-text citations, their names *are* included in the References section (see Chapter 12), except in a listing of a bunch of authors (more than seven)—in that case, discussed in the next paragraph, an author's name might not ever be listed. So whether the first, second, or ninth time you cite the article in the body of your paper, you use only the first author's last name.

If you cite a source with more than seven authors, the rules are the same in the text of your paper, but they change in the References section. In the case of more than seven authors, in your References section you include the names (last names, first initials) for the first six authors, followed by three ellipsis points, and the last author's name—for example, Sleepy, V., Grumpy, I., Bashful, N., Doc, M., Happy, S. O., Dopey, R., . . . Sneezy, T. (2013). Notice there is no ampersand (&) in this type of citation. And notice that the names of coauthors who are seventh, eighth, and ninth may not see their names included in either your text or your References section. Now that is truly a raw deal for the penultimate (next-to-last) authors! (Note: The previous example assumes that an unknown eighth dwarf assisted Snow White and was the seventh, and thus unlisted, author for this reference.)

A Variation on the Theme

The examples of in-text citations shown earlier illustrate the preferred way to write citations within parentheses. You will note that in all cases, the parenthetical citations are placed at the end of the sentence. Sometimes, you may want to cite the author(s) within the flow of your sentence. In such cases, the biggest difference is that you use the word *and* where you used an ampersand (&) in all the previous parenthetical examples. Use the ampersand symbol only in parentheses. You still need to include the publication date in parentheses at the end of the citation:

> Schwartz, Landrum, and Gurung (2016) have certainly written one of the most readable books about APA style ever created in the history of humankind.

Some Curveballs

We have sketched out the most common in-text citations you will need. The previous examples will probably account for more than 85% of your citation needs. That said, here are some interesting citation conundrums you might come across, and we certainly do not want to leave you hanging. Below, we list each issue and then the solution. Then following this section, we also include a table (see Table 8.1) to summarize how to cite all the examples included in this chapter.

Citing More Than One Article in the Same Spot

Sometimes, you need more than one citation to make a point. In such cases, there are two major rules to follow. First, you separate the sources with a semicolon (;), and then you put the articles in **alphabetical order using the first author's**

last name as the main reference point (even if that puts the years published out of chronological order). You then list all the different articles. For example:

> When objectified, a woman's body, or parts of her body, are separated from other personal characteristics (Cheng, Frith, & Shaw, 2005; Moradi, Dirks, & Matteson, 2005; Muehlenkamp, Swanson, & Brausch, 2005).

Sometimes, you may need to provide citations for different parts of a single sentence. No problem. Just add your citation, with author and publication date in parentheses, at every point. It certainly makes for difficult reading to someone not used to APA style, but it is the rule:

> Although objectification is often talked about primarily as something men do to women, fueled by research on pornography (McKee, 2005), both men and women objectify (Strelan & Hargreaves, 2005) and can be objectified.

Before we move on, we break for an important warning about one place a common rookie mistake can be made. Make sure that when you cite a multiple-author piece, you use the exact same order of authorship as found on the first page of the original article. *Do not* alphabetize the authors *within* an article. For example, some of the authors of this guide (Schwartz, Landrum, & Gurung, 2016) would be pretty peeved, or at least mildly offended, if someone cited the book as (Gurung, Landrum, & Schwartz, 2016). Nice alphabetization and good for Gurung (!), but it is not APA style. Alphabetization (by the first author's last name) is key for order of citations and References lists but not for rearranging published author lineups.

Including Two or More Articles by the Same Author and Some Are the Same Year

Using two or more articles by the same author, published in the same year is more common than you think. People often do a lot of research on similar topics and often have a number of publications on the topic you may want to cite. If you do need to cite **different articles by the same author** and they are all single-author publications, list the author's name once followed by the publication years of the different articles in chronological order from earliest to latest, with a comma between publication years.

If more than one article was published in the same year, then use lowercase letters (e.g., *a*, *b*, *c*) to differentiate the different articles. (Note: For articles by the same author published in the same year, the references are alphabetized by article title and lowercase letters are added to the dates accordingly.) If the same author has articles with coauthors, add them to the mix in alphabetical order, using the second author's last name to alphabetize the list of sources (if the first two names are the same, then look at the third name, and so on):

> We now know much about how students study and how they should study (Gurung, 2004, 2005a, 2005b; Gurung & McCann, 2012; Gurung & Schwartz, 2009).

Including Two or More Articles by Authors With the Same Last Name

> Ever wonder what the citation would look like if Indiana Jones and his father published together? Even when relatives are not working together, this question is often relevant when folks with common last names end up working together or publishing separately on the same topic. To cite them in the text, use the initials of each author's first and middle name in addition to the last name and publication year: It is now clear that drinking a lot of caffeine can be linked to a host of problems (C. R. Smith, 2009; P. T. Smith, 2011).

or

> Findings from research conducted by both C. R. Smith (2009) and P. T. Smith (2011) illustrate that drinking caffeine can be problematic.

Citing an Article or Document From a Website or Video

This one is easy as long as you keep website citations to an absolute minimum. There are a few websites that make useful citations. For example, if you want to refer to sociodemographic information (e.g., number of men, women, African Americans, etc.) in a given area, you may want to cite data from the Census Bureau (e.g., U.S. Census Bureau, 2016). That said, if you get the information from a table or figure on a website (even the Census Bureau's website), there will be a table or figure title that you can cite in the text with the date of publication. The actual organization, website, and source will go into the References section (see Chapter 12). Also, when you report the year published from a website, you do not report the year when you retrieved the information but, rather, the year the information was posted to the website. This is difficult to find on many websites and should give you pause about citing that website. If you have to cite a website without a date, use *n.d.* ("no date") in parentheses where the year would normally appear. Again, there are few websites you should be citing (have we said that enough?), but sometimes interesting statistics come in unusual places. For example, did you know this little fact?

> In the Midwest, there are more bars than grocery stores, and in Wisconsin there are 5.88 bars per 10,000 people (Zook, 2010).

For in-text citations, you can treat videos, even those from YouTube, as if they were journal articles and cite the author and the year (e.g., Chew, 2011). The reference for this cited video clip will look a little different. For the Chew (2011) video, it would appear as follows:

> Chew, S. (2011, August 16). How to get the most out of studying: Part 5 of 5, "I blew the exam, now what?" [Video file]. *Samford University.* Retrieved from http://www.youtube.com/watch?v=-QVRiMkdRsU&feature=results_main&playnext=1&list=PLD9129ADF16259237

Referring to the Same Article More Than Once in the Same Paragraph

The first time you cite a source in a paragraph, you use the style rules described previously. What you do the second time or subsequent times depends on how you cited it the first time. If you cited a work without putting the author(s) in parentheses the first time, then the **next time** you cite the article, you need not use the publication date. Note that the year in the first citation is still in parentheses. An example of this is shown here; the ellipses indicate an incomplete sentence/quotation:

> Butler and Geis (1990) found that both genders rated men and women leaders equally but treated female leaders more negatively than they did male leaders. Butler and Geis also found that female leaders . . .

If your first in-text author citation of the paragraph is inside parentheses, then subsequent citations of the same work in the same paragraph *do* need to include the year inside parentheses if you cite the author in the body of the text (yes, we know this may seem silly).

> Researchers reported that both genders rate men and women leaders equally but treat female leaders more negatively than male leaders (Butler & Geis, 1990). Butler and Geis (1990) also found that female leaders . . .

Citing an Article That I Read About in Another Article or Book

Do not (if you can help it) cite a source that you read about in another book or article. Again, we are not asking you to plagiarize but are strongly recommending that you read the original article yourself. It is possible that the article you read (the primary source) that talked about the other article (the secondary source) got it wrong. To some instructors, your use of a secondary source could suggest you did not care enough to go find the original. Why let someone think that of you (it is not true, right)? Importantly, you want to be sure what you write about the secondary source is accurate, and the only way to be sure is to read it yourself. Be especially careful not to use textbooks. Textbooks are great resources and are packed with primary-source citations, but they should not substitute for your finding the primary source. If you really must do it (and we are hard pressed to think of why you would, because you can use interlibrary loans or various online full-text databases to access primary sources), your citation will look like this:

> Butler and Geis (as cited in Gurung & Chrouser, 2007) found that both genders rated men and women leaders equally . . .

Which of the references in the preceding example goes into your References list? Actually, only the reference for the source you have before you (the primary source), which in the example would be Gurung and Chrouser (2007). In other words, you do not include a secondary source in your References list.

Citing a Lecture, an E-Mail, or a Conversation

Sometimes, you may want to use in your paper something incredibly profound that a professor said in class, or you may want to use information from an e-mail (preferably from an authority on the subject). In some cases, you may even want to cite a person's conversation with you. First off, lectures and conversations are not the best sources for your paper. Do not get us wrong; professors and conversational partners have important things to say and are often accurate and credible, but the gold-standard sources for information are peer-reviewed scientific publications. And no, a lecture is not looked on as a favorable secondary source, although the average lecture often discusses primary sources. If you do have to cite a person, the citation should include the person's initials (separated by periods), followed by the day, month, and year of the communication:

> *Baby Blues* in Venice, near Los Angeles has some of the best ribs in the country (R. E. Landrum, personal communication, June 20, 2015).

What If There Is No Author?

Somebody must have written it, right? True, but that somebody may not always be identified. In the event you do run into a piece of work you want to cite for which the author is not identified, cite the first two words of the title of the article, chapter, or webpage you got the information from, surrounded by double quotation marks and followed by the year (e.g., "New Research," 2013). If you got the information from a magazine, book, or technical report of any kind, cite the full title in italics followed by the year (e.g., *Obscure Mayan Numerology*, 2012). Sometimes, the author will wish to remain unknown and will be listed as such. Here, you simply cite the word *Anonymous* and the year (e.g., Anonymous, 2013).

That is it. Master these citation styles, and you will be well on your way to writing a paper in APA format.

8

Table 8.1 Main Examples of In-Text Citations

Type of Citation		Example
In-text citation basics	One author	(Gurung, 2005)
	Two authors	(Gurung & Schwartz, 2009)
	Three authors	First time cited: (Schwartz, Landrum, & Gurung, 2016)
		Second and subsequent times cited: (Schwartz et al., 2016)
	Six or more authors	First and all times cited, use only first author name and *et al.* and year: (Ahrendt et al., 2013)
More than one article	Alphabetical order by first author's last name	(Cheng, Frith, & Shaw, 2005; Moradi, Dirks, & Matteson, 2005; Muehlenkamp, Swanson, & Brausch, 2005)
Citations for different parts of a single sentence	Place the citations in parentheses at the appropriate place in the sentence.	Although objectification is often talked about primarily as something men do to women, fueled by research on pornography (McKee, 2005), both men and women objectify (Strelan & Hargreaves, 2005) and can be objectified.
Two or more articles by the same author	Do not repeat author; add lowercase letters for articles in same year	(Gurung, 2004, 2005a, 2005b)
Two or more articles by authors with same last name	Add author initials	(C. R. Smith, 2009; P. T. Smith, 2011)

8

Type of Citation		Example
Document from a website	Author and year or organization and year	(Zook, 2010) (Centers for Disease Control, 2013)
Secondary sources	Material read about in other material	Butler and Geis (as cited in Gurung & Chrouser, 2007)
Personal communications	E-mails, lecture material, conversations	(R. E. Landrum, personal communication, June 20, 2015)
No author	Title of article, chapter, or webpage (first two words in double quotations, with year of publication)	("New Research," 2013)
	Magazine, book, or technical reports (full title in italics, with year of publication)	(*Obscure Mayan Numerology*, 2012)
	Anonymous	(Anonymous, 2013)

8

A Step-by-Step 9
Playbook of Your
Method

How, What, When, Who, and Where?

When reading about previous research, we are interested in exactly how the authors collected the data. These details are in the Method section of any APA–style research paper. This section of your APA–style paper follows immediately after your Introduction, where you stated your hypothesis in the last paragraph of that section (see Chapter 7 for details on writing your Introduction).

The Method section is where you take that hypothesis(es) and indicate exactly how you will test your prediction(s). You need to be sure that the participants you include and the procedure you use actually test your hypothesis(es). For example, if you predict that test performance will improve when instructors require students to take notes in class rather than receiving the notes from the instructor, your Method section will include how you defined and measured *note taking* (i.e., the operational definition), what the instructor's notes included, and finally how you measured test performance. The clear connection needed between your hypothesis and the methods used to test that hypothesis is included within this part of your paper. By the way, if you have the daunting task of writing an entire research paper in one sitting, sometimes the Method section is a good place to start because its structure and formatting are fairly rigid. However, sometimes you might be starting your writing with the Introduction section, followed by the Method section—the same order as would occur in a research paper.

Where in the Flow of Pages Do You Place the Method Section?

When it comes to the Method section, we see one common mistake—starting a new page in your paper for this section. No new page is needed, and no extra space before the "Method" heading is required. These are the mistakes students first learning to write in APA style make time and time again. Just keep in mind, "when in doubt, double-space throughout!" The same thing goes for the transition from your Introduction to your Method section, which, by the way, is called the Method section and not the Methods section. Drop the *s*. You can talk about your methods, but you need to write the Method section for your paper. The overall goal of the Method section is to provide enough detail that another researcher can understand the meaning of what is being studied, better understand the results, and, if needed, replicate your study. The Method section also allows the reader to understand the *generalizability* of your results, which refers to *the extent to which your findings can be applied to other populations and other situations.*

So after you state your hypothesis at the end of your introduction, the Method section will provide the step-by-step playbook with the details of exactly how you tested that hypothesis. As we tell students, the information in this section of the paper should be detailed enough that the reader can conduct the same experiment to see if the same results are found. You might have learned the term *replicate*, which is exactly what someone is trying to do when using the method from a previous experiment. If you do use the same method as someone else used, you can simply include a brief summary of your method and refer the reader to the original source for details. Be careful, though; your instructor might want you to practice writing a Method section "from scratch," even though you borrowed the methodology from another article. After all, originality counts when it comes to design (even though originality clearly is not allowed much in APA formatting). That said, being aware of past methods used and creating modifications to those methods is a great way to help develop your own research proposals. One of the best ways to become comfortable with APA–style writing is to read as many APA–style publications as you can. One note to remember, however: APA–formatting instructions are meant to provide authors a template for how to submit their research for publication to a journal; what actually appears in a journal, format-wise, is quite different from how the author submitted that work to the journal. In other words, there are no published journals in which the article is presented double-spaced, with 1-inch margins on all four sides, and so on. Technically speaking, the APA *PM* is a manual about how to prepare research for journal submissions, but it's not a guide for how the work will appear in print or on screen.

When writing your own papers, providing the details on how you conducted your research also allows others to evaluate the validity of your experiment. In other words, understanding the details in the Method section about how you

9

collected data can allow readers to figure out if the procedures used really tested the hypothesis in question. So let us say you hypothesize that sleep deprivation leads to a significant drop in test performance—not that we think you are not getting enough sleep (read with a hint of sarcasm). We remember being in college all too well! The Method section includes information such as how much sleep deprivation participants in your experimental group endured, what type of test you had participants take, and how exactly you measured performance. Readers should understand exactly how you operationally defined (in concrete, measureable, and observable terms) sleep deprivation (e.g., 2 hours of sleep or 6 hours of sleep) and how you measured a drop in test performance (e.g., how many tests you used and what type of tests you used). Basically, after reading the Method section of any paper, you should know who participated in the study, what they experienced as participants, what materials the author(s) used, and how the author(s) defined the independent and dependent variables. Note that this is a very good example of the methodology that might be used in a quantitative study about sleep, but keep in mind that there are many different types of methods, which is why most psychology majors complete a "research methods" course. For example, there are qualitative methods, survey methods, case study methods, focus group methods, and so on.

Where in the Method Section Does This Information Go?

9

APA style requires that you include these details in subsections of the Method section: Subjects or Participants, Apparatus or Materials, and Procedure. Sometimes these subsections are combined, depending on how much information you need to include. Sometimes you even see a separate Design subsection. We explain when you can combine some of the subsections; we describe what details you should include within each subsection, with an example for each; and we include information on how to format this part of your paper. You did not think APA would allow you to come up with your own formatting rules, now did you?

Subjects/Participants

We will start with the Subjects/Participants subsection. You might be wondering what the difference is between a *subject* and a *participant*. Although APA used to provide specific rules concerning the use of these two terms, according to the sixth edition of the *PM*, either term is acceptable. You need to use only one term for the subheading. Whether you have participants or subjects, this first subsection begins with details about the participants or subjects included in your research.

Many writers start with how many participants were included, followed by the characteristics of the sample relevant to the question at hand. This usually means including demographic information such as age, sex, and ethnic group, but you should include any aspect of your sample that is relevant to why you included these individuals in your research. If you are conducting developmental research, you might want to include the mean age of your participants as well as the age range; whenever you report a mean (or any measure of central tendency), you will need to report a measure of variability as well—such as range, standard deviation, or standard error. After reading this subsection, a reader should be able to understand why you chose this type of participants in your investigation and why you excluded other types of participants who did not meet your chosen demographic characteristics. Despite the many details you include in this section, you also need to remember to keep the identities of your participants anonymous. Information should be about the group and not about individuals. You cannot state in your Method section that you included the Californian, 18-year-old, Catholic, African American male with the freckle on his right cheek from the fall 2016 section of the social psychology course offered at your school. Too much information. A common mistake—if you collected data from students enrolled in an introductory psychology course (PSYC 1001 Section 14), new writers want to state that participants were recruited from PSYC 1001 Introductory Psychology. The reader does not need to know the college or university or the course name or number to replicate your study—simply writing "Students from the introductory psychology course participated in the study" will suffice.

If you include animals as subjects, you need to include information such as the genus, species, and strain of the animals. Also, you need to include the name of the supplier that provided the animals. Finally, just as you include demographic information about human participants, similar information is needed when conducting animal research, so include sex, age, weight, and any other relevant information that clearly identifies the types of animals included in the research.

Next, you should include how you recruited your participants. Did you go into introduction to psychology courses; did you use an introductory psychology participation sign-up board or a software program such as Experimetrix or Sona Systems; or did you post something on Facebook to recruit for your research? Did you put an ad in the school newspaper asking for volunteers? Did you provide any type of compensation for their participation such as money, course requirement credit, or extra credit? Finally, you need to include information in this section on your *attrition rate*. Attrition refers to the number of participants who began your experiment but did not finish. Many students ask why attrition rate is important. Why do we need to know how many participants did not complete our experiment? Essentially, students who do not complete the experiment might be different from those who are able to see it through to the end. Often, it is unclear what the explanation for not completing the study might be, so simply indicate the number of those who initially participated in your experiment and the number who completed the experiment.

9

Typically, a Subjects/Participants section includes the following:

- The number of participants/subjects included
- Demographic information about your participants/subjects (e.g., age, sex)
- How you recruited your participants/what supplier was used for your animals
- If participants volunteered or if they were compensated (money, course credit, extra credit)
- How many participants did not complete your experiment and why (if known)

In what follows, we provide an example of a participants section (adapted from Wilson, Stadler, Schwartz, & Goff, 2009, pp. 109–110); also see Chapter 21 and the Participants section in the sample paper written by a psychology major in a research methods course.

Participants

Students enrolled in four introductory psychology courses at three institutions in the southeastern United States participated in this study. The courses were conducted during the summer and fall of 2007. Two female and two male instructors taught the courses, with enrollments between 16 and 40 students each. One hundred and five students were present on the first day of class and were randomly assigned to the experimental conditions and completed surveys. Because 15 students indicated that they had met the teacher previously, their data were removed from the data set for final analyses. Ninety students (72 women and 18 men with an average age of 19.50; $SD = 2.34$) who had no previous experience with the instructor ($n = 82$) or who had met the instructor once during new student orientation ($n = 8$) completed the two surveys at the end of the class period. Ethnicities included 44 Caucasians, 44 non-Caucasian (predominantly African-American) students. There were 41 first-year students, 19 sophomore students, 17 junior students, 12 senior students, and one student of unknown classification.

Materials and Apparatus

In this section, you tell your readers the specifics about the materials or equipment used to collect your data. *Materials* refers to tests, surveys, or questionnaires you used or details of information you presented to participants in paper form or on a computer screen (e.g., the Child Behavior Checklist or the Peabody Picture Vocabulary Test—with appropriate citations included). It is important to provide the proper citations for the established measures so that if the reader wanted to follow your intellectual path, the citations become the breadcrumbs for following along. In comparison, *apparatus* refers to an instrument you might have used to measure reaction time (e.g., a stopwatch) or the equipment used to test an animal's memory for hidden food (e.g., a sand maze). It could also be a specialized computer program you wrote or some uncommon software used. Remember, the Method section should let your reader know exactly how you conducted your research, so including the details about the questions asked or the instrument used to measure your dependent variable will be important if, indeed, someone wants to replicate your study. The amount of detail you include depends on how well known the apparatus or materials are. If they are well known, you can simply mention the names for the reader. If they are relatively new and you want to provide a reference where details can be found, you can mention the names for the reader and cite another study that used the same materials and apparatus. If, however, you have come up with an ingenious new way to manipulate your independent variable or measure your dependent measure, then you will need to include the details.

When can you combine this information with the Procedure subsection? When all your materials are from past studies, consider including a description of your materials in your Procedure subsection. So if the materials in your study are relatively straightforward and well established from previous research, combine the Materials and Procedure subsections into one section. We feel compelled to add here that we do not advise students who are just learning APA style to develop their own measures; that entails a great deal of work before you truly know that you have a valid measure. Of course, if there is no measure out there for your dependent variable, then find out what faculty member is most knowledgeable about testing and measurement and all the fun validity and reliability tests that come along with test development. If you are interested in seeing some of the creative equipment used when the science of psychology was a new discipline, check out the Center for the History of Psychology website (http://www3.uakron.edu/ahap/). It is hard to imagine that this equipment was actually used!

Typically, a Materials/Apparatus section includes the following:

- List of common devices or materials
- Citations for common devices or materials
- Description of uncommon devices or materials
- Why a new measure (e.g., survey) was developed
- Reliability and validity data for the new measure developed

Next, we include an example of a Materials subsection adapted from the same article by Wilson et al. (2009, p. 110), which is a stand-alone Materials section because the researchers developed a survey for their study. You can also take a look in Chapter 21 for a sample paper that includes an section labelled instruments, involving a study in which the research included a number of assessment instruments.

Materials

We used a two-page survey. On the first page of the survey, students rated statements about their attitudes concerning the instructor (ex. "The instructor seems like an excellent teacher") and the course (ex. "I expect to learn a lot in this course"), on a 5-point Likert-type scale (*Strongly Disagree* to *Strongly Agree*). Three items (opinion of the overall course, opinion of the effectiveness of the instructor, and overall opinion of the instructor) were scored on a 5-point scale from *Poor* to *Excellent*. Questions about the instructor focused on the teaching skills of the instructor, the degree to which the instructor can motivate or interest the students, and the degree to which the instructor likes or cares for the students. The first page of the survey included questions that requested demographic information about participants (age, gender, ethnicity, year in college, etc.). On the second page of the survey, students indicated their attitudes about touch on a 5-point Likert-type scale (*Strongly Disagree* to *Strongly Agree*). Questions focused on the students' general attitudes about touching (e.g., "Touching is not okay," "Touch is healthy"), their personal preferences about touch (e.g., "I prefer not to be touched often," "I touch people often"), and attitudes about teachers touching students (e.g., "I like it when a teacher touches me," "It is okay for a teacher to touch his/her students"), including three reverse-scored items ("Touching is not okay," "It is not okay to touch people," "I prefer not to be touched often").

9

Procedure

This section can start with a sentence or two that tells the reader the design of your experiment. Did you conduct an experiment with manipulated variables, did you use a correlational design, did you use a quasi-experimental design, or did you observe behaviors in a natural setting? This opening statement informs readers of your independent and dependent variables or, if you used a correlational design instead of an experiment, how you assigned participants to the different conditions or groups in your experiment. If you decide to include this information in your Procedure section, here is an example of what a design sentence might look like:

We used a 2 (gender) x 3 (ice cream flavor) mixed factorial design, and counterbalanced the order of presentation of ice cream flavors in an effort to minimize order effects.

Now that you have included the details of who participated and what materials you used to collect data from those participants, and the design of your research is clear, it is time for a detailed description of exactly what you did during your experiment. Here is the tricky part. You need to include enough information about details of your procedure that would influence the data collected but leave out the irrelevant stuff. So you should include information about how you assigned participants to each condition in your research, but you can omit what types of chairs participants sat in or the size of the lecture hall used. If the size of the lecture hall is presumed to make no difference in the outcomes of the study, then the size of the lecture hall is irrelevant—and should not be included in the Procedures subsection. Really, after writing this section, you should read it (or have someone else read it) to see if the information included allows someone else to conduct the same experiment. The type of detail you need to include really depends on what your research is all about. If you study eyewitness testimony, you will likely not tell your participants that they will need to remember details about an event before the event occurs (we feel compelled at this point to mention the need to follow ethical guidelines when using deception in your research). So if you are not telling your participants that they are about to witness an event they need to remember, what are you telling them? In this case, the specific instructions provided are important for the outcome of your results, and therefore you should include them in the Procedure section. The rookie mistake (made by someone not reading this book) is again providing too much irrelevant detail. Thus, it is OK to say that you tested students in a lecture hall, but you do not need to say you tested students in the Business Building, Room M204-1. That latter level of detail is irrelevant to the outcome of the study.

Typically, a Procedure section includes the following information:

- How you recruited and assigned participants to groups
- What natural observations you made and how you assigned participants to the different groups
- What your independent variable was and how you manipulated or arranged it
- What your dependent variable was and how you measured it
- Where data collection took place
- How informed consent was achieved, if necessary
- What you told the participants regarding the purpose of the research
- What actions the participants performed
- How the researcher was involved in the data collection process
- How long you gave participants to complete the tasks
- How you rewarded participants for their participation
- Whether a debriefing occurred at the conclusion of the study

Once again, using an adaptation from Wilson et al. (2009, pp. 110–111) paper for our example, you will see that when you read the Procedure section that follows, you will know exactly how the researchers collected the data.

Procedure

Before the first day of class, the instructor prepared the two-page survey by folding it in half and taping or stapling it shut. The instructor then made an inconspicuous mark to designate whether the instructor would shake the student's hand before handing the survey to the student. For example, a light pencil stroke was made on the back corner of the survey that was to be given to students with whom the instructor would shake hands.

On the first day of class, the instructor met students as they came into the classroom. As students entered, the instructor greeted the student, using a standard phrase such as "Welcome to the class" or "Welcome, my name is [instructor's name]," using the phrases in a random order. At the same time, the instructor either shook the student's hand and handed the survey to the student or simply gave the survey to the student. The student was then instructed not to do anything with the survey until the end of class. Once the time for class arrived, the instructor finished greeting students and proceeded to start class. General first-day-of-class activities occurred (e.g., handing out the syllabus, giving an overview of the course, introducing some course content). In the last 20 min of class time, the instructor gave instructions to the students about filling out the survey, appointed a student to collect the surveys when everyone had completed them and get the instructor, and then left the room. When the students had completed the survey, and the instructor reentered the classroom, the instructor discussed the study and used it as a tool to introduce research methodology in psychology. Follow-up questions during the discussion indicated that students did not know the nature of the manipulation or the purpose of the study when they were filling out the survey.

Formatting Your Method Section

Now that you know all the information to include in the Method section and you can write this section so that readers can understand your research, we review the APA rules for formatting this section. We have listed the formatting rules for the Method section below:

- Start the Method section immediately after the end of your introduction.
- Double-space the entire Method section.
- The word Method is centered and boldfaced (like your other headings).
- Write the Method section using past tense for completed research.
- Each subsection is started on a new line and boldfaced, but no extra line spacing between subsections.
- The subsection paragraph begins on a separate line and is indented.

Use the following as a mini-checklist to **avoid** these **common errors:**

- Starting the Method section on a new page
- Using the heading "Methods" instead of "Method"
- Including extra space between subsections
- Forgetting to boldface headings and subheadings
- Writing the subsection text on the same line as the subsection headings
- Forgetting to use citations for materials borrowed from others
- Not including enough information about the participants or subjects
- Not including enough details about the procedure

When you read any Method section, you should be able to understand who participated in the research, why some participants did not complete the experiment, what was needed in order for the researcher to conduct the investigation, and what exactly the participants did. There should be no question of how the data were collected.

9

Writing About Statistics and Associated Fun 10

How Did It All Turn Out?

Analyzing data to solve a mystery can be exciting. Eyes scan the statistical readout searching for that significant *p* value. Now it is time to share your findings with your instructor and perhaps with others in a poster or paper at a conference, such as the Midwestern Psychological Association Conference, or even in a journal article, such as in the *Psi Chi Journal for Psychological Research* (www.psichi.org). When it comes to writing your Results section, you will no doubt need to include information about your statistical findings. We will guide you through how to present your statistical information. At times, you will feel as though you are writing in a foreign language. Hang in there; we will help you make sense and let you know how and when to use all the new words and symbols you are learning.

The first question to ask yourself when writing your Results section is "Should I include my findings in a table or figure, or should I include them all in my Results section?" The general rule of thumb is to present your data in a Results paragraph if you have three or fewer sets of numbers. So if you are reporting statistics for three or fewer groups (i.e., means, standard deviations, sample size for each group), you can write the Results section without a table. If you are able to write a sentence that flows well and makes sense, then leave the information in the paragraph. A good way to test the flow of a sentence is to read it out loud. If it sounds like too much information to include in one sentence, then it likely is, and you should consider using a figure or table. Typically, you create a table when you have four or more sets of numbers. Remember, if you present your means and additional statistics within a table or figure, you should not also include those numbers within your text. That would be statistics overlap/overkill. What you do need to do is tell readers in the Results section where they can find your data (e.g., which table or figure) and what they will find there when they turn to that page. For example, if you included the means and standard deviations for each of the eight different groups in your experiment, you might write this:

> Descriptive statistics for both the experimental and control groups appear in Table 1.

Again, you want to be sure to tell readers what information they will find when they read over the table you are asking them to look at so they can better understand your results. Take a look at Chapter 15 for details on using figures and tables in your paper. In that chapter, we cover all the APA–formatting issues, and believe us, there are specific ways that APA wants you to present your findings in tables and figures.

Let Us Talk Statistics

10

When including in your Results section the type of statistic you worked with, there is no need to provide a reference for the commonly used analyses (e.g., *t* tests, multiple regressions). Few (if any) readers will be excited to go find that reference and spend an evening reading all about commonly used inferential statistics. To be fair, there are some pretty exciting books that cover the treatments of statistics using SPSS, a common statistical package. One of our favorites is Field (2014), a real hoot to read (and you think we are kidding?). There are two reasons you should consider including a reference with your statistics, and you will likely need to be concerned only with the first reason we include here. If your paper topic is focused on a particularly obscure type of statistic, you need to include a reference. Or if you use a common statistic in a most unusual way, a reference should be included. But we usually discourage our students from using or creating new and unusual statistics for their research, so it is unlikely you will need a reference for that reason. If you needed to include an in-text citation to a statistical approach, it might look like this: "According to Gorsuch (1982), eigenvalues > 1.0 are generally acceptable for factors extracted after a principle components analysis."

These same rules apply to formulas. There is no need to include the formulas for common statistics such as *t* tests or means. But when you start to use those newfangled, never-before-heard-of statistics, then by all means, present your equations. Now, if you counter that you have never heard of most statistics before, we counter-counter that we mean the statistics not commonly seen in published journal articles. We are guessing you will not be likely to include any newfangled formulas when you are just learning how to write in APA style. For that matter, many researchers who are well versed in APA style are not creating newfangled formulas.

All that said, the important question is how to **present your statistics** within the Results section of your paper. (Note: For general tips on writing the Results section, check out Landrum, 2012.) Having taught research methods, we know that presenting results is often a difficult task for students to learn at first, but we can tell you that once students grasp the way this section is formatted, most future Results sections are a snap. Personally, we think that sometimes students new to psychology skip reading the Results section because they don't think they understand the concepts and the statistics, but during and after a course in research methods, you shouldn't skip this reading anymore. The important idea to keep in mind is that you need to write this section of your paper so the reader can understand exactly what you found when you ran your statistical analyses. For example, you need to write about the groups you compared and the results from each group, and you need to know your means, standard deviations, and effect sizes. In other instances, you may need to report the correlations, sample sizes, or power analyses. The type of numbers presented really depends on the type of statistics you have performed and the complexity of your design. Here is an example from a Results section:

> There was a significant, positive correlation between scores of both the objectification of the models and self-objectification, $r(81) = .64$, $p < .001$, indicating that individuals who objectify themselves also show a tendency to objectify others and vice versa. Interestingly, self-esteem showed significant, positive relationships with objectification tendency, $r(81) = .24$, $p = .007$, and self-objectification, $r(81) = .29$, $p = .001$.

Notice in the examples that follow, you typically include the statistical information after a comma at the end of the sentence, and when you write about the means within your text, you use the words and not the symbols. You would write, "The mean of the experimental group was significantly greater" and not "The M of the experimental group . . . " The symbols are used when reporting the means within parentheses (see Table 10.1 for the most common symbols used). About the correlation example above—note that there is not a leading zero (0.64) before reporting the correlation coefficient—the technique above is correct (.64). If a number cannot be greater than one (or less than negative one), then there is no need for a leading zero. The same is true for p values! Since a p value cannot be greater than 1, there is no need to report $p = 0.007$; just .007 will do. And one more item to note (sorry)—treat the equal sign like a word, that is, there should always be a space on both sides of the equal sign just like there is a space on both sides of a word. Now for some examples.

10

Table 10.1 Typical Statistical Symbols and Abbreviations

Symbol or Abbreviation in English	Meaning of Symbol or Abbreviation
ANCOVA	Analysis of covariance
ANOVA	Analysis of variance
CI	Confidence interval
d	Cohen's measure of effect size
d'	Discriminability, sensitivity measure
df	Degrees of freedom
ES	Effect size
f	Frequency
f_e	Expected frequency
f_o	Observed frequency
F	F distribution
GLM	Generalized linear model
H_0	Null hypothesis
H_1 (or H_a)	Alternative hypothesis
HSD	Tukey's honestly significant difference
M (or $\bar{X}$)	Sample mean
MANCOVA	Multivariate analysis of covariance
MANOVA	Multivariate analysis of variance
Mdn	Median in the sample
MS	Mean square
MSE	Mean square error
n	A part of the sample population
N	Total number in the sample
ns	Not statistically significant
p	Probability
r	Pearson's correlation coefficient

10

Symbol or Abbreviation in English	Meaning of Symbol or Abbreviation
r^2	Estimate of the Pearson product-moment correlation squared
r_s	Spearman rank order correlation
R	Multiple correlation
R^2	Multiple correlation squared; measure of strength of association
SD	Standard deviation
SE	Standard error
SS	Sum of squares
t	Student's t distribution; a statistical test based on the student's t distribution; the sample value of the t-test statistic
z	A standardized score; the value of a statistic divided by its standard error
Symbol or Abbreviation in Greek	**Meaning of Symbol or Abbreviation**
α	Alpha (probability of making a Type I Error)
β	Beta (probability of making a Type II Error)
η^2	Eta squared (effect size)
μ	Population mean
ρ	Population product-moment correlation
σ	Standard deviation (for the population)
σ^2	Variance
χ^2	Chi-square distribution
Σ	Summation
Φ	Phi (effect size for chi-square distributions)
Ω	Omega (effect size for meta-analysis)

10

Incorrect: The M for children using the drawing technique was 72% and was not significantly different than the Ms for children in the verbal condition at 70%, $F(1, 48) = 1.45$, $p = .09$.

Correct: Children's reports when using the drawing technique ($M = 72\%$, $SD = 0.45$) were not significantly more accurate than children's reports when asked just to tell us what they could remember without drawing ($M = 70\%$, $SD = 1.89$), $F(1, 48) = 1.45$, $p = .090$.

Basics and Beyond

One of the more complicated rules when writing an APA–style Results section is whether to use standard, **boldface**, or *italicized* typeface. Typically, the type of statistics you will include should be italicized. So when writing about how many participants you included in your experiment, you use an uppercase, italicized N. You switch to a lowercase, italicized n when writing about a subset of that number (e.g., how many participants were in your experimental group). See Table 10.1, adapted from a similar table presented in the *PM* (APA, 2010a).

If, by chance, you are including statistics that involve vectors or matrices (and we doubt that will be the case), then you will type those symbols in **boldface.** You might need to include a symbol for Greek letters (e.g., β for beta), subscripts (e.g., H_0 for null hypothesis), or superscripts (e.g., r^2 for r-squared). Those symbols—Greek letters, subscripts, or superscripts that are not variables—are typed in standard type. (Note: You can use the Symbols font to insert Greek letters. Most are intuitive, such as b for the beta symbol β, but you can Google for the English equivalent and then "translate" by changing to the Symbols font.) Now, to make things even more complicated, the APA *PM* reminds us that all other test statistics are italicized (e.g., t and F). Again, check out Table 10.1, which illustrates some of the most commonly used test statistics and their abbreviations.

10

Formatting Your Results Paragraph

Once you figure out what language to use when writing about your statistics, keep a few basic rules in mind. First, when writing out mathematical formulas, include spaces in your mathematical copy. In other words, treat each number as if it were a separate word. Do not forget to include punctuation after equations. This is true whether an equation is in a paragraph or standing all alone.

Incorrect: $1+3=4$

Correct: $1 + 3 = 4$

Most equations should fit nicely on one line and are easy to include in your text. When you need to include fractions, just use a slash (/) to present the numerator over the denominator. When you need to include a more complicated equation (e.g., one that requires a square root of a fraction), then you will need to display it on its very own line.

Incorrect: 3 / 4

Correct: 3/4

Finally (and we promise this is the last part), when you are writing about percentages, APA style requires that you use the % symbol when preceded by a number (e.g., 10%); otherwise, use the word *percentage* (e.g., "a large percentage of the sample"). Note: Use the word *percent* only when it follows a number that must be spelled out (e.g., at the beginning of a sentence); do not use it in place of *percentage*.

Incorrect: Less than 10 percent of the sample reported wearing protective clothing.

Correct: Less than 10% of the sample reported wearing protective clothing.

Incorrect: A small percent of the sample reported wearing protective clothing.

Correct: A small percentage of the sample reported wearing protective clothing.

Greek letters, subscripts, and superscripts that are not variables are in standard type; symbols for vectors and matrices are in bold; and statistical symbols are in italics (APA, 2010a, p. 118). If something can be represented by both an abbreviation and a symbol, consult Table 4.5 (pp. 119–123) of the APA *PM*. The fine print on page 123 instructs us, in such cases, to use the abbreviation when referring to the concept and the symbol when referring to a specific number.

Including Effect Size and Power

For many undergraduate research assignments, especially those completed within a single semester, sample sizes are often not very large. As a result, there is also an unfortunate shortage of significant findings. When faced with statistical tests that are not significant, you may erroneously conclude that you have wasted your time. But wait; statistical significance is influenced by two major factors: sample size and effect size. If the number of students in your study is very large, this large sample size can make even small statistical differences significant. In this scenario, a small difference (although statistically significant) may not mean much by practical means—thus, researchers use effect size as a way of assessing practical significance—that is, is the difference truly meaningful (and not just an artifact of a large N)? By the same token, if you have a very small sample, then you may not get a statistically significant difference *even though there may be differences between groups*. Not finding statistical significance with a very small sample might just mean the research study could not detect the existing difference (Gurung & Schwartz, 2009). This is where the size of your effect comes in handy.

Effect sizes are valuable statistics that provide the reader with a sense of the importance of your research results. Essentially, this statistic indicates the strength of the relationship between your variables. So in addition to knowing if the relationship is significant, readers are interested in knowing the strength of the relationship. Correspondingly, including the effect size in your Results section is now an explicit recommendation of the APA *PM* (APA, 2010a). The key is that the size of the effect provides an idea of the real-world significance of the finding. Researchers often use a benchmark established by Cohen (1988) called d' (this is pronounced as dee-prime), and Cohen categorized effect sizes of .20 as small, .50 as medium, and .80 as large. In most psychological research, an effect size of .20 is something to be taken very seriously. Even a small effect size can have large real-world implications (e.g., the effect of aspirin in reducing heart attacks has an effect size of only .06; see Bloom & Lipsey, 2004).

Effect sizes for most statistics are available directly in the statistical program (e.g., SPSS) and are sometimes represented by the letter d. The *PM* also strongly recommends the use of confidence intervals (CIs), a measure of the precision of your statistic, also available in the statistics program. The effect size and confidence interval follow your reporting of the p value. Like all statistics in APA style, the letter d is in italics. Here is what it looks like in a Results section from a study by Prestwich, Perugini, and Hurling (2010, pp. 45–46):

> In a surprise recall task at Time 2, those in the implementation intention + plan reminder condition showed greater plan recall than those in the implementation intention + goal reminder condition, $t(84) = 5.09, p < .001, d = 1.10$, 95% CI [0.63, 1.62], supporting Hypothesis 4.

Statistics can be intimidating. The neat outcome is that if you learn to write them correctly, you will have an easier time reading Results sections as well. Then the fun really starts as those mazes of numbers all make sense and research really comes to life. Have fun.

10

Writing Your Discussion 11

It's a Wrap

Congratulations! You completed your research, and it is now time to tell the world, or at least your professor and perhaps the psychological community, what your results really mean. In Chapter 7, you can learn how to write your Introduction. In Chapter 9, we provide details about how to write the Method section, and Chapter 10 details how to write your Results section. Of course, once you tell the reader how you tested your hypothesis and if you found a result that is statistically significant, it is time to explain what you believe those findings really mean; that is the primary purpose of the Discussion section of your paper. The Discussion section of your paper immediately follows the Method and Results sections of your paper. In this last written section of your paper you get to write about what you believe your results really mean and how those results fit in the literature you reviewed throughout your introduction (although the Discussion section will be followed by your References section, and tables and figures—if you have them). Now, you still need to stick to a scientific writing style, but the Discussion section is where you can include your own opinion. Of course those opinions need to be tied back to the literature and the data; but there is some leeway given that there are multiple interpretations to many research projects. Though you are not about to write poetry or prose about your findings, your Discussion section is where you can let your creative side shine.

Remember, this section needs to cover all of your findings. You cannot just pick and choose those findings that are consistent with your hypotheses or those that are easy to explain. You have to write about the results you expected to find and the results that seem to not make any sense to you given past research. You cannot ignore those unexpected and surprising findings. Instead, here is where you explain possible reasons you found those unexpected results. Keep in mind, it is best to tie those possible explanations to the literature. These explanations should be based on scientific reasoning and not just what you think best explains the unexpected. To be consistent with other chapters, in this chapter we explain what to include in your Discussion, how to format this section of your paper, what you can do to get started, and how to organize your Discussion. To close, we include a checklist of common errors to avoid. To help follow all the information on how to write this section of your paper, we have once again included a sample student paper at the end of this chapter.

Formatting Your Discussion Section

APA formatting requires that this section follows immediately after your Results section. Once again, remember to double-space throughout. No new page, no additional space needed in between sections or headings. You use a bolded, centered, heading titled "Discussion," and that heading is the same font size as the rest of the text in your paper. When discussing the implications of your research you are writing about, use past tense, when writing about your current judgments, use present tense for that material, and when discussing future research . . . you guessed it . . . future tense.

To summarize:

- Start the Discussion section immediately after the Results section.
- Double-space the entire Discussion section.
- The heading here is simply the word Discussion, boldfaced and centered.
- Write the Discussion section using past tense for completed research, present tense for your current judgments, and future tense about ideas for future research.

What to Include in Your Discussion Section

First, let us start with what to include in this section of your paper.
Your discussion section should include the following information:

- A restatement of the purpose and/or the hypothesis of your research
- Did you support your hypothesis?
- What were the overall findings that emerged from your research?
- Did you find anything surprising that you did not expect?
- Are your findings generalizable?
- Did you uncover any limitations concerning your methodology?
- What are the larger implications of your findings?
- How do your findings coincide with the existing literature?
- With the literature in mind, what do you believe your findings tell us about the research question?

11

- What are the alternative interpretations of your findings that should be considered?
- What is the direction one can take when addressing the same topic in future research?
- What gap in the literature does this research fill?
- A final summary paragraph that concludes your paper

Getting Your Discussion Section Started

As you can see from the list above, the Discussion section is where you get to pull it all together. To help you do this, with your findings in mind, we suggest that you read over your Introduction section and your Results section. Given the past studies and the results reported by researchers, think about how your findings fit with the related past research. We do want to warn you to not just rewrite your introduction for this section of your paper. Though the same studies will likely be cited and included in your Discussion section, the way those studies are included in your Discussion should be different. Whereas in your Introduction section you used those studies to justify and provide the rationale for your hypotheses, in your Discussion section you will write about your results, how they fit with existing theories in the field, what are the possible different interpretations of your findings, and what you believe your findings illustrate with regard to psychological theory. We caution you here to avoid what we see many of our students do when first learning to write a Discussion section, particularly if you did not support your hypothesis. Do not simply restate your results, then explain all the limitations you encountered (e.g., not enough participants) that did not allow you to support your prediction and then discuss future research in which you would include more participants to test your hypothesis. You need to dig deeper than that. And, if you answer all, if not most, of the questions listed above in what to include in this section of your paper, you will go beyond that minimal approach to your Discussion section.

Organizing Your Discussion Section

If you read Chapter 7 on writing an Introduction, you will remember the hourglass analogy. The Introduction is the top of the hourglass, starting with a more general focus and moving to a specific hypothesis. Well, your Discussion is the bottom half of the hourglass, starting off very specific and ending with a more general focus on your topic. To do this, start this section by discussing your hypothesis and whether you supported your prediction. Then you start to interpret your results and elaborate how your findings fit in the literature and in the related psychological theory. If you encountered some unexpected results, you should then broaden your discussion. This leads to possible interpretations of your findings, what you believe is the best explanation for your findings, as well as consideration of some limitations you identified after you completed your research. The final paragraph in your discussion should provide a conclusion to your paper. What do we now know about the topic you addressed that we did not know before you conducted your research? What questions are still unknown? Consider finishing your paper with a statement that indicates what we learned. What is the take home lesson? This is often a broad statement that discusses the larger implications of your research, reminding the reader why your topic is important. Take a look at the sample Discussion section included at the end of this chapter to see how these questions are addressed.

Just as we suggested using an outline to organize your Introduction, we suggest the same for your Discussion section. To help us illustrate how to organize a Discussion section, we have included a sample paper of one of our students. You'll notice that we included a number of citations in the outline that can help tie your findings to past research as you write this section. With permission from Diep "Penny" Trieu, the Discussion section from her honors paper from Randolph College is included at the end of this chapter. We will refer to sections of her discussion in her paper, titled *Modes of Instagram's Usage and Levels of Narcissism*, to help us illustrate how to best organize a Discussion section.

Often this section of your paper starts with a statement of support or lack of support for the hypothesis tested. Indeed, that is a common way to start your Discussion section. But why not recapture your reader's interest again at this point in your paper, and provide a brief paragraph that restates why your research is incredibly interesting. Start with a paragraph that restates the purpose. In Penny's paper, that is exactly what she did. Rather than jumping right into her hypothesis and whether she found support for that prediction, she started the Discussion section by writing about narcissism and social media sites again. Not exactly as she wrote in her Introduction, but once again setting the stage to write about what her findings mean. Next, you will see a paragraph that discusses the hypothesis and if the findings that emerged supported that prediction. Notice that when discussing the findings, you need to write about the differences or lack of differences you found, but you do not include statistical information in this section. You simply state if a significant finding emerged, the direction of that difference, and whether that finding supported your prediction. No means, no F, t, z, or p values here.

The paragraphs that follow are where the organization gets a little more challenging and where an outline will be very helpful. If you have multiple hypotheses, you could organize your Discussion around each prediction. Or you could organize your Discussion around the different research questions addressed by your project. You could consider the different analyses conducted or the different variables you included in your study and how your findings compare to similar studies examining those same variables. You need to decide which approach provides the best way to present the implications of your study. Regardless of the approach you choose, many of the paragraphs that follow will state whether your findings are consistent with the past studies you included in your literature review. Be sure to cite those studies in APA style and discuss why your findings are consistent or why your findings contradict the results of others.

To help you introduce your findings in relation to those in the past, to discuss something interesting you found that is unique to the area of research, to note some limitations of your research, and to provide avenues for future research, below we provide some of the typical transitions included in Discussion sections.

When your findings support past research or a particular theory, you could state:

- Consistent with Franklin and Clinton's (2014) findings . . .
- These results are consistent with the findings of Franklin and Clinton (2014) and illustrate . . .
- This was not surprising given the findings of Franklin and Clinton (2014), who also found . . .
- As predicted by researchers using cognitive dissonance theory . . .

Keep in mind that even when your findings do not fit with the literature you have read, there is a great deal you can say about that inconsistency. In fact, one might argue there is more to say when you do not support your hypothesis than when you do. You cannot avoid discussing these findings, and in fact you might enjoy trying to figure out why your findings do not match up with those in the past. Take a close look at methodological differences. Often that is where our students find the key to better understanding the inconsistent finding. When your findings are NOT consistent with past research you could state:

- Contrary to the findings of Franklin and Clinton (2014), our results . . .
- Surprisingly, results from the current study are not consistent with . . .
- This discrepancy between past findings and the current study may be due to . . .
- In contrast to attachment theory . . .
- This inconsistency could be explained by . . .

11

Whether or not your outcomes supported your hypothesis, we are confident you can find at least one interesting contribution resulting from your research. Find that contribution and include it in your Discussion section. Be proud of that contribution, but do not go overboard. Some humility here is important. When you want to point out a result that is unique to your research, consider the following:

- A notable finding in the current study is that . . .
- Distinct from past research, given our findings, it is clear . . .
- Because we defined honor systems according to the specific type of system in place, . . .
- Given the variety of toys included in the present research, our findings . . .
- These findings help refine the existing theory of attachment by . . .

One section of your Discussion will allow the reader to understand what you believe you would do differently if you were to conduct this research again. Often these limitations pertain to issues of control or lack thereof. Sometimes the limitations are related to the limited subject pool available on your campus. In other cases, limitations are created due to the timeframe available to collect data and complete a course assignment by a certain deadline. When you are ready to discuss the limitations of your own research, consider the following:

- Perhaps our findings are due to the way in which we assessed . . .
- Because our methods included only participants from a homogeneous sample, . . .
- Our manipulation of immediacy did not provide the . . .

There are always ways in which you could think of conducting your research differently . . . if you actually have the time to do so before you finish a course or before you graduate. Here again, changes in methodology are often a great place to start. Or perhaps, after conducting your research you came across another study that changes your way of thinking about your topic. This brings up an important point about writing your Discussion. As you consider the implications of your findings, you might start to search for additional research related to your topic that you had not thought of when developing your study. As a result, it is common for writers to include articles in the Discussion section not included in your review of the literature. Just be sure to cite those new studies appropriately, and include the new studies in your reference list. To start a section on future research directions, consider the following:

- To gain a better understanding of the relationship between chronotypes and ethical decision making, researchers could consider . . .
- Given the gender imbalance in the present study, future research should . . .
- In the future, rather than a 2-week delay between event and testing, a longer delay would allow for . . .
- Future research is needed to . . .

Though some research is theoretical in nature and cannot be applied outside, if you are interested in providing ways in which your findings can be applied outside of theoretical theory, you could state:

- These findings provide mechanisms through which educators could consider in order to . . .
- Given the findings concerning significant influence of task complexity on attentional competence, designers considering human factors should . . .
- Clinicians should consider these findings in order to . . .

In the end, your Discussion should leave the reader with a take-home lesson, and that lesson should focus on what we now know about the topic in question that we did not know before you conducted this research. After indicating whether you supported your hypothesis, you need to explain how that take-home lesson connects to what we already knew, what questions remain unanswered, and what direction to take in the future. If you provide this information, your Discussion section should be in good shape.

Common Mistakes to Avoid in Your Discussion Section

Use the following as a mini-checklist to **avoid** these **common errors:**

- A rewrite of your Introduction with little enlightenment about your findings
- Discussing your findings without placing them within the current literature
- Speculating as to why your findings emerged without a connection to scientific findings; just posing opinions without reason
- Only focusing on the results that support your hypothesis
- Presenting a biased interpretation of your findings without considering obvious alternative explanations
- Focusing too much on the limitations of your research rather than on your contributions
- Ending your Discussion abruptly; forgetting to include the take-home lesson from your research
- Not including directions for future research

11

Outline for the Sample Discussion Section Included

I. Restating the purpose of the research (Twenge et al., 2008)

   a. Understanding the possible connection between the rise in social media use and narcissism (Bergman et al., 2008; Davenport et al., 2009)

   b. Different types of social network sites: others- vs. self-focused (Ellison et al., 2009; Steinfield et al., 2013)

   c. Effect on levels of aggression

   d. The findings: Was the hypothesis supported?

II. Strengths of the current research

   a. The use of Instagram (Buffardi & Campbell, 2008)

   b. Experimental examination of social media usage and narcissism

      i. Past experimental studies do not compare pre- and post-levels (Gentile et al., 2012; Horton et al., 2014)

III. Specific findings on narcissism (Buffardi & Campbell, 2018)

   a. The others-focused group results

      i. Self-focused explanation

      ii. Differences between different social media sites

      iii. Change in instructions needed

IV. Specific findings on aggression

   a. The self-focused group results (Toma & Hancock, 2013)

      i. Self-affirmation and aggression (Thomaes et al., 2009)

      ii. Threatened egotism theory (Baumeister et al., 1996)

V. Limitations

   a. Few male participants

   b. Additional time on social network sites outside experiment

VI. Future research

   a. Measure narcissism both pretest and posttest

   b. More specific monitoring of social network site usage

VII. Conclusions

   a. Restatement of overall findings

   b. Use of SNS (social network sites) could lead to increased levels of narcissism

      i. Future research needed to understand the possible mechanisms involved

11

Sample Paper

NARCISSISM AND INSTAGRAM   1

Discussion

Temporally, the rise of narcissism, documented by Twenge and colleagues (2008), and the increasing adoption of social media platforms, have accompanied each other. Such timing, in addition to the propensity for self-expression and self-promotion on the sites, has driven a series of studies investigating the connection between the two. As a result, researchers have repeatedly found a clear relationship between narcissism and social media (e.g., Bergman et al., 2008; Davenport et al., 2009). Compared to non-narcissists, narcissists mostly differ in their approach to social media as a platform for amassing followers and promoting themselves, rather than connecting with others and building connections. On the other hand, social media remain networking sites, where people could easily connect with one another and build social ties (Ellison et al., 2007; Steinfield et al., 2013), which may lead to decreases in narcissism (Giacomin & Jordan, 2014).

Prompted by the two facets of social network sites for both communal connection and self-promotion, I attempted to discover if asking participants to focus on themselves or on others on Instagram would, respectively, increase or decrease

11

NARCISSISM AND INSTAGRAM   2

their narcissism. Aggression, as a principal negative effect of narcissism, was also examined and compared between the self-focused group and the others-focused group, with the self-focused group expected to be more aggressive than the others-focused group. However, my findings did not support any of these three hypotheses and even contradicted the second hypothesis: participants in the others-focused group exhibited a significant increase in their levels of narcissism after the manipulation.

Several strengths of the current research stand out as particularly intriguing and constructive to the current literature. First, through several studies, narcissists consistently expressed a preference for pictures and for self-promotion through the picture medium (Buffardi & Campbell, 2008). Despite this prominence of the role of pictures in narcissistic self-presentations, the existing literature features few if any study of Instagram or any other picture-based social network site, and narcissism. My current research outcomes filled in this gap by focusing on Instagram and the picture medium. Specifically, participants were asked to interact with their Instagram profiles or other people's Instagram profiles and post new picture-based content.

11

NARCISSISM AND INSTAGRAM   3

Second, the pretest and posttest experimental design of the current research demonstrated a change in the levels of narcissism of participants. The majority of studies on social media and narcissism have been correlational (e.g., Buffardi & Campbell, 2008). The researchers in two experimental studies did not compare narcissism before and after the experimental manipulation (Gentile et al., 2012; Horton et al., 2014). Instead, they compared the narcissism scores *between* the others-focused group and self-focused group after the manipulation. With this method, Gentile and colleagues detected higher levels of narcissism for participants using MySpace, compared to participants using Google Map. They did not detect a difference between participants using Facebook and participants using Google Map. As for Horton and colleagues, who investigated only Facebook, they did not report significant differences among agentic (self-focused) thinking-mode participants, communal (others-focused) thinking-mode participants, or control condition participants. In the current research, the increase in narcissism of participants in the others-focused group could be detected only through a *within-group* comparison of their narcissism scores, before and after the manipulation. The others-focused group and self-focused group in the current experiment did not differ in their posttest narcissism scores. Therefore, the inclusion of both pretest and posttest scores in the analysis enabled a more direct comparison and observation of changes in levels of narcissism.

A few factors might have contributed to the findings of participants in the others-focused group increasing their narcissism. First, in interacting with others on social network sites, participants might have somehow engaged in agentic (self-centered) thinking mode. The instructions of the others-focused group explicitly asked participants to think about, comment on, and interact with other people's profiles. However, since these people are either close friends or family members, looking at and interacting with these individuals' profiles may have an unexpected and indirect self-focused effect on participants. In addition, after participants comment and like on others' posts, others may feel the need to reciprocate. As such, for the duration of the experiment, traffic and attention to others-focused participants' profiles may increase and activate their self-focused thinking as well. Another factor might lie in the medium. Horton and colleagues (2014), who examined Facebook, did not detect any differences in narcissism among their participant groups. Gentile and

NARCISSISM AND INSTAGRAM   5

colleagues (2012) discovered higher narcissism in participants

using MySpace, not Facebook. The current study, studying

Instagram, not Facebook, also found higher levels of narcissism

in one participant group. The discrepancy of findings that

emerge when comparing studies including MySpace, Facebook,

or Instagram, attest to the likely differences in functions each

site serves and in turn the effects of using each site on the user.

In other words, certain features about each specific site, such

as Facebook's relatively stronger emphasis on connecting users

or Instagram's exclusive focus on pictures, might account

for the differences in the effects of using these sites on users'

levels of narcissism.

On a related note, in the self-focused condition, though the

instructions explicitly asked participants to reflect on and post

new content on their own profiles, the new content may not, in

nature, be self-focused or even self-promotional. For example,

one participant posted her favorite quote, which, according to

her description, denoted her life philosophy. Furthermore, when

participants reviewed their profiles, the reviewing might have had

a self-affirming effect on their self-concept, as proposed by prior

research on social network sites and self-affirmation (Toma &

Hancock, 2013). Self-affirming processes help individuals fortify stronger self-concepts that deem them less susceptible to the vulnerable self-concepts associated with narcissism.

Moreover, self-focused group participants also reacted to the criticism with lower levels of aggression, although the difference was not statistically significant. This might be additional evidence that self-affirmation took place, as self-affirmation can also alleviate aggression (Thomaes, Bushman, Orobio de Castro, Cohen, & Denissen, 2009). The examination of aggression is another contribution of the current research to the literature. Most studies on the intersection of narcissism and social media so far have examined primarily the construct of narcissism, as measured by the Narcissistic Personality Inventory, but not notable effects associated with narcissism, such as aggression. Not only did my current research include another dimension to narcissism, the findings related to aggression, though not statistically significant, corroborated the significant finding of narcissism. The others-focused group increased their narcissism, and the self-focused group did not experience changes in narcissism. Per the threatened egotism theory (Baumeister et al., 1996), elevated narcissism would lead to stronger reaction to ego threats, such as the criticism of participants' Instagram profiles in the present study. Accordingly, the others-focused

NARCISSISM AND INSTAGRAM   7

group reacted to criticism with higher aggression than the self-focused group.

Some limitations may affect the interpretation of the current research. Gender was not a salient factor of the study, but, the participants, with 91% female, can be more diverse. In addition, I had no control or monitoring of how participants use Instagram outside of the experiment. Thus, though the present experiment monitored and manipulated 45 minutes of participants' usage of Instagram within one week, participants might be spending hours on other activities, neutralizing or undermining any effect produced by the experimental procedure.

The lack of controlling extended to the real nature of participants' experimental procedure. Though the instructions explicitly asked participants to focus on others or on themselves, their actual activities may not correspond to the assigned mode. For example, if, when commenting on someone else's Instagram, the participants somehow drew attention to themselves, the interaction would become self-focused.

These limitations and strengths of the current study lend themselves to several directions. Future studies should attempt to measure and compare both pretest and posttest narcissism scores,

11

NARCISSISM AND INSTAGRAM   8

which might reveal more than comparing just posttest scores between different groups.

Previous researchers did not detect changes within groups of participants but rather compared between two groups. A pretest–posttest design offered a more direct detection of changes in levels of narcissism in participants.

With regard to medium to explore, Facebook, as the most popular social network site, has received the majority of researchers' attention. However, that the current research on Instagram found inconsistent results from previous studies on Facebook signify the diversity of these sites and the necessity for research into sites other than Facebook. More importantly, a design where all of participants' activities, including postings, reactions to participants' postings, likes, and comments, would allow for a more sophisticated analysis of the characteristics of participants' social media usage, including whether the postings are self-focused, others-focused, or neutral. The analysis would enable a more accurate description of which psychological processes occur when participants use Instagram, including whether self-affirmation took place for participants in the self-focused group.

In conclusion following an experimental manipulation of Instagram usage, I demonstrated an increase in narcissism,

NARCISSISM AND INSTAGRAM   9

although the direction of change was unexpected: others-

focused participants increased their narcissism, and self-focused

participants did not experience changes in levels of narcissism.

Thus, the notion that certain approaches to social media may

lead to increases in narcissism is reinforced. As long as probable

increases in generational narcissism remain salient in our society

and social media continues its prevalence, future researchers should

pursue investigations on this subject to bolster our understanding of

mechanisms underlying changes in narcissism and usage of social

media.

11

Everybody Needs References 12

A Helpful Note

The new APA *PM* (APA, 2010a) includes 77 different examples of reference formats. Providing 77 different examples in this chapter would be overwhelming. Frankly, many of the rules in the *PM* will not be needed when first learning how to write in APA style. This section is a great example of working on a "need-to-know basis." There are a small number of commonly used reference sources. These are the ones we feature. We believe the number of details included in the *PM* can overwhelm most students, and we therefore downplay them. By sticking to the basics, we try to minimize the confusing exceptions and details. With each example, we have listed the basic components of that type of reference, allowing you to see the differences between each type of source you are likely to cite. However, we wanted to be up front and let you know that we have included the types of references that are *most likely* to be included in your paper. If you feel compelled to know those extra details, we are confident you know where to look. One more thing. More of our students are using websites that purport to convert your reference into APA style. Be careful. Please do not be lulled into a false sense of security if you are using a database reference—most databases offer an APA–style citation for your reference, *but these are often wrong!!* There is no substitute for knowing the rules yourself.

Creating Your References Section

When writing about that very interesting topic you chose for your paper, undoubtedly you took a look at the past research related to your subject matter to make sure your great idea for an experiment or term paper had not already been completed by someone else. As we explained in Chapter 5, when you include information from any of those other primary sources (those you read on your own), you are immediately in need of a reference list for your paper. You must include most of the items you cite in your paper in your reference list. This way, interested readers who want to take a look at one of the sources you used will have all the information needed to access that source on their own. Think of your reference list as an indication of your academic pedigree; you get to show off your skills in locating sources and analyzing what is relevant and what is not. Your References section recreates the intellectual journey you took to draw the conclusions you made in your paper.

Most of the sources you include in your reference list will be journal articles, books, or chapters from books. We also recognize that you find many of your sources through electronic searches; so we have included a section to cover how to reference those as well. Luckily, if you cited a personal communication in your paper (and we do not recommend that you do so unless necessary), you do not need to include it in your reference list (this is the only instance when a citation in the text does not require a corresponding reference)—though we know that Aunt Susan, who discussed the importance of communication in any relationship, will be upset that she was not given the recognition deserved in your paper. Remember, you need to include only the sources you cited in your paper (i.e., this is not a bibliography containing a list of every item you researched). One common mistake our students make is to list a reference they read because it was related to their topic even though they did not include information from that source in their paper in the end. Sometimes this error occurs because students worked on a number of drafts of their paper and during that time deleted some information (and a citation or two . . . or three) that included sources they had listed in the References section earlier—yet another good reason for proofreading!

One easy way to see if all the sources you have cited are in the reference list and all the sources in the reference list are in fact cited in your paper is to search for each first author's name in the reference list using Word's "Find" function (see the screenshot of the header bar that appears in Word 2013, or in any version of Word, use the keyboard shortcut Ctrl+F). The "Find" function on the right of the header is circled in the screenshot. Simply type in any word or name, and Word will search for that word or name throughout your document. For a more low-tech solution, just print a paper copy and hand check each citation in the text against each source listed in the References section. You can also create a split screen of your Word file so you can see your reference section simultaneously while you proof your paper—a simple way is to just copy your references to a new document that sits side by side with your main file. Make sure every citation in the text has a corresponding reference—and that name spellings, publication dates, and page numbers (for quotations or specific pages you want the reader to see in the source you are citing) match between a citation and its reference; likewise, make sure every entry in the References section is located and cited properly in the text somewhere. Finally, one more common mistake is changing the order of authors in a reference to alphabetical order in the citation of

12

that reference. Always make sure you use the same author order in your citation as listed in the source. We mentioned this in an earlier chapter but believe it is worthwhile to mention it again here. The order of authors' names is something one should never change, because that order is usually determined by each author's contribution to the research.

Let us get to the reason you turned to this chapter. How do you put together a reference list? The reference list is the part of the paper that makes you realize APA style is really different from other styles of writing. So if you are used to writing papers for an English, history, or chemistry course, get ready to learn some new rules. There are *very* specific rules you need to follow. In our many years of teaching students how to write in APA style, we have found that some of the biggest APA–style challenges occur when attempting to create a list of references. This is likely because of the specific rules for each of the different types of sources. The good news is that the rules, though abundant, are very specific. You can nail them, especially with our help. The bad news is that there are many details and ways to make mistakes when creating a list of your references. This is a part of your paper in which you have to pay special attention to detail.

Using Abbreviations

12

For many of the references we describe subsequently, you will need to include information in the form of an abbreviation. Many abbreviations are used in this section, some of which are standard abbreviations (e.g., state names). Additional abbreviations are not as commonly used. To help clarify what abbreviations to use, we have included Table 12.1. For more on abbreviations, see Chapter 18.

The Basics

To simplify this part of APA style, we will start by listing the basic components, a couple examples, and the basic rules for formatting this part of your paper. Then we present some of the more detailed rules based on the type of source you want to include in the reference list. We will warn you now: Where the rules start to get more complicated is in the details about the different types of sources. So once we cover the very basics, we include examples of the most common types of references you are likely to use when first learning how to write in APA style. **HINT:** When using the examples below, pay attention to the placement of

Table 12.1 Using Abbreviations in Your References Section

The Term	The Abbreviation for the Term in Your Reference List (With Accompanying Punctuation)
Digital object identifier	doi:
Edition	(2nd ed.).
Editor	(Ed.).
Editors	(Eds.). or (Eds.),
Revised edition	(Rev. ed.).
No date	(n.d.).
Page (for a chapter in a book)	(p. 18).
Pages (for a chapter in a book)	(pp. 194–201)
Third edition	(3rd ed.).
Volume	(Vol. 3),
Volumes	(Vols. 1–3)

12

punctuation (e.g., commas and periods) and to what is in *italics*. For each source listed in your reference list, APA format has rules on when to use a comma and when to use a period, as well as additional rules on what part of the reference should be italicized.

The basic components of most citations placed in your reference list are these:

- Alphabetize your list of references using the first author's last name. Only the initials of the authors' first and middle names are included (i.e., do not write out the full first name), and there is a space between the initials. For a work with multiple authors, a comma separates each author's name (even when there are only two authors).
- For a work with multiple authors, use an ampersand (&) before the last author's name, with a comma before the ampersand.
- The order of authors for any work listed as a reference should never be changed from the order listed on the first page of the article (i.e., never alphabetize multiple authors within a single reference).
- Date of publication (the real date of publication—not the date you found it—especially pertinent for any citations based on information retrieved from the Internet) is placed within parentheses, followed by a period.
- The title of the work follows the date of publication.
- The entire reference is prepared using a hanging indent and is double-spaced.

| Table 12.2   Where to Find the Different Types of References in This Chapter ||
Type of Reference	Page Number
Journal articles	p. 155
Books	p. 156
Chapter in edited book	p. 156
Online sources	p. 157
Works with seven or more authors	p. 159
Conference presentations	p. 159
Newspapers and magazines	p. 160

Table 12.2 points you to the exact page in this chapter where you can find each of the basic types of references you will likely include in your paper.

Journal Articles

Now on to the details determined by the type of source you are including in your References section. Let us start with a journal article, which is the most common type of reference you will be expected to use. This is an example of a journal article:

> Gurung, R. A. R., Ansburg, P. I., Alexander, P. A., Lawrence, N. K., & Johnson, D. E. (2008). Scholarship of teaching and learning strategies and tactics: The state of the scholarship of teaching and learning in psychology. *Teaching of Psychology, 35,* 249–261. doi:10.1080/00986280802374203

In this example for a journal article, notice the following:

- Both the title of the article and the title of the journal are included.
- The only words capitalized in the title of the article are the first word and the first word after the colon. If there are any proper nouns in the title, they are always capitalized.
- Except for conjunctions (e.g., *and, or*), short prepositions (e.g., *at, as, of*), and articles (e.g., *an, the*), all the first letters of major words (i.e., longer than three letters) in the journal title are capitalized.
- The title of the journal is italicized.
- The volume number is included and italicized.
- The issue number of the volume is not included, which is true in most cases because most journals are not paginated by issue.
- The page numbers of the journal article are included. Note that inclusive page numbers are followed by a period (without using "pp.").

12

- The publisher's name is not included for journal articles.
- The doi (digital object identifier) number is included (list it whenever available, whether you got the article online or in printed form).

Books

At times, you will want to include information found in a book rather than a journal article. When you do this, keep in mind the important difference between primary and secondary sources, as discussed earlier in this chapter. A book is a great source for a review of a topic, but you will need to get the actual journal articles discussed in the book to really understand what the research entailed AND to include it in your paper as a primary source. On that note, you should discuss with your instructor whether secondary sources are allowable in your paper. Oftentimes, only primary sources are permissible in research papers, given that when you include a secondary source, you are reading another person's interpretation rather than reading the original source yourself.

If we change the example to a reference for a **book**, you will notice some of the basics remain, with some changes:

> Schwartz, B. M., Landrum, R. E., & Gurung, R. A. R. (2012). *An easyguide to APA style* (2nd ed.). Thousand Oaks, CA: Sage.

- The book title is italicized.
- The only words capitalized in a book title are the first word, the first word after a colon, and proper nouns.
- The book title is followed by a period.
- The publisher's location is included (city and state abbreviation), followed by a colon and the name of the publisher.
- A period is placed after the publisher's name.
- If the author and publisher are the same, place the publisher where the author is listed and use the word *Author* where you would provide the publisher name.

Chapter in an Edited Book

Instead of citing an entire book, you might want to cite just a **chapter in a book**. In this example, the chapter is in an edited book, which means the chapters were written by different authors and the book was edited by one or more individuals. The reference would look like this:

> Halpern, D. F. (1999). The war of the worlds: Why psychology helps bridge the gap between students' and professors' conceptual understanding. In B. A. Pescosolido & R. Aminzade (Eds.), *The social worlds of higher education: Handbook for teaching in a new century* (pp. 91–94). Thousand Oaks, CA: Pine Forge Press.

In this example, for a chapter in a book, notice the following changes to the reference:

- The author(s) of the chapter are listed first.
- The title of the chapter is provided after the date of publication.
- The editors of the book are listed with their initials **before** their last names.
- After the editors' names, the abbreviation "Eds." (or "Ed." for a book with only one editor) is included in parentheses, followed by a comma.
- A period is placed after the abbreviation for *editor(s)*.
- The title of the chapter is not italicized.
- The title of the book is italicized.
- The only words capitalized in each title are the first word, the first word after a colon, and proper nouns.

Online Sources

Fortunately, many sources for your paper are available with a few taps on your keyboard, without ever having to get up from where you are. We will not discuss here how fortunate you are to have these online resources, because we are confident you have heard from many of your professors all about the days when we actually had to go to the library to read past research or had to wait for days or even weeks for the library to receive an interlibrary loan from another college or university before we could even read the article. APA quickly became aware that many of our print sources are accessed online, and many additional sources are available only online. Consequently, more APA rules were created to guide citation and referencing of these documents. APA even published an additional APA style guide to unpack all the diverse sources of electronic sources (APA, 2012).

You should notice that most of the same information included in the reference for a book or article is needed when you access the source online. When you find the book or article online, present most of the source information in the same order as in the typical reference. The part of the source information we need to add for these electronic resources is either the URL (uniform resource locator) or the doi. Online information can be moved; we have all experienced typing in a URL only to receive a message that the information can no longer be accessed in that location. As a result, many sources now have a doi that will not be affected if the source is moved to another site; however, not all publishers include a doi. We expect more and more sources to have a doi, so knowing how to include these sources in your References section will become more and more relevant. To find a doi, look at the source information listed online with most articles or in the upper-right corner of an online version of a printed article. At times, "doi" will appear before the numbers; other times, you will find a long list of numbers (and sometimes letters) that start with the numbers *1* and *0* (*10*). One general rule of thumb to keep in mind: When a book or article is available only online, you replace the publisher information with the online retrieval information (see examples for details). Some of your sources will have just the URL, and some will have both a URL and a doi. We provide examples for all these possibilities.

12

158 SECTION III WRITING WITH (APA) STYLE

If you obtained an **electronic** version of a paper that is available in a printed version, you reference it as follows:

Reaser, A., Prevatt, F., Petscher, Y., & Proctor, B. (2007). The learning and study strategies of college students with ADHD. *Psychology in the Schools, 44,* 627–638. doi:10.1002/pits.20252

Notice the following about the reference with the doi:

- Most of the parts of the reference are the same as for the printed source.
- The acronym "doi" is printed in lowercase letters.
- There is no period at the end of the series of doi numbers.
- There is no space after the colon following doi.

The following is an example of an online source using a URL but no doi:

Wilson, J. H., Stadler, J. R., Schwartz, B. M., & Goff, D. M. (2009). Touching your students: The impact of a handshake on the first day of class. *Journal of the Scholarship of Teaching and Learning, 9,* 108–117. Retrieved from http://aca demics.georgiasouthern.edu/ijsotl/v4n1.html

Notice the following about the reference with the URL:

- The reference includes the same basic information as other references do.
- The words "Retrieved from" appear before the URL.
- Retrieval dates are needed only for material that changes over time.
- A period does not follow a URL.
- The URL is not in a blue font, nor is it underlined; you may need to use the "remove hyperlink" function in Word to format URLs properly. (On a PC, either right-click on the URL and select *Remove hyperlink* or select the URL and press Ctrl+Shift+F9 on your keyboard; to quickly remove all hyperlinks in the same file, press Ctrl+A to select the entire document, and then press Ctrl+Shift+F9 to deactivate all hyperlinks at once. On a Mac, use COMMAND+A to select all.)

Given all the many electronic resources available these days, you might come across webpages, blogs, data sets, online encyclopedias . . . honestly, the list goes on and on. Because there are so many types, it would be too lengthy to list an example of every type here. We have picked some of the most used below. In general, keep in mind that for most of these sources, you need to include the following:

- The author's name (or authors' names)
- The date (if not available, use "n.d." for "no date" in place of the date in parentheses; if the date includes a month and year, type the year first in

parentheses, followed by the month and day of the month—e.g., 2006, October 7)

- The title of the document (if no author, start with the title)
- The words "Retrieved from" followed by the URL of the document

The following examples show how you would list a reference for a webpage and a blog post:

American Psychological Association. (2015). *About APA*. Retrieved from http://www.apa.org/about/index.aspx

Martin, R. (2015, June 2). Anger quotes: Sigmund Freud [Web log post]. Retrieved from http://blog.uwgb.edu/alltherage/

Works With Seven or More Authors

Though you will typically find that most of your articles and books are written by a smaller group of authors, you might come across a source that includes more than seven authors. You might recall reading about these details in the chapter on citations, where we discussed how to cite and reference articles with different numbers of authors. Most of the reference format for sources with this many authors is exactly the same as what we have described already. However, because the APA *PM* added a new rule in the sixth edition, we want to make sure you are aware of how to include this type of source in your References section.

When a reference has seven or fewer authors, you can include **all** the authors' names in the reference list. However, for articles with more than seven authors, you include only the first six authors' names, followed by three spaced periods (ellipses) and then the last author's name. In this case, there is no ampersand before the last author. (Hint: Try not to be an author whose name comes after the sixth author's unless you are the last author on a research team; otherwise, you will never see your name in a reference list.) What follows are two examples of this type of reference; the first example is a print version, and the second is an online version (with, we kid you not, 17 authors).

Halonen, J. S., Bosack, T., Clay, S., McCarthy, M., Dunn, D. S., Hill, G. W., IV, . . . Whitlock, K. (2003). A rubric for learning, teaching, and assessing scientific inquiry in psychology. *Teaching of Psychology, 30,* 196–208.

Lennertz, L., Grabe, H. J., Ruhrmann, S., Rampacher, F., Vogeley, A., Schulze-Rauschenbach, S., . . . Wagner, M. (2010). Perceived parental rearing in subjects with obsessive–compulsive disorder and their siblings. *Acta Psychiatrica Scandinavica, 121,* 280–288. doi:10.1111/j.1600–0447.2009.01469

Conference Presentations

We often tell our students that the most up-to-date research is found at conferences at which researchers present their findings before publishing them in a journal or book. Keep in mind, often if you e-mail researchers known for research in a specific area, they will share these presentations with you. To include such a source in your References section, you would format the reference as follows:

> Schwartz, B. M., Tatum, H. E., Coffey, C. C., & Mandarakas, A. (2010, August). *Classroom interactions: The influence of gender of professor and gender of student.* Poster presentation at the annual meeting of the American Psychological Association, San Diego, CA.
>
> Tatum, H. (2007, August). Barbie, Goldilocks, and other stories for the psychology of gender. In B. M. Schwartz (Chair), *Using stories from our personal lives to teach psychological theories and concepts.* Symposium presented at the annual convention of the American Psychological Association, San Francisco, CA.

The two examples above illustrate a poster presentation at a conference and a paper presented as part of a symposium at a conference. In these types of references, notice the following:

- Following the year, the month of the presentation is included within the parentheses.
- For the poster presentation, italicize the title of the presentation and indicate that the research was part of a poster presentation at a conference.
- For the paper presented at a symposium, the chair of the symposium is included, first initial and last name followed by the word *Chair* in parentheses.
- The title of a presentation at a symposium follows the year and month and is not italicized; instead, the title of the symposium is italicized.
- For both poster presentations and papers presented at a symposium, the name of the convention or meeting and its location are included.

Newspapers and Magazines

We are confident that your professors will advise you, if at all possible, to avoid citing information from newspapers and magazines. Instead, find the reference cited in that newspaper or magazine article and consult the original source of the information discussed in the article. Some of the time, newspaper and magazine articles report on the primary source (see also Chapter 8 on citing sources). Primary sources are the articles or books that present the original text by the author of the investigation. In contrast, secondary sources refer to articles or books that discuss another article and the findings from that source. For example, let us say we discuss information in our paper that we read about in one article, a primary source we will call Source A. We would include Source A in our References section. As you read Source A, you will likely find information about another related study, which we will call Source B. Again, Source B is called a secondary source if we do not actually find the article and read it (and

12

that would not be a good idea). However, if you are unable to read Source B yourself and you really want to include information from Source B in your paper, then you will need to cite where you read about Source B, which in this case would be Source A. You do not include Source B in your References section. In the following example, you have read the Gurung and Schwartz (2009) chapter, in which they discuss Hattie's work; however, you never read Hattie's work directly from his book.

> Hattie's (as cited in Gurung & Schwartz, 2009) work on visible learning makes an important contribution to the literature.

Notice that you include the author for the secondary source and for the primary source but do not include the year for the primary source. The year is included only for the secondary source.

Should you find that you are unable to access the primary source, the following are examples of reference items for magazine or newspaper articles from which information was obtained.

> Goldstein, R. (2010, March). Major developments in undergraduate psychology. *Observer, 23*(3), 23–26.

> West, K. (2010, February 2). Some odd thoughts about thinking. *The News and Advance,* pp. B1, B3.

Notice a few things about these examples: Most magazines start with page 1, so the issue number should be included if available. Many articles in newspapers are on multiple pages in specific sections of the paper. Include the exact pages of the article's location, and include the section as well.

12

Basic References Section Formatting Rules

Next, we fill you in on some of the basic reference list formatting rules (e.g., headings, margins, order of references). We have noted all these rules on the sample reference page included in Chapter 12.

- Start your reference list on a separate page at the end of your paper.
- Place the reference list before any footnotes, tables, figures, or appendices.
- Use 1-inch margins for top, bottom, left, and right sides of the page.
- Center the word *References* at the top of the page (not italics or bold).
- Double-space your references, with no extra line space between references. (See Chapter 14 for how to make sure these extra spaces are not included.)
- Use hanging indents (and set it up in Word rather than using a hard return and spaces or tabs)—first line for each reference starts at the margin, and all other lines are indented about 1/2 inch (in Microsoft Word, highlight the reference and hit Ctrl+T).

- Alphabetize the reference list by first author's last name.
- Use each author's full last name and only initials for first and middle names.
- Italicize the title of the work (title of the book or journal title).
- Start with one-author works and earliest publication year when you include multiple sources with the same first author.
- When you include sources with the same author and same year of publication, place lowercase letters after the year (e.g., 2009a); articles with identical authors are alphabetized in the reference list according to title. When you have two sources by different authors with the same last name but different first names (e.g., Schwartz, B. and Schwartz, R.), alphabetize by first initial.
- Include all authors listed for each source, up to seven names total (see the section in this chapter titled "Works With Seven or More Authors").

Some Not-So-Basic Rules You Might Need

- When no author name is available, alphabetize using the first major word of the article or book title or the first word of the organization's title.
- When no date of publication is available, use "n.d." (for "no date") in parentheses directly after the author names.
- As a general guideline, in every APA–reference format, some part of the reference will be italicized.

By now, you recognize that the References section of your paper is by far the most complicated when it comes to using APA style. And, as stated at the beginning of this chapter, this summary of details is only the tip of the iceberg; our goal here is to present the most commonly used sources in an attempt to avoid what is often overwhelming in the *PM* (i.e., a list of 77 different types of references). APA provides guidelines on how to reference everything from a map to a video blog post to a letter from a private collection. However, our experiences with teaching students how to write in APA style have taught us what sources students typically use when writing their papers. Those are the sources we included in this chapter. Should you need to cite a more uncommon source, such as a court decision, a patent, or an archival source with a corporate author, you are just going to have to find a copy of that *PM*.

12

SECTION IV

Presenting Your Work in APA Format

The Numbers Game 13

*How to Write Numbers
(and When the Rules Change)*

When writing an APA–style paper, you will need to know the rules for how to express numbers, which could mean writing *10, 11,* and *12,* or *ten, eleven,* and *twelve.* In fact, numbers are everywhere in APA–style writing. Whether you are writing how many participants you included in your experiment, how old the participants were, the dosage of a drug used, or what percentage of a population demonstrated a behavior, you will need to know how to properly include that information in your paper. You will not be surprised to find out that the APA *PM* has specific guidelines on this matter, with *many* exceptions to those guidelines. The big distinction here is whether to use numerals (e.g., *15*) or words (e.g., *fifteen*) to express numbers. Table 13.1 allows you to look up the type of number notation you need to include and how to express that number. In that table, you will also find examples for each rule. Keep in mind when using the table that you should look for the specific type of number you want to include by skimming the far-left column. It starts with the very general rule and moves to more specific rules. The rules that follow apply when writing both ordinal (e.g., 12th grade) and cardinal numbers (e.g., the 12 seniors). You use ordinal numbers in reference to rank or order (e.g., the first grade). On the other hand, use cardinal numbers to indicate the number of something (e.g., 40 participants).

13

Table 13.1 Expressing Numbers in APA Format

Type of Number	How to Express	Example
10 and up	Numerals	300 apples
Less than 10	Words	Three apples
Numbers in an abstract	Numerals	3 students
Mathematics	Numerals	Divided by 3
Numbers with a measurement	Numerals	3.57 cm
Numbers in a graph	Numerals	$M = 86$
Numbered series	Numerals	Column 4
Time, dates, ages, scores, points on a scale, exact sums of money, numbers as numbers	Numerals	\$4.17; 1 hr 20 min February 12, 2009, at 2:20 p.m. 4 years old 3 on a 5-point scale the number 7
Approximation for days, months, and years	Words	We landed on the moon about forty years ago.
Numbers beginning a title or heading	Words	Fourteen Hundred and Ninety-Two: A Year to Remember
Numbers beginning a sentence	Words	Seventy percent of the sample
Common fractions	Words	one third of participants
Universally accepted usage	Words	Thirty Years War
Lists of numbers	Numerals if list includes four or more numbers; words if list includes three or fewer numbers	Subjects could choose among 1, 2, 3, 4, or 5 pathways. Subjects could choose among one, two, or three pathways.

13

When You Use Numerals

So what is the general rule for numbers in APA style? Good question, because you will likely find that APA rules for numbers are different from the rules you follow when writing, for instance, an English literature paper in MLA format. Too often, students find that out the hard way. So we are going to help you avoid the dreaded red ink and/or tracked changes/comments on your APA–style paper.

The general rule of thumb is to use numerals (10, 11, 12, etc.) for numbers 10 and up. Did you notice that we used the numeral *10* and not the word *ten*? Yup, we followed APA style. So if you are reviewing the methodology used in past research and you need to write in your paper, "We gave participants 18 vignettes to review," you express the number as a numeral. However, if the participants were given only eight vignettes, you now need to use the word *eight* instead.

Incorrect: We presented all participants with ten different questionnaires.

Correct: We presented all participants with 10 different questionnaires.

You might be thinking, "That is simple enough. Numerals for 10 and up; words for anything less than 10!" Not so fast. There are times when you use numerals regardless of the number. For instance, when you are writing your **abstract**, you use numerals only. Hooray! One place not to have to stop and think about number rules. When the number immediately precedes a **unit of measurement**, use a numeral. So when your research includes information about number of yards, inches, pounds, milliseconds, lumens, hertz, and the list can go on and on . . . you should include a numeral before the unit. By the way, there are entirely separate rules for how to abbreviate units of measurement, such as inches, pounds, and seconds. See our tips in Chapter 18 on how to present units of measurement correctly.

13

Incorrect: The rats received five-hundred mg of Prozac. The rats in the control group receiving zero mg were envious of those in the experimental group.

Correct: The rats received 500 mg of Prozac. The rats in the control group receiving 0 mg were envious of those in the experimental group.

When writing about your results, you might need to write about **mathematical functions**—statistics, quantities, ratios, percentiles, or quartiles, for example. In that case, you need to stick to the numerals. Using numerals is relevant for your Results section because that is where you include all your statistical results. You might come across these numbers when discussing prevalence of a behavior, in which case you would write, for example, "Less than 9% of the population agreed with the local election results" (see Chapter 10 of this book for more details about writing your Results section).

Here is an easy rule to follow: When you include numbers in **graphs**—and this is common—you use only numerals and not words. You have likely come across bar graphs that include the mean score presented above each bar; that number would be expressed as a numeral.

Research papers often include information about parts of a **numbered series.** You might need to refer to "Chapter 3" in a book or "Table 4" in your paper. This is another exception to the rule, and you need to use a numeral. Your paper might also include a list of items. When the items in a series are separate paragraphs, then each item is preceded by a numeral that is followed by a period (e.g., 1.). In this case, parentheses are not used to enclose the number. However, when the series is within a sentence or a paragraph, you do not use a number at all. Instead, your list includes a series of letters, "The following insects were presented to each participant: (a) ants, (b) bugs, (c) spiders, and (d) moths." This type of ordered listing is called seriation, and we tackle it in Chapter 17.

The exceptions to the rule do not end there (see Table 13.2 for a list of all the exceptions). When a number represents time, dates, ages, scores, points on a scale, or exact sums of money, use numerals. For example, "The participants were 3- to 4-year-olds." Regardless of how young or old your participants are, use numerals to express their ages. You will likely include in your Procedure section information about the length of time your experiment required (e.g., 3 hr 47 min), and you might also include the time of day when you conducted your research (e.g., at 3:12 p.m.). Finally, if you are fortunate enough to have funds to compensate your participants, you will express the exact sum of money offered using numerals and write, "All participants received $8 for participating." Of course, APA style would not be complete without an exception to this exception, and that brings us to the next section of this chapter.

13

When You Use Words

There are times when you are writing a research proposal and do not have exact time information. In those cases when you must write **approximations**, you need to use words rather than numerals. In this case, you would write, "Participants returned to the laboratory for Session 2 about ten days following their first visit." This is the first of several rules that requires you to use words rather than numerals to express numbers.

APA style suggests that you **do not start a sentence** with a number (e.g., "Ninety-six percent accuracy ratings emerged for the group that received the study guide."). However, when you feel the need to do so (and you never know when that need will emerge), you always use words to express those numbers (rather than using numerals). But perhaps that exception to the rule should be avoided, and you should just not start sentences with numbers.

The same rule also applies to **titles** and **headings**. Those numbers at the beginning of titles and headings should be expressed as words, but again, whenever

Table 13.2 Exceptions to the Number Rules

Type of Rule	Exception	Example
Express numbers 10 and up as numerals	Combine words and numbers for back-to-back numbers	Twelve 3-year-olds
Report statistics to two decimal places	Report to three decimal places for p	$p < .001$ or $p = .036$
Express abbreviations in lowercase letters	Use uppercase letters for liters, ambiguous abbreviations	7 L (for liters)
Insert a space between the symbol and the number it refers to	No space in measures of angles in degrees, minutes, seconds, etc.	45°; 11'; 2"
Include commas in figures of 1,000 or more	Page numbers	p. 3084
	Binary digits	0010001110
	Serial numbers	37194058
	Degrees of temperature	4013°F
	Acoustic frequency designations	1000 Hz
	Degrees of freedom	$F(1, 2900)$
Capitalize words in a title	Abbreviations for measurement in a title	An Examination of 35 mm of the Brain

13

possible, create a new title or text heading that does not begin with a number. In this case, you can use many of the same words in a title and just reorganize the words to avoid starting off with a number. So instead of using the title "Fifty-Nine Years After the Depression: How Much Will Seniors Remember?" you can use the title "How Much Will Seniors Remember 59 Years After the Depression?" So in this case, you would stick to the original rule of using numerals for numbers greater than 10 when the number is in the title but is not the first word of the title.

When reporting your results, you might need to include **fractions**. APA style requires that you use words for these numbers. These types of numbers are found in about one fourth of the papers you read in scientific journals. Get it . . . one fourth? We actually made up that fraction for this example, and we must admit that before going on to the next exciting APA rule for numbers. We have no idea how many journal articles include common fractions. Well, at least two thirds of the authors of this book have no idea. You may have noticed that the fractions in this paragraph are not hyphenated. That is another APA rule for numbers; hyphenate fractions only when they are used as adjectives—for example, "a three-quarter turn" (see Chapter 14 for more details on when to hyphenate).

We have one more APA rule to present that tells you when to use words for numbers. Numbers are sometimes found in **commonly used phrases**. In this case, words are used for the numbers. So if you state, in an APA–style letter to your roommate, that using your toothpaste without permission violates one of the Ten Commandments, you will indeed use the word *ten* rather than the number *10*. Or if you bring a friend back to your room to have a private conversation, you might need to post a note on your door (of course, in APA style) that states, "Two's company; three's a crowd." You might be writing your younger sister on her birthday and wish her a happy "sweet sixteen!" We would love to include more examples, because these are fun to write about, but we are confident you get the point.

Using Both Numerals and Words

To jazz things up a bit, APA style includes some writing-with-numbers rules that require you to write with both numerals *and* words at the same time. This applies when you are writing **back-to-back numbers**. Huh? You might be asking yourself, "When would I write two numbers back to back?" In your Method section, you might write about the types of scales you used to collect your data. Let us say you needed to include two different scales, both of which were 5-point Likert scales. You would state that **two 5**-point Likert scales measured participants' opinions. Think about experiments that include multiple independent variables. You might find multiple interactions in that experiment. In this case, you would write in your paper that "3 four-way interactions emerged." Notice that those sentences include two different numbers back to back (side by side) and that one number is written as a word and the other number is written as a numeral.

We need to tell you about one **exception** to the back-to-back numbers rule. If writing with both words and numerals makes it more difficult to understand what you are trying to get across to readers, then by all means, use words in both cases. So instead of writing, "The first 10 questions on the exam were not used when calculating a grade," you would write, "The first ten questions. . . . " Also, if you are using ordinal numbers (e.g., first), then you should use only words.

Incorrect: The study of social interaction included twelve four-person groups discussing stress speaking only in Pig Latin.

Correct: The study of social interaction included 12 four-person groups discussing stress speaking only in Pig Latin.

Exception: The first four-person group talked about stress only in Pig Latin.

How to Use Decimal Points

When to Include a Zero Before the Decimal Point

One question students often ask is when to include a zero before the decimal point when writing numbers using numerals. We are excited that we have an easy-to-follow APA rule for that question. You use a zero before the decimal point when the statistic reported is less than 1 but **CAN** exceed 1. For example, if you are measuring the distance between the index finger and the middle finger and the measurement is 0.83 cm, you will include the zero because that measurement can exceed 1. In your Results section, you will likely be asked to use Cohen's d to measure effect size (see Chapter 10); this would be reported as Cohen's $d = 0.54$ because the Cohen's d can exceed 1. However, if the number cannot exceed 1, then no zero is used before the decimal fraction. You will come across these numbers often in your Results section when writing your alpha level (e.g., $p = .028$). This is also true for correlation coefficients that are always between -1 and +1, inclusive—for example, $r(59) = .63, p < .05$.

How Many Numbers Should Be Written After the Decimal Point?

This question really answers the question often heard around the world: "How should I round my numbers?" The answer: Round your answers to two decimal places as often as possible to make statistics easier to understand. Sometimes this means changing the scale (e.g., 41234 millimeters = 41.23 meters). By changing the scale, you make reading the number easier but still provide precise information. You should be able to report most data using two decimal places and still maintain precision. So when reporting your r, t, F, and X^2, you would use only two decimal places.

But wait . . . an exception to that rule! When reporting p values, report the exact p value using two **or** three decimal places and the equals "=" sign ($p = .034$). Any p value less than .001 should be written as $p < .001$ (with the less than "<" sign). For those of you who remember older APA rules, this is a change. We used to write p values out to two decimal places (e.g., $p < .05$). This is no longer the case with most statistical calculations conducted using statistical software, unlike in the olden days when statistics were calculated by hand and tables of critical values were used to determine statistical significance.

13

Additional Rules for Including Numbers in Your Paper

Numbers are sometimes expressed as **Roman numerals**. If that is the common way to express those numbers, use the Roman numbers (e.g., Type I error); if not, do not use Roman numerals (e.g., Table 1, *not* Table I).

When expressing numbers, **use commas** in figures of 1,000 or more. Once again, it sounds simple, if only. . . . But this rule does not apply to the following: (a) page numbers (e.g., p. 3084); (b) binary digits (e.g., 0010001110); (c) serial numbers (e.g., 37194058); (d) degrees of temperature (e.g., 4013°F); (e) acoustic frequency designations (e.g., 1000 Hz); and (f) degrees of freedom, $F(1, 2900)$.

At times, you might need to include **plurals of numbers**. Many writers have an urge to include an apostrophe when using plurals even though this is not correct in any style of writing. Instead of that apostrophe, just add an *s* or *es* (e.g., 1990s, fives and sixes, 30s).

Metrication

In your papers, you will sometimes need to express numbers in terms of **physical measurements**. For example, if you are studying spatial learning and memory in rats using a sand maze, you will want to include a detailed description of the maze so others can replicate using the same apparatus. In doing so, you will need to include the physical measurements. APA style requires that all these measurements be expressed in metric units rather than in standard units. When discussing the policy on metrication, the *PM* states that metric units should be used if possible. Yes, you read it correctly . . . **if possible**. However, that section also states that if you include measurements using nonmetric units, you need to include metric equivalents *immediately* after in parentheses. For example, "To study pain perception in children, a total of 3 gal (11.36 L) of water was poured over the ice for the cold pressor task." So in other words, it is *always* possible to express your physical measurements in metric units. So much for the flexibility. To find conversions of standard measurement to metric measurement, we suggest you check out http://www.sciencemadesimple.net/conversions.html. On this site, you will also find how to express these units of measurement in full names and abbreviations. This brings us to the next APA rule.

13

When Do You Use Abbreviations?

When you **write your measurements** using metric units, you can use the **abbreviation** for the unit of measurement after the numeral; remember that these abbreviations do not include a period unless they are found at the end of a sentence (e.g., 5 cm). Abbreviations are expressed in **lowercase letters**, though there are exceptions to this rule because, for example, you want to avoid the abbreviation for liter (L) being misread as the number 1. When you use a symbol, you need to insert a space between the symbol and the number it refers to (e.g., 10 m). Warning! There is an exception to this spacing rule, too. When you write about measures of angles in degrees, minutes, and seconds, no space is required (e.g., 60° angle, 10', 5").

When circumstances call for you to describe what metric unit you used for your measurement, you no longer use abbreviations. In those situations, you should **write out the measurement term**; the term should not follow a numeric value (e.g., "Distance was measured in centimeters"). Notice that you use **lowercase letters** to write out the names of units. The typical exceptions apply here (e.g., used in a title, beginning of a sentence). And our favorite type of APA rule, an exception to an exception, is next. Lowercase letters are still used in titles when you include a symbol rather than the full name of the metric unit. Honestly, we think the better idea is not to use the symbol but instead just to spell it out. Including a symbol in your title is awkward to begin with.

You might also need to express these **units of measurement** in plural form (e.g., centimeters). Did we just include an example to illustrate a plural form of a measurement? We apologize for that. APA style requires that when writing out the full name of the measurement, you express the term in plural (e.g., "length was measured in centimeters"). Yes, we just gave that same example again. However, when you use the abbreviation for a metric unit, even when there is more than one of that unit, it is *not* expressed in plural units. This means stating that you used "50 cm" and not "50 cms."

To summarize, we have just one thing to say: If you are shocked by the number of rules that apply to expressing numbers in an APA–style paper, you are not alone. Most people feel the same way, and we sure did when we first ran into these rules. But we all know the rules, and we can be stronger writers in APA style because of that—sometimes it is all about attention to detail.

13

Formatting 14

*Organizing, Headings, and Making
Your Work Look Good to Print*

After your hard work creating the scientific story for your paper by reading the literature, writing your paper, creating logical arguments in your introduction to support your hypothesis with findings from the literature, and developing methodology to test your hypothesis, it is time to take a different focus and examine the formatting of your paper. As you read in Chapter 1, APA format is what makes a journal article consistent with scientific norms. This may sound trivial, but you are probably not surprised that the APA *PM* provides answers to almost all your formatting questions. And keep in mind, following instructions and paying attention to detail are important skills that employers value highly. So no matter what career path you plan to take (e.g., butcher, baker, candlestick maker), the ability to follow these detailed writing rules is a marketable skill in and of itself. Following these instructions will create a paper that makes a good impression even before one starts to read it. Although the quality of your writing is of utmost importance, together with the rigor of your research, even these small details can make a difference when deciding between an A and an A-.

So read on to learn the order of the parts of the manuscript, the headings you should use, the size of your margins, and when and when not to indent. In Chapter 16, we provide instructions for how to use Word to format the different sections of your APA paper. In Chapter 21, you will find a sample paper that provides an illustration of exactly what your paper should look like before you turn it in. You do need to keep in mind that some colleges and universities require that you use formatting rules different from those for APA style, so be sure to check with your institution before starting to format your paper. In other words, check local listings.

14

What Goes Where?

Let us start with ordering the parts of your manuscript. Just use the following order for the different sections of your paper, and you will already be on the right track. We have also noted when you need to start a section on a new page.

Title page

Abstract (new page)

Introduction (new page; the word *Introduction* not needed, but the title from page 1 is repeated)

Method

Results

Discussion

References (new page)

Table/s (new page)

Figure/s (new page)

Appendix (new page)

A common mistake we see our students make is to start a new page for the different sections in the main text of their papers. For example, many students often feel compelled to start their Method section on a "fresh" page just after the introduction. We think this is somewhat of an automatic behavior—the need to separate the big sections of the text physically. As we tell our students, "When in doubt, double-space throughout!" We have also seen our students thinking "green" and, in an attempt to conserve paper, beginning some sections that *do* require a new page (e.g., References) directly after the preceding section. As long as we are on the topic, APA style does not allow you to print your paper on both sides of the page. You can check with your instructor to see if double-siding is permissible; we understand the waste of using only one side of each page. We will say that it is easier to edit/grade a paper printed on one side compared with one printed on both sides.

14

What Your Paper Should Look Like

Fonts, Margins, and Indents

Let us start with the rules that influence how your paper looks. When you start writing your paper, you need to pick a **font** and **font size** that are easy to read. APA recommends Times New Roman in 12-point size. This is not a place to flaunt your individuality. In Word 2013, Calibri in 11-point size is the default when you first open any document. We suggest that you change the default to Times New Roman in 12-point size. The one place you can use a different font is your figures, with APA recommending sans serif type (e.g., Arial, Helvetica, Tahoma, Verdana). Check out Chapter 16 for details on how to change fonts in Word, and see the sample paper in Chapter 21 for an example of these different fonts. Really, you just want to avoid the fonts that make it difficult to read your paper. Leave the calligraphy to those greeting cards and fancy invitations. Whatever font you choose, use the default spacing between letters and words, but be careful not to use the default spacing between paragraphs. Sometimes in Word 2010 and Word 2013, the default spacing is 1.15 (we know . . . an odd choice), when it should be 2.0—double-spaced. Regardless of the version of Word you are using, you should know how to change the line spacing.

Next, we need to cover setting your **margins**. We know this is an issue when you want to achieve a particular page length, and you may have played with your margins in the past to get your paper to span the correct number of pages. We need to break the news . . . APA requires 1-inch margins throughout. That means the top and bottom margins, as well as the margins to the left and right, are uniform (see Chapter 16 for instructions and screenshots on how to set margins). For your instructors who do not yet use Word to track changes and provide feedback, those margins provide enough room for them to give you all the information you need to improve your paper or a place to write their rave reviews. Be sure to justify the margins only on the left. This means all lines on the left of the page will be even, and the lines on the right of your paper will be uneven. See Chapter 16 for details on how to correctly justify the left margin and maintain a ragged right margin using Word.

Within these margins is where you get to read all the comments in red ink that some instructors love to use when marking sections that need to be reviewed. Do not take all that red ink personally. Two ideas to share here: (a) Red ink (or any color ink) on your paper in general means that your instructor cares enough to give you detailed feedback to help improve your writing, and (b) every writer's writing can be improved; your authors marked up one another's chapters continuously throughout the revision of this book. Remember, the ultimate goal is to communicate as clearly as you can. If you remember that goal, you may come to appreciate the red ink. But, honestly, red is just a color that can be easily seen in contrast to the black ink on your paper.

When writing your paper, be sure to **indent** the first line of each paragraph using the typical five- to seven-space indent; normally, just using the "tab" key will do. You can also set up the indents by using the ruler function in Word. Detailed instructions on how to set this up are provided in Chapter 16 under the heading "Tabs, Centering, and the Ruler." APA style does have a few exceptions for indenting. You *do not* indent for the following parts of your paper: (a) the first line of the abstract paragraph, (b) block quotations, (c) titles or heading Levels 1 and 2, (d) table titles, and (e) figure captions. Sometimes the software you use will automatically make this indent the right size, around five to seven spaces. You may remember from Chapter 12 that you use hanging indents for the

14

reference list, which means that for each separate reference item, all lines except the first line are indented five to seven spaces. Again, the "hanging" part of that term refers to the first line hanging to the left of the rest of the lines. Skip ahead to Chapter 16 for the how-to on formatting with hanging indents, but do not forget to come back so you can read about a head that runs.

Running Head

Although the text of your paper needs to have 1-inch margins, you need to place your running head within that 1-inch space at the top of the page; place the page header information at 0.5 inches. The words *Running head* appear on only page 1 of your paper (see Chapter 16 for the Word instructions on how to do this). Note only the first word "Running" has a capitalized first letter. Including a running head is important given the possibility that your professor could throw your paper and those of other students into the air (hey, it's possible), resulting in a confetti of pages. How many people today own a stapler anyway? Once the professor's excitement passes, the realization will set in that these papers need to be placed back in the proper order, with the correct pages going with their respective papers. That is where the information in your running head comes into play. Each page of your paper includes an abbreviated title (a short description) in the upper-left corner and the page number in the upper-right corner (see the sample paper in Chapter 21). Your abbreviated title needs to be 50 characters or fewer (including all spaces and punctuation) and in all uppercase letters, placed flush with the left margin. This is what will allow all pages of your paper to be identified as part of your paper. Typically, this shorter title is your longer title with fewer words. For example:

> **Title:** Effects of Type of Lineup on the Accuracy of Children's Person Identification

> **Abbreviated title:** ACCURACY OF CHILDREN'S PERSON IDENTIFICATION

14

On your title page, you include the words *Running head*, followed by a colon and your abbreviated title in all capital letters. For all pages that follow, include only your abbreviated title (i.e., NOT the phrase "Running head"). All pages of your paper are numbered (also called paginated), including your tables and figures, starting with the first page. Place the page number in the running head you create, flush with the right margin. If you use the *Header* function under the *Insert* tab in Word 2013, you will not need to type this information separately on each page. Instead, you can type it in the header space one time, create a different first page (by selecting *Different First Page* in the *Design* tab in Word 2013; see Chapter 16 for instructions) so you can include the words *Running head* only on the first page, and you are good to go for the whole paper.

Headings

To help organize an APA–style paper, five different heading levels are used. There are rules about when to use these different headings. You will see that choosing the headings depends on the section of your paper and the number of experiments you are writing about. We have included a list of these headings in the table that follows; a separate table tells you when to use each of the heading levels.

Table 14.1 How to Format Headings	
Level	How to Format
1	Centered, Boldface, First Letter of Important Words Capitalized
2	Flush Left, Boldface, First Letter of Important Words Capitalized
3	Indented, boldface, first letter of first word capitalized, end with a period.
4	Indented, boldface, italicized, first letter of first word capitalized, end with a period.
5	Indented, italicized, first letter of first word capitalized, end with a period.

In case you are wondering what makes a word "important" enough to be capitalized in headings and titles, here are a couple things to remember: (a) Capitalize *any* word of four or more letters (e.g., *with, from, into*), and (b) capitalize all verbs (e.g., *are, be, can, is, was*), nouns (e.g., *end, gun, ink, net*), pronouns (e.g., *it, he, she, him, her*), adverbs (e.g., *far, if, not, too*), and adjectives (e.g., *big, few, low, new*). Here are some words that should *not* be capitalized in headings and titles: conjunctions (e.g., *and, but, or*), articles (e.g., *a, an, the*), and prepositions of fewer than four letters (e.g., *in, at, to, off, for*).

There are two **exceptions** to the Level 1 heading rules. You *do not* use boldface for your abstract or reference headings. Why? Good question. We dug around for an answer but came up empty. If we were in charge of APA style, we would have made all headings boldface. Not using boldface for the abstract and reference sections just seems like an easy way to confuse everyone. But, obviously, we are not the ones writing the rules—just trying to make them easier to understand. When typing the paragraph that follows heading Levels 1 and 2, start the paragraph on a new line. For Levels 3, 4, and 5, start the paragraph on the same line as the heading. Always remember to continue to double-space your paper when using the different heading levels. Next, we will go over when you use each of these headings.

Typically, you will use only two heading levels in your paper. In Chapter 21, you will see a sample paper written with two heading levels. Take a quick look to understand how these headings appear within a paper.

14

Table 14.2 Headings With Multiple Experiments in Your Paper

Level	When to Use
1	For the start of each separate study (e.g., Experiment 1)
2	For each of the main sections of each study (e.g., Method, Results, Discussion)
3	For the subsections of the Method section (e.g., Participants, Procedure)

Table 14.3 Headings With One Experiment in Your Paper

Level	When to Use
1	For each of the main sections of your paper (e.g., Method, Results, Discussion)
2	For the subsections of the Method section (e.g., Participants, Procedure)
3	For the subsections of subsections of the Method section (e.g., Surveys, Software)

One common mistake we see when students are first learning APA style is that they use the word *Introduction* as a heading rather than simply retyping their title above the introduction of the paper. For that heading, you use Level 1 whether you have a single experiment or multiple experiments.

Spelling Matters: Spelling and Capitalization Rules

14

We have all gotten used to the wonderful spell-checker provided by Word. We believe that Bill Gates usually provides the correct spelling for us. However, sometimes Bill is wrong and we need additional guidance—or Bill does not have an extensive knowledge of your discipline and its jargon. Additional spelling guidance should come from *Merriam-Webster's Collegiate Dictionary* (2005), in which spelling conforms to standard American English. At times, the word you are looking up (and we always love looking up words we cannot spell) might not be in *Webster's Collegiate*, in which case you will need to look in *Webster's Third New International Dictionary* (2002). Yes, you will need to be a global speller! Finally, when it comes to psychological terms, you can also refer to the *APA Dictionary of Psychology* (VandenBos, 2007). In some cases, you will find that a word has multiple spelling options. Always use the first spelling option provided in these sources (e.g., use *color* rather than *colour* and *toward* instead of *towards*).

Plural Words

Sometimes just adding an *s* or *es* to a word is not the way to go when changing the word from singular to plural. This is particularly true for the plural forms of **words of Latin or Greek** origin. Given that we spend a great deal of time collecting data, this is one word to be familiar with when it comes to the plural form. One of the most common mistakes relates to the word *data*. This is the plural word for the singular *datum*. We rarely talk about the datum from our research, because we typically collect findings from multiple participants or multiple observations per person; therefore, you will use the word *data*. Just remember that this word is plural, and the verb that follows should also be plural. So this is an example of the *um* becoming an *a* when the word is made plural. Another example: Sometimes an *x* becomes *ces* (e.g., *appendix, appendices*). For other words of this origin, the singular *non* becomes *na* (e.g., *phenomenon, phenomena*).

Plurals are often needed when using the possessive form for a group of individuals. The common question asked in this case is whether to add the **apostrophe before or after the s**. The easiest way to make a singular name possessive is to add an apostrophe and an *s* (e.g., Little Albert's). But when forming the possessive of a plural name, add an *s* before the apostrophe (e.g., the Pavlovs'). An **exception:** If the singular noun ends in an unpronounced *s*, you use only an apostrophe after that *s* (e.g., Descartes'). No need for another *s*. Keep in mind that when you do pronounce the *s* of a name, you add an *es* before the apostrophe (e.g., the Ebbinghauses').

Finally, the other issue with regard to plurals concerns the confusion about when to use just an *s* or an *es* to indicate the plural form for a name. The rules are very simple: To indicate a group of people whose name ends in *s*, add *es* (e.g., the Calkinses). If the name does not end in an *s*, then you add an *s* (e.g., the Horneys). OK, clearly a table will help out here, so see Table 14.4 for more examples of the rules for singular and plural spelling of words.

14

Table 14.4 Examples of Some Singular and Plural Words Demonstrating Key Rules

Singular	Plural
Datum	Data
Stigma	Stigmata
Wells	Wellses
Lanning	Lannings
Smith's (possessive)	Smiths' (possessive)
Doe's (possessive)	Does' (possessive)

Hyphenation

When should you use a hyphen? This question is raised when dealing with compound words, which can be written in a number of different ways. Although not something we think of often, using a hyphen can dramatically change the meaning of a sentence. When you write about a dirty-movie theater, you are addressing a different issue than when you write about a dirty movie theater. In the first case, you are discussing the type of movie the theater shows; in the second case, you are addressing the cleanliness of the theater itself. So you see, a little hyphen can make all the difference in the world. Therefore, correctly using the hyphen can make your writing more clearly express your intended meaning. Often, the use of a hyphen for a compound word will be determined by the context of the sentence. Some compound words can be spelled both with and without a hyphen. In those cases, simply use the first spelling found in the dictionary. There you will find whether to use the compound words as a single word (e.g., *overachiever*), with hyphens (e.g., *over-the-counter*), or, finally, as separate words (e.g., *work group*). In other cases, you need to follow the APA principles for hyphens. Tables 14.5 and 14.6 differentiate when and when not to use hyphens. In both tables, you will find a list of the rules followed by examples to illustrate each rule.

14

Table 14.5 When to Hyphenate	
The Rule	**An Example of the Rule**
Hyphenate . . .	
To make sure compound adjectives are not misread	Iced-tea cup (vs. cup of iced tea); thrill-seeking teenagers
To help the reader understand the intended meaning of two or more adjectives that act as one idea and precede the noun	First-class seat; top-notch idea
When the combination of an adjective and a noun precedes the noun	Same-sex marriage
When prefixes are followed by	
capitalized words	neo-Freudian
numbers	post-911 years
abbreviations	non-APA members
more than one word	post-20th-century invention

The Rule	An Example of the Rule
When using the prefix *self*	Self-report; self-confident
When the prefix can create a word with a different meaning	Re-cover the sofa; re-lease the apartment
When using two or more compound words with a common base used only once in the sentence	2-, 3-, and 4-year-olds
To avoid doubling a vowel	De-emphasize
When using cardinal numbers	Twenty-seven
When using fractions as adjectives	One-third minority

Table 14.6 When Not to Hyphenate

The Rule	An Example of the Rule
Don't hyphenate . . .	
A compound with *-ly*	Happily married couples
A compound with a comparative or superlative	Higher optimism scores
Chemical terms	Sodium glutamate compound
A modifier using a phrase from a foreign language	a priori argument
A describing phrase that uses a numeral or letter in the second part	Type I error
Fractions as nouns	Three fourths of the students
When using most prefixes	Pretest

14

Capitalization

Compared with whether to include a hyphen, you will likely find that an easier decision is whether to use an upper- or lowercase letter. But . . . think again. APA has so many rules related to when to capitalize that we decided it was best to list the many times when you should capitalize the first letter of a word. You will find the different rules listed in Table 14.7. Though some of the APA–format rules will seem obvious and follow what you would expect when typing a paper, you will see there are a few instances specific to APA format.

Table 14.7 When to Capitalize	
The Rule	An Example of the Rule
The first word of a sentence	We have capitalized the first word of this sentence.
The first word of a complete thought following a colon	Two basic instances in which you capitalize: The first word of a sentence is capitalized, and the first word of a complete thought following a colon is capitalized.
All words of four letters or more in the title of your research paper	Passive Social Support's Influence on Pain Threshold
All words of four letters or more in titles of books or articles when they appear within a paper	In his book *Undergraduate Writing in Psychology: Learning to Tell the Scientific Story* (2012), Landrum presents students with a step-by-step guide for scientific writing.
The first word of titles of books and journal articles in your reference list; all major words of a journal title	Wilson, J. H., Stadler, J. R., Schwartz, B. M., & Goff, D. M. (2009). Touching your students: The impact of a handshake on the first day of class. *Journal of the Scholarship of Teaching and Learning.*
When you reference a section of the paper you are writing	As you see in the Method section, all participants were less than 6 years old.
Proper names	Margaret Floy Washburn
Specific department name at a specific university or college; specific course offered	The Department of Psychology at Randolph College offers Health Psychology as an upper-level lab course.
Brand names of drugs, food, equipment	Paxil, Cheez-Its, Kleenex
Nouns followed by numerals	In Experiment 4; as shown in Table 3; as illustrated in Chapter 13
Exact titles of tests/assessments	Peabody Picture Vocabulary Test; Beck Depression Inventory
Names of conditions or groups in your experiment (when the number/letter of the condition follows)	Condition A; Condition 2
Variable names with multiplication signs	Suggestibility × Age × Sex

14

We see the most capitalization errors when our students are preparing their References section. For book titles and journal article titles, you capitalize only (a) the first word, (b) the first word after a colon, and (c) proper nouns (see Chapter 4 for a review of what constitutes a proper noun).

Final Touches

We have a few final words of advice before you hand in your paper. Take a close look at Chapter 20, which provides you with some proofreading how-tos, and Chapter 19, which reviews how to use a rubric to make sure you have covered all the guidelines provided by your instructor. We assure you that both steps can significantly improve your writing and your grade. In addition to your instructor's rubric, we have also provided a checklist for you on the back flap of the book. The checklist will help you make sure you have avoided the most common errors we come across in student papers, and it reviews some of the APA style and format rules you will want to double-check before handing in your masterpiece.

14

Table That Motion 15

*The Special Challenges
of Tables and Figures*

D id you use some interesting visual stimuli in your research study? Do you have so many numbers (e.g., means and standard deviations) from your statistical analyses that writing them out in the text of your paper would be cumbersome? These are just two of the reasons you may have to use tables or figures in your paper. Some undergraduate papers that are not associated with reporting research do not need either figures or tables. That said, we know that some instructors and professors require a table in papers for their research methods classes, precisely so students can practice formatting a table. Papers assigned for experimental or research design classes typically do require some display of results, and such assignments are often designed explicitly to give you training in table and figure design. You may be surprised to note that even literature reviews can sometimes use a table and even a figure.

What Is What

A well-designed table can actually save space compared with repetitive paragraphs presenting a boatload (a technical term) of numbers. A figure can help tell a story that words in text cannot communicate as well; perhaps a picture can be worth a thousand words at times. Tables and figures can be extremely effective writing tools when used appropriately—which is what this chapter is all about.

Tables are most often rows and columns of descriptive data (e.g., means, standard deviations), the results of inferential analyses (e.g., correlations or other analyses), or sometimes even words (e.g., sample items from a scale or questionnaire or outcomes from a content analysis of open-ended survey items). Figures are essentially everything else: line graphs, pie charts, histograms, bar charts, photographs of stimuli material, or even flowcharts and models to illustrate key variables and hypotheses. Often, a bar graph or even a pie chart can illustrate your data in a clearer way than could writing it out as text in your Results section. In fact, when you are presenting a poster for a conference, it is preferable to use a figure to illustrate your data because your findings are typically more quickly absorbed if done right and space is not a problem. Space? Yes, one of the reasons researchers are often urged not to use figures and sometimes even to avoid tables is that tables and figures take up more space on the printed page where, for journals, every page costs money to produce. This is not something one has to worry about when turning in a paper for a class assignment. The primary consideration is this: *Does a table or figure describe your results more clearly?*

Although adding figures and tables provides a nice visual to your paper, use them in a paper only if they are going to help the reader better understand your results and what you did. For example, it is clearly easier to create a table describing the results of correlations than to list each and every correlational coefficient, sample size, and p value in your text. If you are listing means and you have fewer than four means to list, do not use a table; instead, describe the means in your Results section (APA, 2010a). In fact, a cursory scan of journal articles over the years shows that what was often presented in a table in older journal articles is now presented directly in the text. A good example is the reporting of results of statistical significance tests (e.g., reporting whether many different t tests or an analysis of variance [ANOVA] was significant). If you are testing the relationship between variables (e.g., is the amount of sleep one gets correlated with how many pages of notes that person takes in class?) or whether two or more groups are different from each other (e.g., did the group of students who drank two cans of an energy drink pay more attention to the lecture than the group of students who did not?), you need statistical tests to establish whether findings are at chance levels or beyond chance levels. If the results are beyond chance levels, then we start to think about whether the independent variables can explain the results (see Chapter 10).

A simple way to check whether you need a table or figure is to see if you can describe what you want to put into a table or figure clearly and simply in your text. Of course, another consideration is if you have been explicitly required to include a table or figure as part of your assignment. Bottom line: The main goal of tables and figures is to help you present a lot of information efficiently and to make those data easier to understand (APA, 2010a). If you can achieve these two goals without tables and figures, avoid them (and more power to you). Similarly, if a table or figure is redundant (i.e., adds nothing more to the text), avoid them as well. By the way, this is a good time to look again at our chapter on Results sections (see Chapter 10).

Getting the Look Down

Like many other key elements of an APA–style paper, such as in-text citations, it is easy for a reader to see if you have used correct APA style for your table or figure. Even more important, make sure you know how to use your word-processing program to set up your tables correctly using tabs and indents where needed. In other words, do not just use your space bar and enter key to replicate the look of our sample table or a journal article table. It is also a good idea to avoid using the tables provided by statistical programs such as SPSS (Statistical Package for the Social Sciences) or Excel, as these programmed options are often not exactly APA–style compliant, and tweaking them will probably take more work than creating the table from scratch. The next chapter (Chapter 16) shows you how to create APA–style tables in Word.

Let us start with tables. Take a look at the sample in Table 15.1 (adapted from Gurung & Johnson, 2013). Table 15.1 shows you a basic way of reporting correlations and also includes descriptive data. Note that the numbering of tables for chapters in a book is different than for papers or articles; you will not see decimal points in table numbers in articles. And yes, we really needed a table here to illustrate the format for an APA–style table. Another note: We are following our convention of using a different font to show examples of what *you* would do when writing your paper; however, just remember that this table would be in a Times New Roman 12-point font in *your* paper.

Every table has a number identified at the top of the page (e.g., Table X, where X is the number of the table). The table title is next, typed in *italics,* with the first letter of each major word (i.e., not *of, the, and*) capitalized. Your titles should provide the reader with a clear sense of what the table holds.

Incorrect: *Descriptive Data*

Correct: *Mean Values, Standard Deviations, and Intercorrelations of Control Variables*

Each column of data should have a clear heading that is not too long. Sometimes two columns—and, correspondingly, two headings—may need an additional and higher level heading that describes both columns (e.g., see Table 15.2).

Table 15.1

Mean Values, Standard Deviations, and Intercorrelations of Control Variables

Measure	M	SD	1	2	3	4	5
1. Objectification	4.07	11.03	—				
2. Self-objectification	3.92	12.37	.64***	—			
3. Self-esteem	4.54	0.82	.24**	.29***	—		
4. Benevolent self-esteem	3.21	0.87	−.15	−.02	−.06	—	
5. Hostile sexism	3.26	0.91	−.11	−.01	−.07	.50***	—

*Note: *p < .05. **p < .01. ***p < .001.*

Some common abbreviations such as *M* for "mean" or *SD* for "standard deviation" can be used without your having to define them in the Note section, but statistical symbols and notations, including *M* and *SD,* should be italicized in the table. There is one exception: If those items appear in the italicized table title, then "un-italicize" them; the whole point is to emphasize the statistical notation.

The title is followed by an underline (or "rule"; "__") that runs horizontally across the top of the table. There are several ways to create this line: Press the shift key and the key between the 0 and = keys (do not use the underline function of your word processor), and hold them down until your line is the desired length, or you can insert a line by hitting that same key—the hyphen key—three times at the beginning of the line and then hitting Enter. Cool trick, eh? These underlines appear under the title and headings, as major dividers in the table itself, and at the bottom of the table above the Note. There is no line under the Note. Feel free to use white space instead of a line to separate sections or blocks of data. You can also use some of the tips presented in Chapter 16 to use Word to create a table, but no matter which method you use, be sure to follow the rules of APA format for tables.

In Table 15.1, notice that the numbers line up below the decimal point. Remember to report your results in tables using two or three decimal places. If you are reporting correlations, you do not need to use a zero in front of the decimal point, because correlations cannot exceed 1 and no zero is needed for any statistic that cannot be greater than 1 (see Chapter 13). **Important error to avoid:** Probability values to your table Notes should use $p < .01$, $p < .05$, and $p < .001$ (with periods between each *p* value), even though your results section should use exact probability values (as discussed in Chapter 10). Speaking of numbers, report correlations of a variable with itself as a dash ("—"), as seen in Table 15.1. This dash is called an "em dash" (it is the length of an *M* in whatever typeface you are using); press Ctrl + Alt + the minus sign on the number keypad to insert an em dash.

Table 15.2 shows you a basic table representing means for an experiment with three conditions. With the data for all three conditions in one table, the reader can easily compare the means across conditions. It also represents a clear case for when a table can save a lot of space. Of note is that when Valerie Johnson (from whose paper the table is taken) first created the table, she had a separate table for each category of variables (e.g., Objectification, Competence). Although it did seem to be less cluttered than what you see in Table 15.2, it precluded a reader's comparing means across category *and* condition. Always combine tables when you can. If you have a really long table that will not fit on one page (Table 15.2 did not fit on one page when this chapter was first written in Word and not yet typeset on the printed page you see now), you need to repeat the title on each page. After the first page, add the word *continued* in parentheses at the end.

The tables you see here represent the most common tables needed for students learning to write their first papers in APA format. As the complexity of the research design increases, the complexity of the tables and formatting increases

15

Table 15.2

Mean Values of the Control Variables and Dependent Variables Separated by Condition

Variable	Control[a]		Athletic		Academic	
	M	SD	M	SD	M	SD
Competence						
Competent***	5.81	1.23	6.90	1.17	6.42	1.44
Determined***	5.99	1.31	7.84	0.96	6.71	1.45
Independent***	5.58	1.54	6.99	1.18	6.22	1.56
Intelligent***	5.66	1.08	6.87	1.19	6.92	1.64
Responsible***	5.51	1.41	7.10	1.21	6.15	1.62
Studious***	5.33	1.42	6.60	1.28	6.68	1.73
Talented***	6.08	1.08	7.93	0.98	6.55	1.37
Objectification						
Attractive	6.74	1.12	6.78	1.31	6.49	1.52
Desirable***	6.33	1.39	6.72	1.22	6.10	1.50
Promiscuous***	6.12	1.65	4.71	1.54	5.59	2.13
Sexy*	6.42	1.59	6.41	1.40	6.03	1.65
Short-term fling***	6.61	1.70	4.62	1.66	5.70	2.21
Uses body***	6.26	1.80	4.80	1.84	5.65	2.25
Personal characteristics						
Feminine***	7.85	1.07	7.13	1.36	7.38	1.23
Fit/healthy***	7.27	1.22	8.20	1.63	6.32	1.63
High self-esteem***	6.95	1.36	7.17	1.25	6.39	1.63
Honest***	5.57	1.27	6.32	1.21	5.84	1.46
Shallow***	5.12	1.77	4.12	1.47	4.74	1.84
Vain***	5.51	1.79	4.77	1.54	5.30	1.79
Fillers						
Appropriateness***	5.36	1.77	6.63	1.66	4.82	2.29
Likeable***	6.47	1.22	6.78	1.19	6.14	1.28
Popular***	7.07	1.19	7.01	1.25	6.32	1.52
Revealingness***	5.24	1.86	4.10	2.10	5.33	2.32
Trustworthy***	5.49	1.21	6.47	1.24	5.87	1.58

15

Note: Table used with permission from Valerie Johnson, University of Wisconsin–Green Bay.

[a]Models in the control condition wore the same outfits as those in the two experimental conditions.

p < .05. ***p* < .001.

as well. Some tables will need divider lines or spaces between blocks of numbers. Remember, there are never vertical lines in an APA–formatted table, only horizontal lines when needed.

A Note on "Notes"

If a table has a note, that note is placed at the very bottom of the table, and the word *Note* or *Notes* is italicized (see Table 15.2). There is an order to what goes in this section. First, and right after the period (use a period, not a colon or semicolon), you list definitions of abbreviations, if any, and "general" information that pertains to the entire table. General notes may include the source of your information. On a separate line, list a "probability note," which explains what the asterisks in the table mean. Sometimes you may need to use a "specific" note (on its own line between the general and probability notes) if you have information that relates only to specific columns or rows. For example, you may want to indicate that the means in a certain column or for a certain variable were different. You do so using a superscript lowercase letter (e.g., [a, b, c]).

Figuring It Out

It is rare to need a figure for most papers written for undergraduate classes, because the data represented in most figures can be more easily and effectively written in the body of the paper. Figures are particularly helpful for illustrating the results of complex statistical analyses and intricate research designs. Neither of these situations is common when you are first learning to do research and write in APA style. However, your design could easily include two variables. In that case, a figure might be best to illustrate a finding that includes an interaction of those variables. An additional possible use of figures is when you use photographic stimuli and a description will not suffice or when you have a really complex research design and want to use a chart to illustrate the research design. Mind you, these exceptions can be common. The tables used as examples (Tables 15.1 and 15.2) refer to a study in which participants saw photographs of students provocatively attired and in different contexts (e.g., at a swimming pool, in a classroom, against a blank wall). The researchers measured the extent to which the student models were objectified (Johnson & Gurung, 2010). Describing the clothing and contexts—the main experimental stimuli and variants—does not provide a reader with a good idea of the experiment. This is one place where it may be necessary to include photographs (and the authors did so in their paper). Although using photographs may imply brightening up your paper with color, use only black-and-white versions of photographs and all other figures. Some journals allow color figures, although most do not. Ask your instructor what he or she prefers in this regard.

15

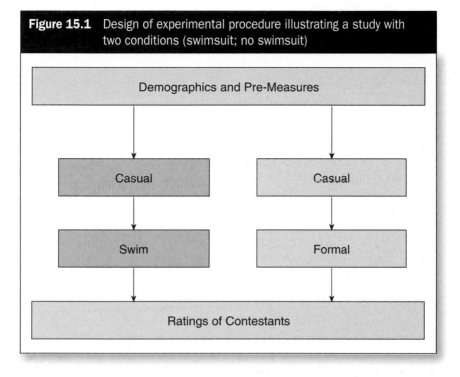

Figure 15.1 Design of experimental procedure illustrating a study with two conditions (swimsuit; no swimsuit)

Demographics and Pre-Measures

Casual | Casual

Swim | Formal

Ratings of Contestants

Figures are also very useful for depicting the relations between different variables. Figure 15.1 illustrates how the complex relationship between variables in a study can be easily represented by a figure (Gurung, Morack, & Bloch, 2005). Note that the figure has a "caption," which also serves as a title ("Design of experimental procedure illustrating a study with two conditions [swimsuit; no swimsuit]"). Figures do not include a separate title.

Get *Legendary* (and Use Captions)

Tables have titles; figures have "captions." Also in contrast to tables, the caption is placed below the figure (not shown in Figure 15.1) and in many ways combines the title and notes sections of tables. A caption always starts with the word *Figure* in italics and has the number of the figure, followed by a period (e.g., *Figure X.*). Again, use whole numbers, similar to how tables are numbered. Follow the number with a clear but concise description of what the figure shows.

A legend is the descriptive information within a figure that identifies key components of the figure. For example, a graph with x (horizontal and always the independent variable for an experiment) and y (vertical and always the dependent variable) axes should have the axes labeled. In Figure 15.2, the vertical axis

15

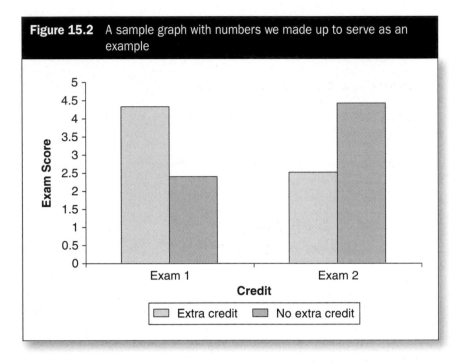

Figure 15.2 A sample graph with numbers we made up to serve as an example

represents scores on an exam. The horizontal axis represents Exams 1 and 2. The legend explains how the shaded bars represent the students who either did an extra-credit assignment or not. For legends, as for table titles, capitalize only major words.

Where to Place Tables and Figures

So you know you need a figure or table but wonder where to place it in your paper. If you were submitting a manuscript for review for publication in a journal, your tables and figures would be the last pages of your paper. Your table or tables would follow your references and footnotes (if applicable), and your figure or figures would go last. Most instructors also want your tables and figures to be similarly placed. In the published article, your tables and figures will be placed in the text. Some instructors actually like the tables and figures to be placed within your manuscript closest to where they are described (and this is what we did when we first wrote these chapters). Although this organization is incorrect according to APA format, be sure to ask how or where your instructor would like the tables and figures placed, and then follow your instructor's guidelines. If your paper does include a figure or table, you need to include a reference to the table at the appropriate point in the paper, almost always in the Results section. You need to use only the table or figure number; do not worry about (or include) the location (i.e., *above* or *below* or on *page X* of your paper). As we described in

Chapter 15, references to your tables/figures can be directly within the sentence or within parentheses, as in the examples that follow, and should tell the reader what is presented in the table.

Incorrect: Results are presented in Table 1.

Correct: Means and correlations between the major variables appear in Table 1.

Correct: There were significant correlations between the major variables (see Table 1).

But I Am Doing a Literature Review: Could I Use a Table or Figure?

We began this chapter by suggesting that, indeed, you could use a table or figure even when doing a literature review; so the answer is yes. Mind you, the emphasis is on *could*. You rarely *have* to, but often, a table summarizing key findings or research articles/citations can come in handy. A figure can be used to visually map out theoretical ideas or links between variables and concepts described in the paper. Figure 15.1 provides a good example of this.

Do Not Forget

- If you revise your paper and redo some analyses and find you have to change your table, make sure to go back to your Results and/or Discussion section(s) to update related material.
- Watch your formatting. Pay close attention to the labels and positioning of labels in relation to the rest of your material.
- Avoid abbreviating material unless absolutely necessary, and if you do, make sure you explain your abbreviation in a table note.
- Number your tables/figures in the order in which they are needed in your paper, and use only whole numbers (e.g., Table 1, Table 2—not Table 1.5 or Table 1a, Table 1b). In case you are wondering, tables are numbered in this book by chapter plus the order in which the tables appear in the chapter—for example, Table 15.1, Table 15.2—but your paper won't have chapters, so you need only whole numbers.
- Plagiarism rules still apply (see Chapter 5). Do not copy a table or figure from another published work without getting permission (yes, tedious, but needed even if you have adapted the material) and also citing the source.
- Do not go table/figure crazy. Most 10- to 15-page papers (a guess as to the average undergraduate paper length) need not have more than one or

15

two tables/figures. Consolidate where appropriate, while always follow-ing the teacher's instructions.

- Tables and figures should not duplicate material in the text.
- Tell your reader, in the text, exactly what is presented in the table or figure you include.

Tables and figures can break up the monotony of text and illustrate what you did. Although you may not need to create one for your research paper, it may be good practice to include one if you can. There are a lot of details to pay attention to, but relevant tables and figures truly make an article more palatable.

15

Make Microsoft Word 2013 Work for You

16

APA Formatting

Every job, every occupation, and every career has tools of the trade. One of the key skills you can acquire during your undergraduate career is the ability to write clearly and succinctly. One of the tools of your trade will be Microsoft Word (Word from here on). There may be times when you attempt to get by with substitutions (Pages, OpenOffice, WordPerfect), but to achieve the attention to detail that an APA–formatted paper requires, Word is your best bet (and no, we do not receive royalties from Microsoft for this quasi-endorsement). In this chapter, we present some of the common tasks you will need to master when preparing a paper in APA format; we show you the menus and guide you through the process of making all this happen. As you try to achieve any of the tasks in this chapter, you may want to lay your book flat next to your computer, with Word open, so you can follow our instructions step by step.

Word 2013 Tabs and Drop-Down Menus

You should note that all the instructions in this chapter are designed for Word 2013. Some folks may still be using Word 2010, and maybe even Word 2007, which is fine. However, the menus and the screenshots look different; in other words, the organization and appearance of the features changed sometimes from 2007 to 2010 to 2013, but all the functionality remains if you are still using Word 2010 or 2013. For Mac users, some of the Office for Mac functions are a little different, and the tabs and menus often look different from Word 2013 in Windows.

16

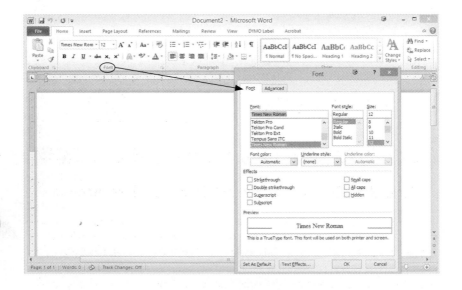

This is the header bar at the top of Word 2013 screens. In this screenshot, you may see choices that are not on the version you are using; do not worry about that. We have installed some "add-ins" for our versions of Word that you will not need for preparing APA–formatted papers, such as DYMO Label and Acrobat. Word is organized on the basis of tabs listed across the top of the screen. Your tabs probably look like this: *File—Home—Insert—Page Layout—References—Mailings—Review—View—*and perhaps other add-ins if you have them. Clicking on a tab presents many other options and choices, which will appear just below the lineup of tabs.

If at some point you needed to customize (beyond the options provided), clicking on the Home tab will give you access to a menu where you can adjust anything.

There are certainly other methods of accessing particular functions in Word, including shortcut keys and drop-down menus. Sometimes these complete menus can be handy if you have to make a set of complicated changes, such as changes to the font size, font, and other details, for more control. If you just need to change one feature quickly (e.g., the font alone), the tabs across the top of the page work well.

16

Setting the Margins

APA format is consistent about margins: 1-inch margins on all four sides of the paper (top, bottom, right, left). If you set your default document properly, you will never have to change the margins. But you should know how to anyway, because you might be swapping documents with classmates or merging two files into one. To set the margins, start by clicking on the *Page Layout* tab indicated in the next graphic.

When the page layout options appear, click on *Margins*, and then click on *Normal*; the drop-down box also indicates that *Normal* is 1-inch margins on all four sides of the paper, which is exactly what you want for APA format.

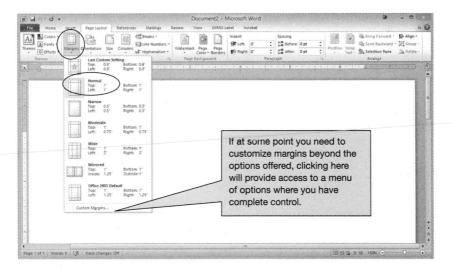

If at some point you need to customize margins beyond the options offered, clicking here will provide access to a menu of options where you have complete control.

Line Spacing and Spacing Between Paragraphs

Throughout the text of your APA–formatted paper, you will need to use double-spacing. If this is not how your default document opens in Word, you will have to change it for the document you are working on. Click on the *Home* tab and then on the icon circled in the next screenshot; when you hover over it (i.e., leave your cursor over it for a second), a box will show that it is called *Line and Paragraph Spacing*.

16

Clicking on the *Line and Paragraph Spacing* icon will give you access to the drop-down box presented next. For double-spacing, select 2.0—which stands for double-spacing.

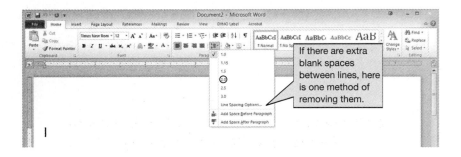

Sometimes in Word 2013, you will see extra spaces between paragraphs; in APA format, you do *not* want this. You want regular double-spacing throughout the entire document, with no extra spacing added, for example, between paragraphs. There are at least two ways to fix this. If there is extra spacing between paragraphs, the drop-down box presented in the previous screenshot will offer the options *Remove Space Before Paragraph* or *Remove Space After Paragraph*. Clicking on the relevant choice is one way to remove the extra space. Another way to remove the extra space is to use the more complete drop-down menu shown in the next screenshot. There should not be any need to use the *Add Space* option if the rest of the formatting is correct.

You can quickly access the drop-down box by clicking on the icon circled in the next screenshot. Make sure that under the heading *Spacing*, both *Before* and *After* are set at 0 pt.

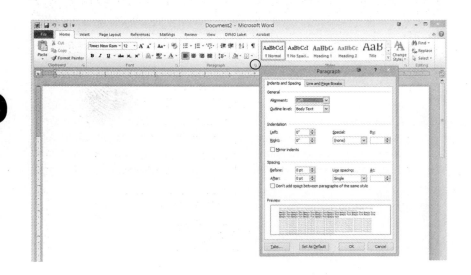

Then, in the *Line Spacing* section, change the menu option to *Double*, which will give you double-spacing. If you want that to apply to the entire document, press Ctrl+A before choosing *Double* in the *Line Spacing* menu, and the entire document will be double-spaced. As you can see, typically, you can achieve formatting changes in Word 2013 in one of several ways. You do not necessarily have to do it the way we are showing you here, but we want you to have at least one method that you know (and we know) works! Also in this box, you can remove the extra spaces between paragraphs by making sure it says 0 pt in the boxes labeled *Before* and *After*.

Page Headers (First Page and Subsequent Pages) and Page Numbering

To be honest, the page header system is a bit confusing and difficult to master at first. Many of our students try to do it manually without using the special Word settings—not a good idea. The page header (the information inside the top 1-inch margin of your APA–formatted paper) is different on page 1 than on the remaining pages of your paper. So here, through a series of screenshots, we will show you how to make the page 1 header different from the headers in the rest of your document. This is one of the most common questions we have from our students; by getting this down, you will be way ahead of the game.

The easier part is to insert the page number, which will appear in the same place on every page of your paper; you also want to make sure that the inserted page number matches the font you are using—usually Times New Roman 12-point font. To insert the page number in the header, start with the *Insert* tab and then click on the *Header* icon (circled in the next screenshot).

16

Because you have multiple tasks to achieve in the page header, rather than going one step at a time, you can access menus that allow you to complete many steps at one time. Under the *Insert* tab and keeping with the *Header* selection, choose *Edit Header* instead; see the circled portion in the next screenshot.

Document2 - Microsoft Word
Edit Header

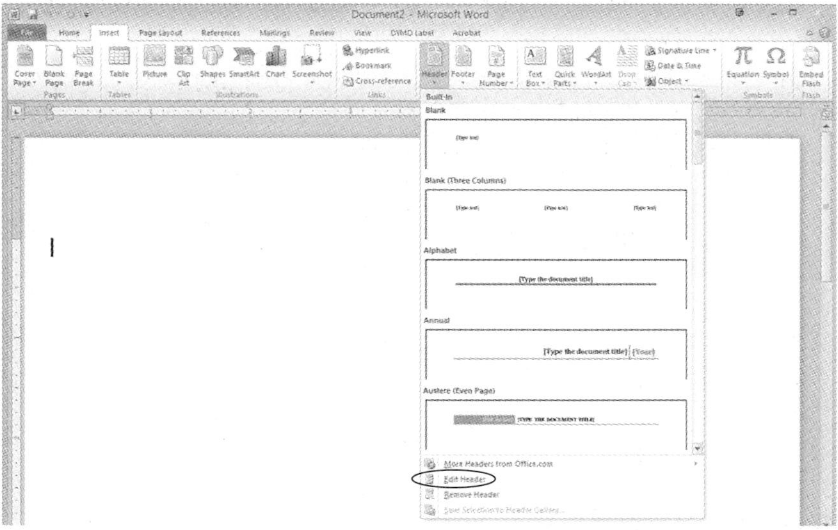

When you click on this option, a whole new set of advanced controls will be available to you, called *Header & Footer Tools* (see the top menu in the next screenshot).

Document2 - Microsoft Word
This is a helpful reminder that you are working in the header space; the main text of your document will appear gray.

First, insert your page number, which must appear in exactly the same place on every page. As you can see in the next screenshot, you first place your cursor exactly where you want the page number to appear (rightmost margin of page header, using tabs or the keyboard shortcut Ctrl+R). Then click on *Page Number*, as shown in the screenshot; select *Current Position* (circled in the screenshot);

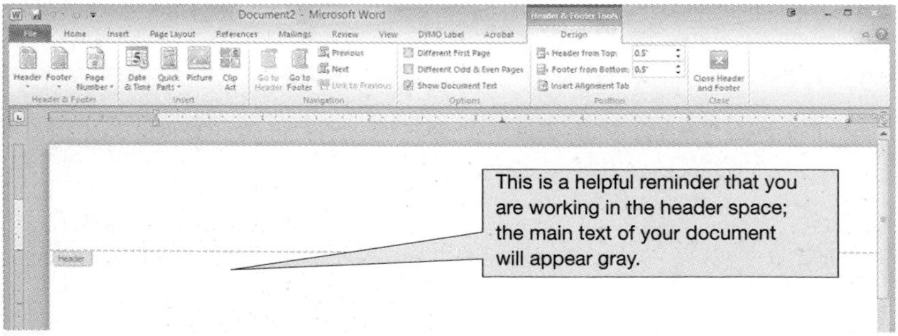

and, finally, click in the first box, labeled *Simple* followed by *Plain Number*. That will insert the page number, and you will not need to add any more page numbers. This feature will number every page in the file for you, and the number will automatically change when you add or subtract pages.

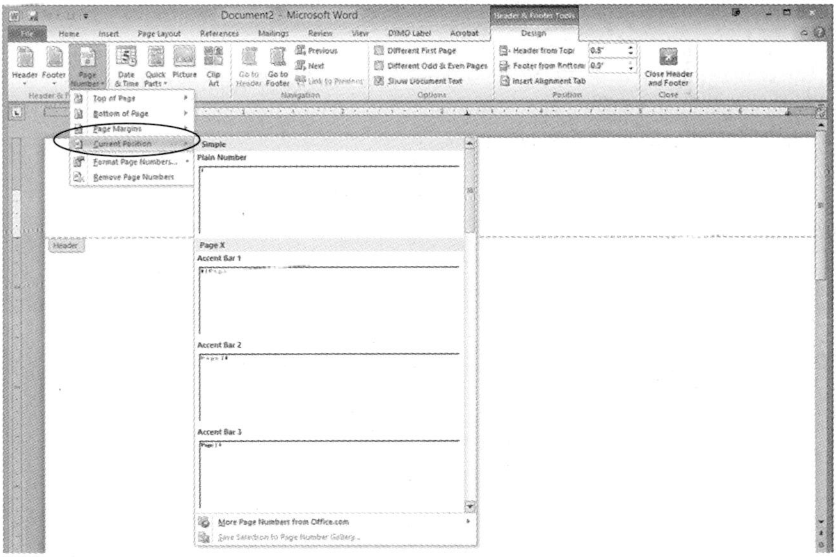

On the first page of an APA paper, inside the top 1-inch margin, the words *Running head* should appear, followed by a colon and a short title in all capital letters (50 characters or fewer, including spaces). On every subsequent page of the manuscript, only the short title (i.e., without the "Running head" label) in capital letters appears at the top of the page inside the header region. To differentiate the first-page header from all the other page headers, click on the option labeled *Different First Page*, circled in the next screenshot.

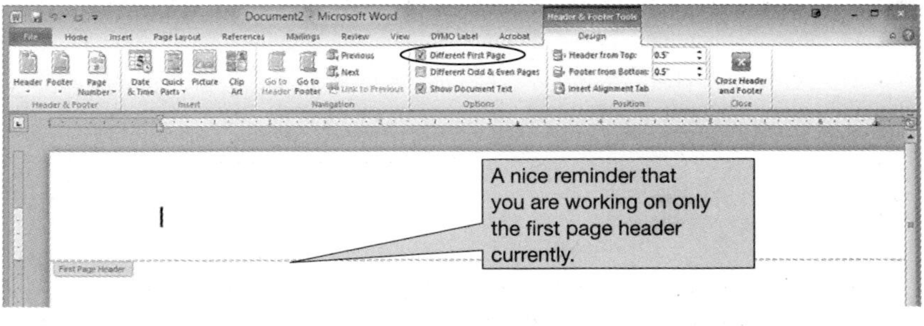

On page 1, you will include the "Running head" indicator, followed by a colon, followed by the short title (in CAPS), with the page number at the end of the line, but on page 2 (and all subsequent pages), you will have just the short title (in CAPS) with the page number at the end of the line. The sample paper in Chapter 21 provides a nice illustration of this feature in use.

Tabs, Centering, and the Ruler

Typically, the default tabs in Word 2013 will work just fine—one-half inch (0.5) with each time you press the tab key. You can gain greater control over tabs, and centering as well, but first you will need to make sure you are viewing the ruler, because the ruler is essential for setting tabs. In the next screenshot, there is no ruler; we will show you how to activate it.

You will want to select the small icon on the rightmost side of your screen (circled in the next screenshot), located a little below the larger options above your document (when you hover over it, you will see that the icon is labeled *View Ruler*).

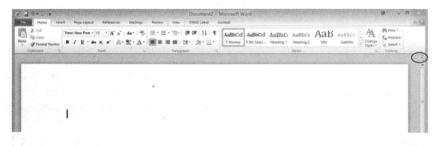

You will see that two rulers appear—the horizontal ruler at the top of the page (you will use this one most often) and the vertical ruler down the left side of the page (visible in Print Layout view only).

16

One method of inserting tabs is to use the tab icon at the top of the vertical ruler, circled in the previous screenshot; you can rotate through different types of tabs (by clicking repeatedly on this icon) and then place (and move) them along the horizontal ruler.

To access the more complete drop-down menus, click the *Paragraph* icon on the *Home* tab, circled in the next screenshot, and then select the *Tabs . . .* button at the bottom of the menu.

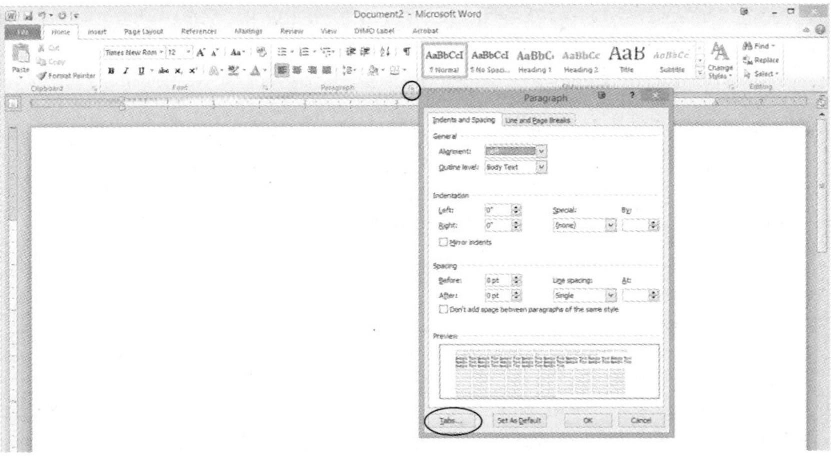

Now you can set your tabs with precision, using exact locations rather than the drag-and-drop feature on the ruler bar. The alignment feature can be handy when you are trying to line up decimal places for a table. Although you probably will not use this in an APA–formatted paper, say an instructor asked you for a table of contents with a dotted line leading to the right where the page number is listed. To accomplish that function, you would use the *Tabs* menu shown in the next screenshot. Under *Leader*, you could select the type of line you want to use to "lead" the reader across the page to the page number (in a table of contents).

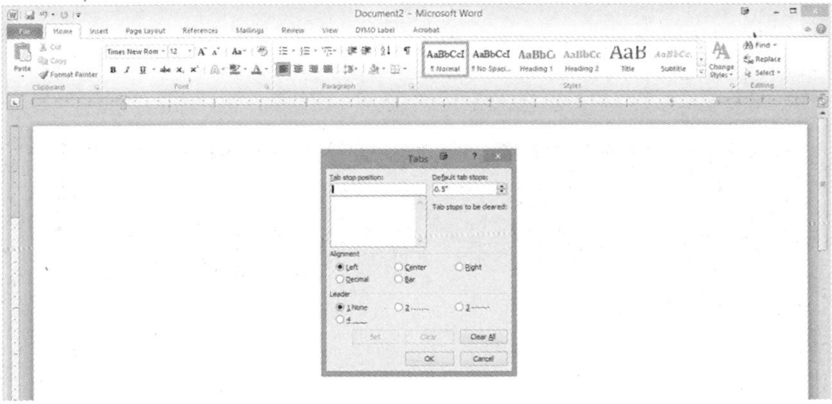

16

Centering using Word is very straightforward. Typically, you highlight with your cursor whatever you want to be centered (or even place your cursor within the word you want centered), and then you click on the *Center* button in the *Home* tab, circled in the next screenshot. Sometimes this is trickier than you might think. If you have a tab (indent) on the line and you type in your heading ("Method," for example), this centering feature will center **Method** with the 0.5-inch tab included—meaning that the Method section heading really is not centered at all. Make sure there are no other tabs or spaces on the line you wish to center. One easy way to spot this is to click on the paragraph symbol in the *Home* menu, also circled in the next screenshot. This will reveal within the text of your paper where there are spaces and other pagination symbols so you can easily spot unnecessary tabs and spaces.

One more problem that occasionally occurs with student papers (and is easily fixable) is when you accidentally hit the wrong formatting button. In the next screenshot, you can see that the button circled looks as though it might be used to center, but it is really for justification. Justification means that Word will insert spaces in between words so that the right and left margins of the paragraph are exactly even; this is the way most newspaper columns are formatted. You do *not* want this in APA format; instead, you want your paragraphs to be left justified, with a jagged right margin. If you hit the *Justify* button by mistake, you can (a) click on the *Undo Typing* icon (the backward-facing arrow on the far left of the toolbar); (b) highlight what is justified and hit the *Align Left Text* button (to the left of the *Center* button); or (c) press Ctrl+Z, which works the same as clicking the *Undo Typing* icon.

16

References and the Hanging Indent

Your References section will appear toward the end of your APA–formatted paper; it starts at the top of its own page (you can easily achieve this by inserting a page break, which we will show you how to do a little later in this chapter). References are double-spaced just like the remainder of the paper, but they have a special format, called a "hanging indent." The first line of the reference is flush left, but all the subsequent lines of the reference are indented. You do *not* want to insert a bunch of spaces or tabs to achieve this, because if you do, and then you have to reformat your paper, you will have to redo the formatting for every individual reference. Believe us, we have learned this the hard way. There is an efficient shortcut for this.

First, type all your references in APA format, including double-spacing, proper italicization and capitalization of titles, and correct punctuation—all this without the hanging indents (see Chapter 12 for reference styles). The next screenshot shows an example of a book reference before formatting. Hit *Enter* at the end of each reference, as if to start a new paragraph. In fact, you can insert all your references this way and then use the hanging-indent trick once (after you "select all" by pressing Ctrl+A), or you can use it on individual references. (Do not worry if squiggly lines appear under the author names. Word often does not recognize names as properly spelled words, but that is OK; the squiggly lines will not print.) After adding your references, apply the hanging-indent format by highlighting all the references with your mouse, as indicated in the screenshot.

With all the references highlighted, let go of the mouse and press Ctrl+T on your keyboard; you will see the hanging indent applied as shown in the next screenshot. Click anywhere in the document, and the blue highlighting will go away. You are now ready to resume your other writing tasks, with the hanging indents easily applied to your references. If you have to copy and paste or change reference styles later, the hanging indent will remain; you do not have to add or subtract spaces or tabs to achieve the hanging-indent format.

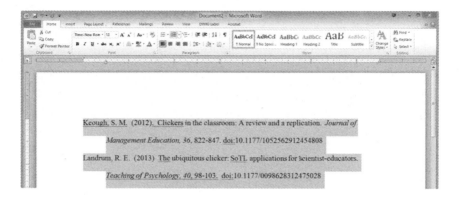

Keough, S. M. (2012). Clickers in the classroom: A review and a replication. *Journal of Management Education, 36,* 822-847. doi:10.1177/1052562912454808

Landrum, R. E. (2013) The ubiquitous clicker: SoTL applications for Scientist-educators. *Teaching of Psychology, 40,* 98-103. doi:10.1177/0098628312475028

Preparing a Table
(Rows, Columns, Lines, Centering)

Depending on the type of writing you are doing for an instructor, you might need to prepare a table. Rules for tables are very precise in APA format, and there is a section of your *PM* dedicated to preparing tables. You can also find additional books (e.g., Nicol & Pexman, 2010) that will give you tips on how to prepare a basic table. Here, we will just get you started with the basic Word commands to start a table; you can see an example of an APA–formatted table at the end of the sample paper in Chapter 21 and more instructions on how to create tables for data in Chapter 15.

If you know the size of the table you want to insert (i.e., the number of rows and columns needed), you can start on the *Insert* tab, click on *Table*, and then *Insert Table*, circled in the next screenshot.

Drag your cursor across the matrix of rows and columns presented, and when you let go of the mouse button, it will insert a table of those dimensions into your Word document. For example, in the next screen, the cursor has been dragged to make a 3 × 5 table, and you can see the three columns and five rows that were inserted into the document.

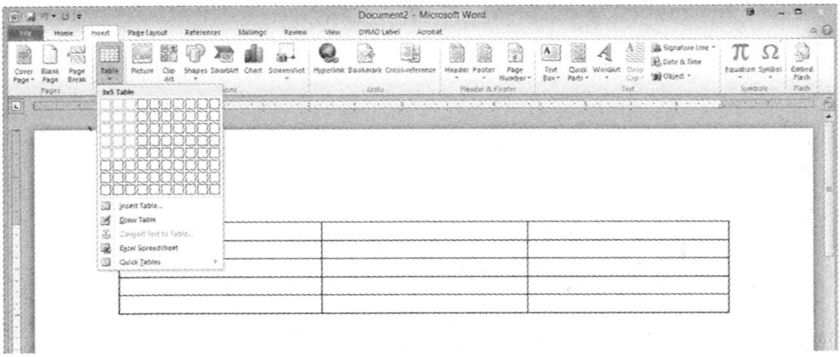

For this table, you still have much formatting to do. Space in this book does not permit step-by-step instructions, because the rules are precise, but you can see an example table at the end of the sample paper in Chapter 21. To format your table, click anywhere inside it, and an entire new set of tools will emerge—*Table Tools.*

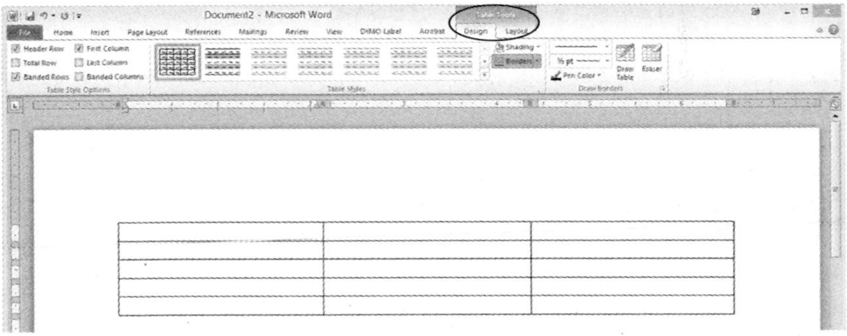

From this menu, you will be able to erase the lines you do not want and draw the lines you do want in the table. For example, a properly APA–formatted table has no vertical lines. In the previous screenshot, four vertical lines need to be removed. As you remove the drawn lines, you will still see the outline of the table displayed as gridlines; dotted blue lines show the shape of the table, but the lines will not print. To format your table properly, make sure you are using gridlines; to do this, select the option labeled *View Gridlines,* circled in the next screenshot.

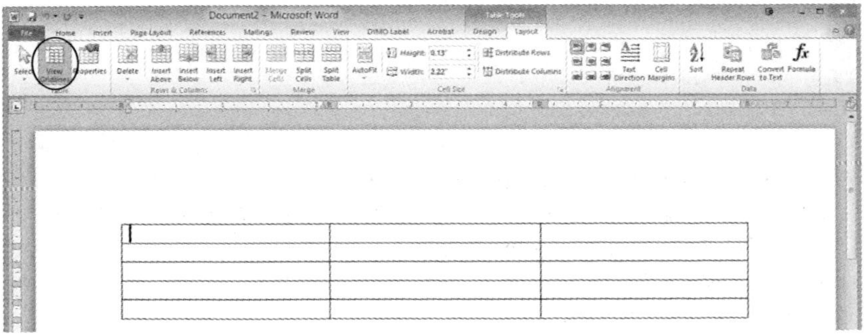

16

As you change the characteristics of different rows and columns, you can right-click on a cell or row or column, and a context-specific drop-down box will appear, as shown in the next screenshot. A number of handy table-editing features are available to you in the drop-down box, such as inserting a row or column, deleting a row or column, merging cells, aligning text within cells, changing the measurements (dimensions) of rows and columns, or determining how tables break across pages. As we mentioned previously, these details only scratch the surface of what you can do with the tables feature in Word. Even though this feature may seem a bit daunting, learn how to use it. Do *not* prepare tables by drawing in lines by hand or by using tabs. Show your instructors that you are learning to master the tools of your trade.

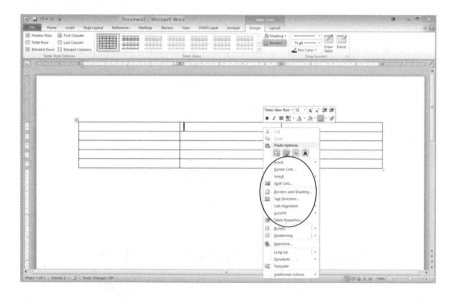

Fonts and Font Variations (Italics, Bold, Superscript)

Technically, there are three levels of Word formatting—the font level, the paragraph level, and the section level (Krieger, 2005). Section-level formatting can be useful in Word, but it is probably not necessary for the APA papers you will be preparing. Given that you will be using the same font throughout your paper, font-level formatting will be perfectly appropriate for you. Most of the time, just accessing the *Font* section (circled in the next screenshot) from the *Home* tab will achieve most of the functions you need.

16

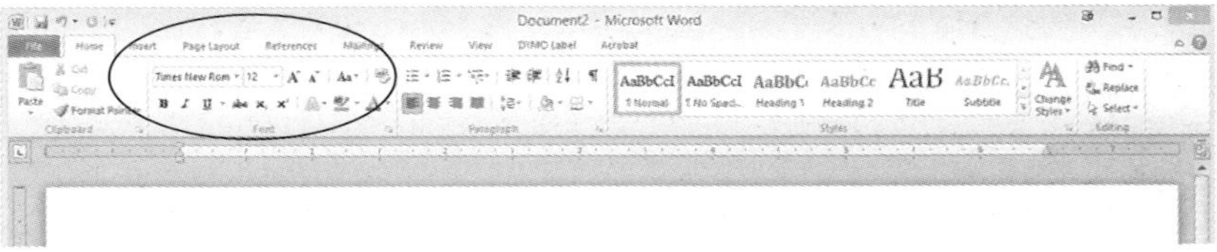

In cases where you may need a bit more control or options for special features of font sets, you can access the more complete Word menu by clicking on the icon circled in the next screenshot.

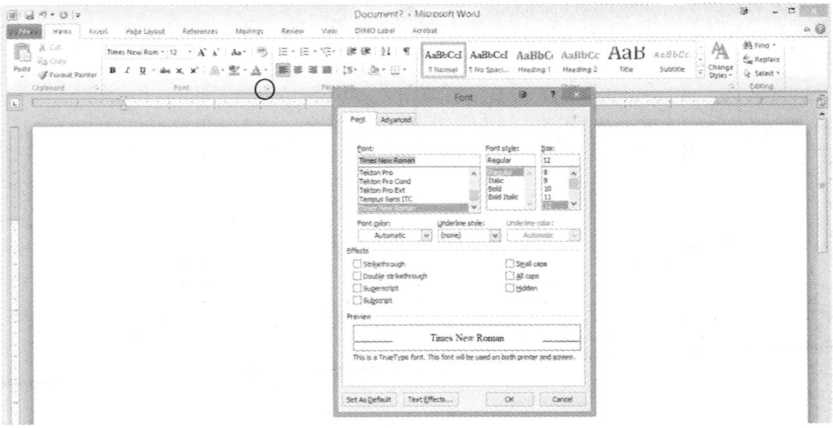

Page Breaks, Orphans, and Widows

Certain parts of an APA–formatted paper, such as the abstract, introduction, References section, and each table, start at the top of the page. On the other hand, the end of the Method section just flows into the Results section, with regular double-spacing. At the end of the Discussion section, the References section starts at the top of the next page. To start a new page, you could just hit *Enter* a bunch of times on your keyboard, or you could insert a page break, which will immediately move the cursor to the top of the next page. Just as you can insert page breaks, you can remove them as well.

To insert a page break, all you need to do is access the *Insert* tab and then select *Page Break* (circled in the next screenshot), or you can use the keyboard shortcut Ctrl+Enter. An easy way to remove a page break is to backspace from the line following the break or click to the left of the page break and hit the Delete key on your keyboard.

16

Widow and orphan control is another feature you should be sure to use. The setting described here and mentioned in Chapter 21 will help keep related text together in a document. For example, if the Results section heading in a research paper is "alone" at the bottom of the page (no other text underneath the heading on that page), you should insert a page break to bump the heading to the top of the next page. That type of separation is called a *widow*—that is, when a heading for a new section or the first line of a paragraph is separated from the text that follows the heading or from the rest of the paragraph. Even though adding a page break to move the "widowed" Results section heading to the top of the next page may leave a large margin at the bottom of the previous page, this is preferable to separating the Results heading from the rest of the Results section.

Another type of formatting to keep in mind concerns the last line of a paragraph that appears at the top of the next page of your document. This type of separation is called an *orphan*. In this context, avoid orphans and widows. Most of the time, the *Widow/Orphan* control box, when checked, does a good job of keeping first and last lines of paragraphs on the same page, but you may occasionally have to insert a page break to avoid widows. The next screenshot shows you where to find the *Widow/Orphan* control box.

Spell-Checker and Grammar Checker

Although they are not perfect, we recommend that you use the spell-checker and grammar checker that accompany Word. Suspected spelling errors will be identified by a squiggly red underline, and suspected grammar errors will be identified by a squiggly green underline. Hovering the cursor over the identified item and right-clicking should bring up a context-specific box in which suggested replacements are offered. On those occasions when you know you have spelled a word correctly, you can simply click the *Ignore* button to make the squiggly line disappear.

To make sure these features are activated, click on the *File* tab, as indicated in the next screenshot; then click on the *Options* button at the bottom of the menu, which will bring up the display you see next.

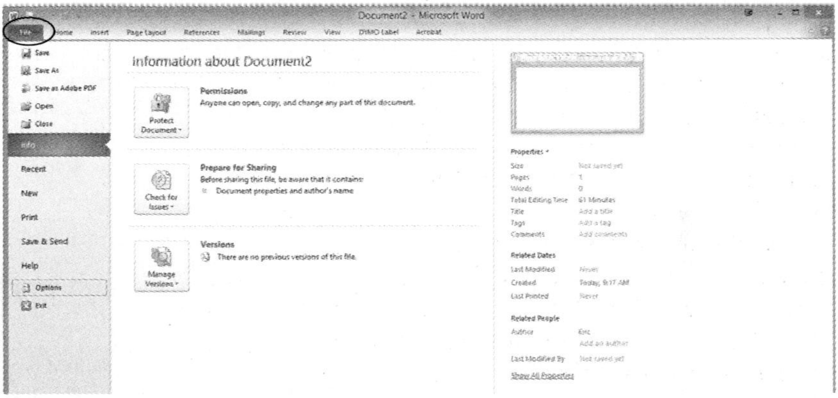

To make sure your spell-checker and grammar checker are activated, click on the *Proofing* option (circled in the next screenshot), and select the spelling and grammar options you want.

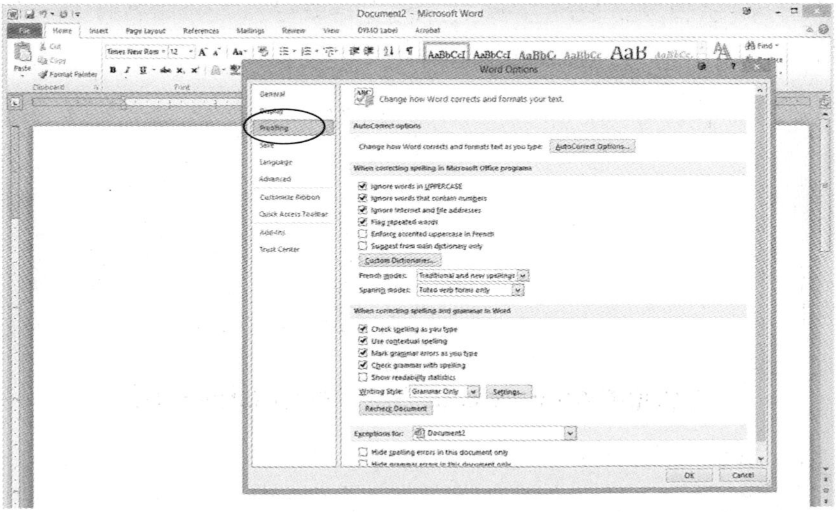

16

Note that this feature will not catch all spelling and grammar errors; you are responsible for your own work, especially proofreading it. Many other parts of this book (including Chapter 20 on proofreading) can help you avoid those obvious mistakes that can be irritating to your instructor when grading—and you do want to avoid that. After you have worked on a paper for a while, it might be hard to see your own mistakes, so swap with a classmate; offer to proofread his or her paper while your classmate proofreads your paper. A new set of eyes can do wonders for finding errors that you have looked at over and over again.

Developing Good Habits: Autosaving, File Naming, File Storage, Frequent Backups

One of the important details of using powerful tools such as Word 2013 is letting the tools help you do your job better. Part of that process is the ability to save and retrieve your work. That might sound like a simple task, but have you ever lost a file? Has the power ever gone off while you were working on a computer, or has your laptop battery ever died unexpectedly? Word provides an autosave feature that can minimize work losses; you may have seen these AutoRecover screens before when you rebooted your computer after a power loss.

Starting from the *File* tab, select the *Options* button, and then the *Save* option (circled in the next screenshot), and review what is checked there. You can see that the default is 10 minutes for autosave; that is, if the computer crashes, the most that will be lost is 10 minutes' worth of work. But if you are a speed typist and can crank out 500 words in that time, that might be too much work to risk losing. You have the option of making the minutes value smaller—say, saving every 5 minutes. You can also have the backup files saved to a web location if you do not want to save backups to your computer's hard drive.

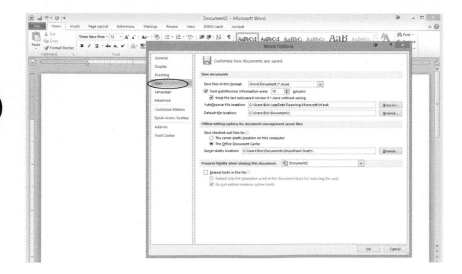

By paying attention to a few more details, you can make your interactions with this powerful Word tool go more smoothly. First, use descriptive file names; this way, you will be able to figure out what is in the file faster, and any search engines you use to find files will have to search only the file names and not within each file (which could be a slow process). Be systematic about your file names. When working on a paper with multiple drafts, save each draft with a different file name—for example, "Developmental psychology paper Version 1.1," "Developmental psychology paper Version 2.0," and so on. Or embed today's date into the file name (02_09_2015) so you will have an additional guide to knowing what day you worked on each draft of the paper. It is also a good idea to include your last name as part of the file name. This becomes helpful if you need to submit your paper electronically. Your instructor would probably prefer not to open, grade, and save a class-full of papers all titled "Developmental Psychology Paper."

Be consistent with where you store your important files; perhaps they are always stored on your laptop or copied to a trusted USB memory stick/flash drive or saved in "the cloud." If you establish some consistent file storage routines, you will spend less time looking for where your work *is* and more time actually working on your paper. If you work on many different computers throughout the week, you might want to think about using a large USB drive or perhaps a reliable cloud storage system such as Dropbox (www.dropbox.com).

Finally, you have to back up your files on a consistent basis; we recommend backing up at least once a week. Pick a convenient time; maybe every Thursday morning you will back up your hard drive while getting ready for class. Once a month, back up your backups. These are all mechanical devices, and they will eventually fail. You do not want to experience that sinking feeling of putting hours and hours into a paper or project only to find that all your work is lost and you now have to recreate it; that is not an efficient use of anyone's time. Develop a consistent backup procedure now, and invest in some backup hardware; you will be happy you did.

If you can learn and master these tools of the trade, writing in APA style (knowing the rules and proper formatting) will allow you to concentrate on the psychological story you wish to tell.

16

SECTION V

Some Nitty-Gritty Details

Making a List, No Apps Required

17

Enumeration and Seriation

Ever had an argument in which you were so irritated that you spouted off at the mouth and could not wait to get all those reasons you were mad off your chest? Perhaps you wanted to tell someone who wronged you all the ways you were right and they were wrong. Well, in scientific writing, there are also times when you have much to say. You have hypotheses to support, findings to list, possible explanations to line up. For each of these reasons, regardless of which section of your paper you are writing, you need to know the APA rules on the different ways to order, list, and present your ideas. Knowing how to list in APA style is a useful skill. Knowing how to properly list items using APA format might even encourage you to use lists more often (if appropriate).

Why Bother?

Knowing how to order your points in a series, hence the word *seriation*, is a key writing skill that enables your reader to better understand your main ideas. Many individuals may not have heard the actual term before but still have presented ordered lists of information. Seriation is designed to make your key points clear. The problem is—and the three of us have seen many examples of this—many writers use a variety of erroneous techniques to present lists. We have seen students use different fonts, different font colors, and even different font sizes to order points (remember, your entire paper should be prepared in the same Times New Roman 12-point font). We have also seen students use a variety of symbols and bullets. Word may have some funky symbols for use, but they do not belong

17

in an APA–style paper. Another consideration: Be careful with lists and seriation. Too many lists in a student paper can make it look as though the student did not really write the paper but instead cobbled together a bunch of lists. Our advice is to use lists sparingly, and when you do use a list, follow the seriation rules precisely so you can show your professors your attention to detail.

Keeping Order at the Section Level

An empirical paper is organized into major sections such as Introduction, Method, Results, and Discussion. The Method and Results sections have their own natural order of presenting information and normally do not require seriation. For example, the Method section has the Participants, Apparatus or Materials, and Procedure sections. However, you may want to order steps when describing your procedure, or you may want to have a list of conclusions in your Discussion section. A variety of options are available for including lists in your APA paper. You just need to be sure you use the appropriate labels for the list you choose to include.

When your lists are separate sentences or separate paragraphs, you use numbers (not Roman numerals) followed by a period, with each sentence in the series also ending with a period, not a semicolon (;) or comma (,). You do not need to use parentheses with the numbers, either—for example, "(1)" or even "1)." Several seriated paragraphs would look like the list shown below.

A variety of first-year seminars exist on a wide range of college campuses. Barefoot (2005) classified freshman seminars into five major types:

1. Extended orientation seminar. Sometimes called a freshman orientation or student success course. It often covers issues of campus resources, time management, academic and career planning, and other topics.

2. Academic seminar with generally uniform academic content across sections. An interdisciplinary or theme-oriented course, which may be part of a general education requirement. Focus of the course is on the academic theme but will often include academic skill components such as critical thinking and writing.

3. Academic seminars on various topics. Similar to number two above, except the academic content varies from section to section.

4. Pre-professional or discipline-linked seminar. Designed specifically for students within a specific major or discipline.

5. Basic study skills seminar. Offered typically to academically underprepared students. Focus is on basic skills such as grammar, note taking, and test taking. (Gurung & Wilson-Doenges, 2010, pp. 97–98)

17

Now sometimes you may look at a list like the preceding one and assume, because of the numbers, that the first item is better than the second one and much better than the last one. To avoid this tendency, you can use a bulleted list instead of a numbered list. If you are submitting your paper to a journal for publication, the "look" of the bullet will depend on the style used by the journal. For a class paper assignment, it is best to use either small squares or circles. We know this seems designed to squash your individuality, but keep in mind that the creative ideas emerge in the content of your paper and in the way you combine ideas rather than in your font choice or the size of your margins. There are better battles to fight. Go ahead, be square. Or do not (use the circles). We do not see too many student papers that require a bulleted list or that even use one, but it is nice to know your options.

Order Within Paragraphs or Sentences

If you do not use seriated paragraphs too often (or have never even thought about doing so), you will probably have more use or more occasion to seriate within a sentence. In this case, you need to use lowercase letters enclosed in parentheses (APA, 2010a). The simple version looks like this:

> In a comprehensive, nationwide study, Landrum, Gurung, and Spann (2010) assessed how student attitudes toward (a) learning, (b) their textbooks, and (c) their instructors influence their own learning as measured by exam scores.

In the example above, none of the segments following the letters in parentheses (e.g., "learning," "their textbooks") have commas themselves, so the three parts can be separated by commas. If segments of a sentence do include commas, then you need to separate the segments with semicolons. We can tweak the sentence to illustrate what this would look like.

> In a comprehensive, nationwide study, Landrum, Gurung, and Spann (2010) assessed how student attitudes toward (a) learning, school, and success; (b) their textbooks, computers, and notebooks; and (c) their instructors influence their own learning as measured by exam scores.

Although most instructors likely prefer the seriated examples just presented, you could also use bullets to separate the elements of a sentence. In this case, because all the bulleted items are still part of one sentence, you treat the construction as exactly what it is—a sentence. Hence, there is only one period at the end. Again:

17

> In a comprehensive, nationwide study, Landrum, Gurung, and Spann (2010) assessed how student attitudes toward

- learning, school, and success;
- their textbooks, computers, and notebooks; and
- their instructors

influence their own learning as measured by exam scores.

On a Related Note

There are a few other circumstances when you should order items. If you have to order a set of tables or figures, the enumeration of these items is discussed in Chapter 15. You may decide to use footnotes or endnotes, information that expounds on portions of the main text of your paper (but that you think would be of interest to only some readers). As a matter of fact, few undergraduate student APA–style papers need to use footnotes or endnotes (and not just because many students need all the text they can get to reach their assigned paper length). If you do use footnotes or endnotes, number them in the order you use them, identify them with a superscripted number, and then either include the corresponding numbered footnote text at the bottom of the page where you need it or order all your footnotes on a separate page at the end of your paper. Unless your assignment requires footnotes, here is our advice: Avoid footnotes at all costs!

Much of this chapter may appear to be a cosmetic flourish. In some ways, it is. But good seriation and accurate enumeration can make a long list of information much easier to comprehend. Careful attention to detail may mean the difference between getting noticed and not.

17

Abbreviations, Signs, Symbols, and Punctuation

18

The Devil Is in the Details

When most people think about APA style, they may imagine it has to do with the technical aspects of psychology and science. That APA style informs writers about the ways to cite sources, write a reference section, and describe data makes sense. Not as many people recognize that APA style also relates to the somewhat smaller things in life: abbreviations, signs and symbols, and punctuation. Once you have graduated from elementary school, you may think that you have punctuation conquered. From the ways we see simple punctuation misused, especially commas and exclamation points, we recognize that some guidance cannot hurt and will make papers stronger. In this chapter, we address some of those underappreciated paper components; remember, for some instructors, it is all about these details. Given that many of these rules will be common knowledge for most of you, we use more of a checklist format in this chapter (see Chapter 14 for more on punctuation).

OMG: To Abbreviate or Not?

18

We have all used abbreviations in everyday life, whether in e-mails or text messages. We have BFFs (best friends forever) and often LOL (laugh out loud), and sometimes we may even exclaim in abbreviated form (*#@!*; you fill in the blanks). Clearly, *these* abbreviations do not belong in an APA–style paper. Many others do. There are a number of types of abbreviations, such as Latin and scientific abbreviations, and there is a simple tip for writing a clear paper: Limit the use of abbreviations. If your paper is packed with abbreviations, your reader may stumble. Ask yourself if you really need them. A good rule of thumb is that if you will not use the word too often, not more than three times, do not abbreviate unless the term is very long (APA, 2010a). If, for example, you are using a questionnaire with a long name (e.g., Multidimensional Body Self-Relations Questionnaire), you may want to use the acronym after the first use of the questionnaire name. Specifically, you *must* spell out the full name the first time you use it, followed by the abbreviation in parentheses; after that, you can use MBSRQ in the rest of the paper. Sure, you may think abbreviations make your paper look technical and impressive, but abbreviations are more likely to confuse than to impress.

Now here is something you may not have known: Some abbreviations are listed in the dictionary as regular word entries (e.g., REM, AIDS, HIV). You do not need to explain these or spell them out, and the *PM* does deem it acceptable for you to use any such abbreviations in your papers. OK, so it will probably be faster for you to type out the abbreviation than to check a dictionary to see if it would be OK not to spell it out, but we thought this was an interesting quirk to share anyway.

Blinding You With Science and Latin

We talked about statistical abbreviations in our chapter on reporting data analyses in your Results section (Chapter 10). The rules for the use of scientific and Latin abbreviations are similar. Most Latin abbreviations (for example, *e.g.*), which we use in abbreviated form naturally, are used only within parentheses. If you want to use the same phrase outside parentheses, you should use the English translation, which of course means you should know what the translation is. A major exception is the Latin for "and others," *et al.*, which is always written in the Latin whether within parentheses or not (APA, 2010a). Don't forget the period after the *al*; *et al.* is actually an abbreviation for the Latin phrase *et alia*.

When using scientific abbreviations such as those for time and units of measurement, some basic rules apply. Abbreviate all units that follow or are used with a number, and if using a series of numbers, you need to use the abbreviation only after the last number in the series.

> **Incorrect:** Students in the three conditions drank 5 ml, 10 ml, and 25 ml of high-caffeine soda, respectively.

> **Correct:** Students in the three conditions drank 5, 10, and 25 ml of high-caffeine soda, respectively.

18

The exception is certain units of time (day, week, month, and year). Those terms are never abbreviated, even if they accompany numbers. All other units of time are abbreviated. Table 18.1 presents the most typical abbreviations you are likely to use.

Table 18.1 Some Common Abbreviations and Their Meanings	
Abbreviation	Meaning
etc.	and so forth
e.g.	for example
i.e.	that is
cf.	compare with
vs.	versus
hr	hour
min	minute
s	second
°C	degrees Celsius
°F	degrees Fahrenheit
g	gram
IQ	intelligence quotient
L	liter
m	meter
a.m.	ante meridiem
p.m.	post meridiem

Some other dos and don'ts:

- Do not start a sentence with an abbreviation in lowercase—or with any abbreviation if you can help it.
- Add an *s* to make an abbreviation plural (no apostrophe needed).
- Do not make an abbreviation of a unit of measurement plural (e.g., 5 min, 100 mg).

Punctuation

18

By the time you reach college, most of you have written a fair number of papers. In college, you often have to take composition or expository writing classes. In most of these classes, you learned how to use punctuation well. This next section presents the major punctuation rules to keep in mind for APA style:

- Use one space after all punctuation, including periods—except when periods are used in abbreviations (e.g., *a.m.*, *p.m.*) or to end sentences in a draft paper; APA now suggests two spaces after a period at the end of a sentence in a draft paper.
- Do not use periods for abbreviations of state names (e.g., WI, VA, ID) or capital-letter abbreviations (e.g., APA, APS, IQ).
- Use a period for initials of names (e.g., R. A. R. Gurung) and Latin abbreviations (e.g., *a.m.*).
- Use a comma before the *and* or the *or* in a series of three or more items (e.g., Tom, Dick, and Harry).
- Use a comma to set off a descriptive part of your sentence. A tip: If you take the descriptive part out, the sentence should still make sense. Try this tip with the following sentence, and also look at your sentences that have more than one comma:

Correct: I always take my good-luck shirt, a colorful bowling shirt in black and blue, with me on holiday.

- Limit your use of exclamation points (!); in fact, in formal writing (such as an experimental paper), you should not use exclamation points at all.
- Limit your use of dashes, and try to use en dashes (–) rather than em dashes (—). More often than not, a comma or semicolon will work.
- Use double quotation marks to set off buzzwords or coined expressions, titles of articles mentioned in text, and examples from a questionnaire:

Correct: Eric really "raised the roof" with tales of his hijinks.

- Do not use double quotation marks for key terms; use italics instead.
- Use single quotation marks only when you need to include, within your text in double quotation marks, any material that was itself double quoted in the original document. If you are quoting a source that itself quotes another source, that other source material will be within single quotation marks in your document (and again within double quotation marks). Good news: This is rarely called for. Yes, for the most part you will not be using single quotation marks.
- Use colons (:) to separate an independent complete clause and a supporting clause (e.g., There are three major types of BBQ: Kansas City, Texas, and Carolina), in ratios and proportions (e.g., 2:1), and in reference lists between location of publisher and publisher name (e.g., New York, NY: Worth).
- Use semicolons to separate two independent clauses with no contraction (e.g., Carolina BBQ sauce is vinegar based; Texas BBQ is tomato based).

18

There is more to know about punctuation, of course, some of which we discuss in Chapter 17 on seriation and enumeration.

SECTION VI

In Closing

Important Considerations

Using Rubrics 19

*Knowing What It Means
to Write a Good Paper*

In this chapter, we hope to present two strong points: To improve your work, (a) follow rubrics when provided, and (b) avoid common errors in APA style and format. Writing improvement comes with practice (and more practice and still more practice), and you will see evidence of your enhanced writing skills as you learn to make fewer errors and tell a clearer story when writing in APA style.

Follow Rubrics When Provided

As a student writing a paper in APA style, you might be feeling that it is a logistical nightmare to make sure you have followed all APA rules. After all, who would have thought you would need to know whether to use spaces between numbers when including an equation in your paper? If possible, imagine having to grade these papers! We know what you may be thinking: "I would rather grade them than have to write them!" When we describe how these papers are graded, you might just change your mind. This chapter will help you better understand the way many professors grade APA–style papers and how this approach can help you avoid common errors and receive a higher grade on your assignments.

To help provide clear expectations and grading criteria for an assignment, to create a fair and unbiased grading system, and to provide detailed feedback to students, many instructors use grading rubrics. What is a rubric? A grading rubric provides students with detailed information on what the instructor is looking for when grading assignments and how grades will be determined. Typically, rubrics include qualities and descriptors for each performance standard and a point system that indicates how well a part of your paper fits the predetermined guidelines; essentially, the rubric is the scoring system the instructor will use to

19

grade your work. Implicitly, this scoring system communicates what is important in an assignment and the most difficult parts of the assignment. For instance, if you were writing a research paper including actual data, the instructor might decide that the Introduction section is worth 100 points but the Method section is worth 25 points. The higher point value might indicate that the Introduction is more important, more complicated to write, or both.

Whenever possible, ask instructors if they would be willing to share any grading rubrics they may be using. Rubrics come in all shapes and sizes. Your best bet is to read over the criteria carefully to make sure you understand what is expected. Read the description of what is included in the rubric and understand the guidelines before you start to write your paper. After you read over the rubric, ask questions you have about any part of the rubric (i.e., ask your instructor for clarification). Then, after you have written a first draft, go over the different parts of the rubric, and as honestly as possible, compare your paper to the grading criteria. Pair up with a classmate and compare each other's papers to the rubric. The following is an example of a rubric you might see when writing different parts of an APA–style paper. Keep in mind that rubrics are used for many types of assignments, so our recommendations regarding the use of rubrics are applicable to all papers, not just APA–style papers.

Example Rubrics

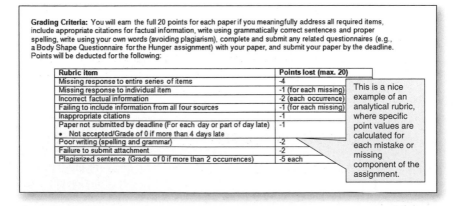

Grading Criteria: You will earn the full 20 points for each paper if you meaningfully address all required items, include appropriate citations for factual information, write using grammatically correct sentences and proper spelling, write using your own words (avoiding plagiarism), complete and submit any related questionnaires (e.g., a Body Shape Questionnaire for the Hunger assignment) with your paper, and submit your paper by the deadline. Points will be deducted for the following:

Rubric item	Points lost (max. 20)
Missing response to entire series of items	-4
Missing response to individual item	-1 (for each missing)
Incorrect factual information	-2 (each occurrence)
Failing to include information from all four sources	-1 (for each missing)
Inappropriate citations	-1
Paper not submitted by deadline (For each day or part of day late) • Not accepted/Grade of 0 if more than 4 days late	-1
Poor writing (spelling and grammar)	-2
Failure to submit attachment	-2
Plagiarized sentence (Grade of 0 if more than 2 occurrences)	-5 each

This is a nice example of an analytical rubric, where specific point values are calculated for each mistake or missing component of the assignment.

The preceding analytical rubric is from Dr. Pam Marek's (Kennesaw State University) General Psychology syllabus. You can find more rubric examples at Project Syllabus, which is part of the Society for the Teaching of Psychology website (http://topix.teachpsych.org/w/page/19980998/Grading%20Rubrics). Better still, if you are curious about rubrics and want to make your own, check out Rubistar (http://rubistar.4teachers.org/). What is useful about Dr. Marek's rubric is that you have beforehand specific explanations about what the instructor will be "looking for" when grading, and the point values do imply which mistakes are more

19

heavily weighted. Thus, if you received 12 of 20 points, by reviewing your work, you should get a clear indication of why you lost points in particular areas of the writing assignment. Importantly, this review of the rubric and the points you received will also tell you what part of the paper you need to focus on even more for future assignments.

Again, this type of rubric is called an analytical rubric because it provides specific criteria for different parts of a paper. In contrast, you might be given a holistic rubric, which does not separate grading criteria for the different parts of a paper and therefore may be less definitive in spelling out how many points a mistake is worth. An instructor using a holistic rubric relies on a global perception of quality rather than accumulating the number of mistakes—for an example of a rubric that combines the qualities of an analytical rubric and a holistic rubric, see the example below. With either system, it is always important to pay attention to the rubric *before* turning in your assignment; ask questions if you are unclear about what a plagiarized sentence is or if you need an example of being too colloquial (too informal). And be sure to value and follow the feedback that instructors provide to you. We suggest you go through each comment made on your paper; if you are unclear about any suggestion provided to improve your writing, set up an appointment with your instructor for clarification—and do not forget about other writing resources, such as classmates, teaching assistants, and your campus Writing Center and Academic Services Center.

Below is the rubric for the final manuscript in Eric, one of your co-author's research methods course—yes, we are happy to report that all three authors teach or have taught research methods (and APA style) on a regular basis—we do more than just write books about the subject. As you read this, you need to realize that it is very specific, that is, idiosyncratic to one instructor—your instructor might not share these same idiosyncrasies—and have others not represented here. One size does NOT fit all, and your results WILL vary. Consult your instructor to help learn about what his/her idiosyncrasies are.

Rubric Details for the Final Draft (200 points)

Completion of the Assignment (100 points)

Title Page

- Page header inside 1" margin, number every page

- Running head inside top margin on every page; actual running head in CAPS. Limited to 50 characters. Page 1 format is different from page header format on subsequent pages.

- Title, name, and affiliation block are horizontally and vertically centered

- Everything double-spaced

- Title is no longer than 12–15 words

- Author underneath title

- Author affiliation underneath author

- In the end, your paper should look EXACTLY like the example paper starting on p. **41** of the *Publication Manual*, except you will not have author notes. You can find more examples in Chapter 2 of your PDF textbook.

Abstract

- Starts on its own page (page 2), "Abstract" centered on line 1

- Everything double-spaced; Abstract paragraph not indented

- No longer than 120 words

- At the end of the Abstract, keywords, indented (only the word "Keywords" is italicized)

Body of Manuscript

Introduction

- Starts on its own page (page 3)

- Repeat the exact title from page 1 at the top of page 3

- Everything double-spaced—the hourglass shape

  • Introduce the reader to the issue in the first paragraph. Convince the reader that this is an important issue. Perhaps it impacts a large number of people, or it is an essential component of daily life. Try to impress upon the reader the importance of the issue. Using some general statistics (with citations) here can be very persuasive.

  • Review the available literature on the topic. If there are studies related specifically to your topic, review them here. If there are no specific studies, then broaden your review of the literature to include related areas. Show that you have done your scholarly homework. You are providing a context for your study. There should be multiple studies cited in this section of your Introduction. Start broad and end narrow.

  • Within this context, identify a problem or area where the knowledge is incomplete. This turns into your statement of the problem to be addressed by this research. You have reviewed the literature, but there is a gap in the literature—an unresolved problem or issue. The goal of your study is to fill that gap by conducting your study. Provide a clear statement of purpose for the current study. In fact, you might think about a sentence that starts with "The purpose of my study is to . . ."

19

- Then give a brief overview of the methodology that will be used to address the knowledge gap. Just a snapshot of the participants, materials, and basic procedure used in the study. This is a preview—"coming attractions."
- Conclude your Introduction section with specific hypotheses to be tested or expected outcomes. What do you expect to happen? Develop your working hypotheses based on your expectations about what is to happen and your review of the literature. The more specific you are here, the easier it will be to write survey questions, and the easier it will be to select the appropriate statistical analyses later. Your hypotheses might examine differences between certain groups, associations or relationships between variables, etc. I recommend that you start each hypothesis sentence with "I hypothesize that . . ."

Method

- "Method" centered and boldfaced, everything double-spaced

- Continues directly after the end of the introduction (no new page)

- The Method section tells the reader exactly how the study was conducted. You will be describing your Participants, Materials, and Procedure in three separate subsections of the Method section (each of these subsection headings is boldfaced).

- Three labeled subsections using APA heading rules

  - **Participants**: Tell the reader who participated in your study. Provide the overall number of participants, how the participants were recruited, and other general demographics (Age? Youngest? Oldest? Gender? Year in School?). Summarize how participants were selected and how rewarded.
  - **Materials**: Describe all the materials used to conduct the study. How were the survey questions developed? Did you borrow questions from others? If so, give credit. Were the materials pilot tested? How so? Then refer the reader to Table 1, where you will list in APA format the questions that are your part of the overall (omnibus) survey. Your goal is to provide enough information so that another researcher could replicate your study.
  - **Procedure**: Give a complete account of how the study was conducted. Under what conditions were participants tested? Individually or in groups? How much time were participants given to complete the research, and how much time did they actually use? Were the participants debriefed? Provide a step-by-step, chronological account of how your data were collected from start to finish.

19

Results

- "Results" centered and boldfaced, everything double-spaced

- Continues directly after the end of Method (no new page on purpose)

- The major purpose of the Results section is to report the findings. In the first section of your Results section, your task is to report on your specific hypotheses that you tested. Recap each hypothesis for the reader, and then follow that sentence with the statistical results. It is helpful here to provide some *context* for the means and standard deviations you may be reporting in these sentences. For example, prior to a *t* test result, you lead in with "For the following items, respondents used a scale 1 = *strongly disagree* to 5 = *strongly agree.*"

- In the next section of your Results section, report here any interesting findings or statistical outcomes that were not part of your original hypotheses. Maybe something interesting happened that you didn't hypothesize about, but report it in this next section of the Results. This could be descriptive statistics, such as percentages.

- Follow APA format for the reporting of descriptive and inferential statistics; include exact *p* values. Systematically report all the significant statistical findings from your SPSS analyses. Remember, no interpretation here; just the facts. Whenever you report a mean, report its corresponding standard deviation. Use APA format in presenting statistical information, including the italicizing of statistics and *p* values, correct degrees of freedom, etc.

- This part is hard—do not discuss or interpret what your results mean; save that level of analysis for the next section of your manuscript. This section is typically dry and not very exciting. You are presenting just the facts. Do NOT tell the reader what the differences/relationships/associations/predictions mean.

Discussion

- "Discussion" centered and boldfaced, everything double-spaced

- Continues directly after the end of Results (no new page)

- In the Discussion section, you finally get the chance to interpret all the results presented in the Results section. Here is where you have the opportunity to finish telling the story that you started in the Introduction section. What happened? What worked and what did not work? What will the reader be able to conclude from your study? The Discussion section starts out very specific and gets broader until you finish with generalizations and conclusions.

- Start your Discussion with the most important finding of the study—what is your **big bang?** What happened? Did you find anything that was unexpected, unusual, fascinating, interesting, unique, or counterintuitive? The first paragraph of your Discussion section should have the "take-home" message for the reader—if the reader is only to remember one piece of information from this study, what is it?
- Briefly restate the hypotheses from the end of your Introduction section, and discuss whether they were supported based on the outcomes of the study. Be specific (e.g., "Significant gender differences were found for the questions regarding X, Y, and Z. In all cases, males were more favorable toward these questions than females. This means that . . .").
- Place your study in the context of the studies that were published before yours. This means revisiting the literature cited in the Introduction section. Re-cite some of that literature here. Did you fill that knowledge gap that you identified early on? Although you might have answered one question, perhaps your study raised three new questions. If your study contradicts previous research, then you need to speculate about why that happened—perhaps it was a different participant population or the methodologies were dramatically different, etc.
- Now generalize a bit about the results of your study. Look to a broader context than just tested. Here you get to speculate on the greater impact of your research, but be sure to label the speculation as such. What do the results of your study mean? In other words, could the results of your study be useful in setting policies about human behavior—could the results of your study lead to some practical application? How might they be interpreted in a broader context (beyond general psychology students at Boise State University)?
- Present the limitations of your study, but don't beat up on yourself too much. What went wrong—what do you wish you had done differently? What should be the next study? Make some suggestions as to the direction of future research in this field. What do **you** suggest be done next?
- Conclude your Discussion section with a brief paragraph that (a) restates your take-home message (first paragraph of the Discussion section), (b) the importance of your study in filling an existing knowledge gap in the literature, and (c) emphasizes the general importance of your topic.

19

References

- Starts on its own new page after the end of the Discussion section

- Everything double-spaced

- Every reference cited in the manuscript should be in the reference section. Every reference in the reference section should be in the manuscript. All name spellings should match. I will check. Really.

- References are prepared in APA format, following capitalization guidelines, italicizing rules, indentation, etc.

- References are important. They show off your academic achievement and your grasp of the literature. They provide guidance to those who want to read what you have read. This is your chance to show you are a scholar. If you kept up with your reference notecards, preparing this section should be easy.

- APA rules are sometimes confusing concerning references. Follow the APA *Publication Manual* precisely. Ask questions ahead of due dates, preferably in class so that others can benefit.

Table

- Be sure to follow APA guidelines for table preparation. No vertical lines on a table; only three horizontal lines. Microsoft Word can do this. I'll show you in class.

- Include information about rating scales in the *Note* at the bottom of the table so that the reader can interpret the statistical information presented.

- Remember that it doesn't make any sense to report the mean of nominal scale data. Nominal scale response categories should be reported as percentages.

General Comments

- Follow APA–format guidelines precisely. No extra spacing between paragraphs—regular double-spacing throughout paper. One-inch margins on all four sides of the paper.

- No right justification (ragged right margins)

- References cited correctly in manuscript. Mostly paraphrase. Minimal use of direct quotations (for the final paper, the maximum allowable number of direct quotes is 3).

- When quoting, use proper format; avoid plagiarism. Have paper proofread by someone else; offer to proofread someone else's paper, too.

19

Avoid all spelling mistakes. Include page number or paragraph number with direct quotes only; no contractions, no abbreviations (unless APA approved). Write in complete sentences. Avoid awkward constructions. Avoid being too colloquial (too informal). Your paper is not a conversation between us.

– Use the Times New Roman font with no changes in font or font size; use 12-point font throughout.

– Once you put the entire paper together at the end of the semester, you need to make sure that everything matches with everything else. For example, the spelling of references in the Introduction should be the same spelling of the same references re-cited in the Discussion section. Be sure to properly use "ct al."

Proper Use of APA Style and Clarity of Presentation (100 points)

• One-inch margins on all four sides of the page; running head and page number inside the top margin. No right justification of text, Times New Roman 12 point throughout, no changes in font or font size.
• Double-space everything; no extra spacing between paragraphs.
• Add appropriate headings to your paper as signposts to improve organization—be sure to follow the APA guidelines on levels of headings.
• Be sure to write numbers correctly and follow number rule exceptions.
• Spelling, grammar, punctuation, noun–verb agreement all correctly followed; obvious mistakes avoided (paper was proofread).
• Transitions between sections should be smooth, and you should avoid awkward sentence constructions.
• Write in complete sentences. Each paragraph focuses on a single topic.
• Avoid being colloquial (informal) in your writing. Be formal, and do not write like you are having a conversation—no contractions.
• Avoid passive voice; no "we" or "us"—single-author paper from first person perspective.
• No anthropomorphizing—the results do not show, the data do not indicate, etc.

One more note about this example—this is provided here as just an example and not presented as advice about how instructors should or should not be grading research papers. The goals and skill levels for students vary from department to department, and instructors should always be designing courses and projects that best fit their own students' needs. That is, these examples are just meant to be descriptive, not proscriptive.

19

Proofreading the Entire Paper

20

Get It Right!

W e know how exciting it is to finally finish writing a paper. You just want to step away from the computer and perhaps not see the paper for a while (or ever again if it was a tough one). Although we encourage you to take a break, we also urge you to leave time for proofreading your paper at least once before handing it in. The difference between a proofread paper and one that is not may be the difference between receiving the grade you worked hard for and the grade you hoped to avoid. If you are tired of proofreading your own paper, then swap with a classmate; trade proofreading for proofreading. A fresh set of eyes looking at your work is a good idea in any case. Ask any professor who grades papers, and he or she will tell you how frustrating it can be to see minor errors in a paper, especially repetitive errors. These minor errors can be so much of a nuisance that they are often included as part of the grading rubric or may simply be one component of the paper considered when grading without a rubric (see Chapter 19 for more on rubrics). At the end of this chapter, we include some sample pages on which we have **purposely embedded many APA errors.** How many can you find? We encourage you to test your APA knowledge and find the errors. To check how many you were able to find, compare your list of errors to what we were able to find, presented in Appendix A.

Why is proofreading necessary? When writing a paper, we usually focus on the content to create logical arguments and paragraphs that present thoughts that flow smoothly from one sentence to the next. The components of the assignment run through our heads. Thoughts such as "Do not forget you need to include at least five references" or "How can I be sure this will be between 8 and 10 pages in length?" are distracting. With all that going on, you are left with little mental energy and little attention to focus on the details, which is particularly true if you have limited time to complete your assignment (do not procrastinate; start early!). But even when time is available, it is easy to overlook misspellings, punctuation mistakes, and grammatical errors, not to mention all the APA format and style rules. Perhaps we have convinced you at this point that proofreading is a good idea.

Convinced or not, we offer some foolproof steps to take when proofreading your paper. A key factor in proofreading that should be stated up front is the time needed to make this process work. You must build in the time to write multiple drafts of your paper; in other words, writing assignments completed at the last minute leave no time for proofreading and review. And you are wasting your time if someone reviews your paper and you do not give yourself the time to incorporate the feedback and comments to produce an improved draft. Some students make the cardinal error of asking an instructor to please comment on a draft (not an error), and then they do not make any of the changes (that's the error!) that the instructor spent time and energy to provide. When a student does not make changes based on feedback, it can be very frustrating indeed for the instructor.

We can all tell you that few people write an error-free paper in the first draft. Even your professors continue to write multiple drafts when submitting their work for journal reviews or papers for conferences. First, leave time between your writing and your proofreading. You might have had the experience of writing a paper and just feeling wiped out. Rather than proofing in that state, you are better off taking a look at your paper when you can reread it with "fresh eyes." Sometimes it is hard to make changes to a paper that you have just worked on for many hours, and you may feel that no changes are needed. Time between writing and proofing can make all the difference.

Next—and this may seem obvious to many of you—we strongly recommend that you use the spell-checker and grammar-checker tools. Do not rely on those squiggly red, green, and blue lines to find errors. It is very common to mentally fill in the missing letters or change words to fit the sentence (i.e., to perceive things that are not really there) when reviewing a paper, simply because of our experience with the English language. This leads us to overlook errors. One easy way to find mistakes is to read your paper slowly out loud. The words that are not misspelled but do not fit the sentence will pop out when you actually hear the sentence spoken rather than just reading it in your head (e.g., "Writing in APA style is always fan"). This way, you are more likely to identify awkward phrases, extra words, or misused words. In fact, you might consider reading out loud to a friend who can help you find awkward-sounding sentences. Better yet, you could have the friend read your paper out loud to you, in which case you might hear something different from what you thought you had written. When it comes to grammar, one surefire way of finding grammatical errors is to read your paper for each type of common error. These errors include sentence fragments, subject–verb agreement errors, unclear pronoun references, run-on sentences, words you have typed twice, words you have completely left out, and use of apostrophes.

20

Here are a few suggestions for searching your reference list for three common errors:

- The period after an author's initial before the ampersand should be followed by a comma (e.g., Landrum, R. E., & Gurung, R. A. R.). Search for a period followed by a space followed by an ampersand (. &), and add the missing comma where necessary.
- Search for a closing parenthesis followed by a space; unless the parenthesis is part of a title, it should be followed by a period or a comma, depending on where it is in the reference (i.e., the ending parenthesis after the publication date is followed by a period; the ending parenthesis after "Ed." or "Eds." in a reference for a chapter in a book is followed by a comma).
- Search for a comma before an opening parenthesis and delete it; a comma should not appear before an opening parenthesis in a reference.

Keep in mind that although proofreading can mean reading your own paper to remove errors, it can also mean having someone else proofread to find the errors that you as the writer might overlook. After you have spent all that time and energy working on a paper, it is difficult to imagine that you have made mistakes. That is exactly why it is in your best interest to have someone else take a look at your paper before you hand it in to your professor. Of course, because we are not talking just about proofing for grammar and logic but also for APA style and format, it would be best to have someone with knowledge of APA guidelines and requirements do the proofing. But whom? Sometimes this is determined for you, with peer review included as an assignment in your class; that makes it easy to find someone to read your paper and also provides an incentive for additional proofreading. However, even when it is not included as an assignment, you might consider making a deal with someone else in your class—the old "I'll scratch your back if you scratch mine," though you will be reading papers instead of scratching backs. To increase the chances that the proofer is reading with specifics in mind, you might consider giving your proofreader a copy of a rubric from the class or even the quiz from Chapter 22 that covers the most common APA errors.

Whether you or someone else is doing the proofing, you want to make sure that the paper is read with the audience in mind. Proofreading your paper will be most effective when you switch from reviewing your paper as the writer to reviewing it as a reader. Of course, for most of you, the audience will be the person who assigned the paper. Using a rubric, as mentioned in Chapter 19, can definitely help with keeping the audience in mind, considering the expectations provided by your instructor, and knowing what differentiates a strong paper from a weak paper. Just so you know, each of the three authors of this book read each revised draft of these chapters a number of times before we let anyone else see them. Over and over. Again and again.

20

Although some like to review papers using a printed copy, the easiest way to obtain feedback for your paper is by using the Track Changes tool in Word. See the next screenshot.

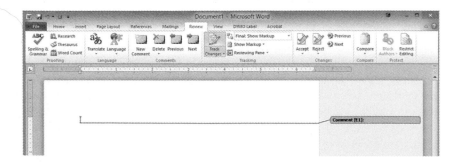

Simply click on the *Review* tab and then on the *Track Changes* option, and you can provide feedback within the paper, letting the author know when any changes have been made.

Another helpful tool when proofreading is the *Comment* option, also available under the *Review* tab (as shown in the next screenshot). Using this tool, you can write comments in the margins of the paper to let the author know something about the paper without making a mark within the paragraph itself. Be sure to save the document with your comments and changes, using a new file name to differentiate it from the original draft. We find that adding the date and your initials is an easy way to keep track of multiple drafts of any paper under revision.

When you are unable to find someone to review your paper, you should also consider using a resource available on many campuses—the writing center or writing lab. Keep in mind that the services provided by the center are typically available to students free of charge. These centers include professional staff members and/or peer tutors who have been trained to assist students with writing. Some centers even train their tutors in APA style and format. One of the best uses of this center would be to bring along the professor's grading rubric to make the reviewer aware of the expectations for this assignment. That will allow the reviewer to really focus on the details and what differentiates a strong paper from a weak one.

20

Then there is the paid source of feedback always available through the Internet. We have never tried this ourselves, but we have seen the offers out there. Remember, if you are going this route, you need to make sure that the reviewer knows you are writing an APA–style paper. You know for yourself how an APA paper differs from other papers. You certainly do not want to pay someone to suggest changes to your paper that are not in accordance with APA style. There are sites that are specific to writing in APA style and plenty of YouTube videos to show you how to format papers for APA style. So if you learn APA style and format well enough, you have just opened up a career option you never dreamed about—editing APA–style papers. We also suggest that you check with your instructor regarding the use of this type of resource. At some schools with honor codes, it is not acceptable to use this type of help on any work. In particular, note that we are *not* suggesting you pay someone to write your paper. You obviously need to do your own work.

So when do you know you have proofed your paper well enough? If you have reread your paper and/or had someone else read through it at least one time, you have checked your paper against the rubric for the assignment, you have gone through the checklist provided at the end of this book that gives you a list of the most common APA style and format errors, and the deadline is here . . . it is time to stop proofreading and hand in your paper! Or you may e-mail it as an attachment or upload it to the course website. Deliver it to your instructor following his or her preferred method.

As we mentioned earlier, the next section of this chapter includes sample pages from **a paper with *many* APA errors.** You will be surprised how easily you can miss these errors the first time you review the pages. We encourage you to try this exercise and note the errors that are easy to find when proofreading a paper and the ones that are easy to overlook (see the answer key in Appendix A). Determining the ones that are easy to miss when using this sample paper can help remind you what style and format rules not to overlook when reading through your own paper.

20

Sample Student Paper for Practicing Proofreading

THE PHARMACOLOGICAL   1

The Pharmacological Effects of Caffeine

Cire Murdnal

PSYC 101 Section 001

April 21, 2011

20

THE PHARMACOLOGICAL   2

Abstract

This paper is about caffeine and how it is pervasive in our culture. This paper talks about the pharmacological effects, the cardiovascular effects, and the behavioral effects that caffeine has on humans. Although much is known about how caffeine works in the body, not much is know about the impact caffeine has on behavior.

20

THE PHARMACOLOGICAL   3

Caffeine is probably the most consumed psychoactive substance in the world (Graham, 1978). Interestingly, its origins derive from all parts of the world as well. Caffeine exists naturally in a number of forms, including the coffee bean, kola nut, cocoa bean, ilex (holly) plant, and from the cassina or Christmas berry tree in North America (Stephenson, 1977). The coffee bean was first found in Arabia, the tea leaf in China, the kola nut in West Africa, the cocoa bean in Mexico, the ilex plant in Brazil, and the cassina in North America.

Caffeine is currently consumed in a number of forms, including coffee, tea, cocoa, cola beverages (pop), chocolate, and it ts often used in a number of over-the-counter preparations, such as Dexatrim, Anacin and Vivarin. Unless consciously monitoring caffeine consumption, most Americans consume from 200–250 m.g. caffeine daily, and many may not even know it. (Stephenson, 1977; Graham, 1978)

Caffeine is an alkaloid compound which belongs to a class of drugs called methyl xanthines. The technical (chemical) structural name for caffeine is 1,3,7-trimethylxanthine. Two other closely related compounds also exist in the methylxanthine

20

THE PHARMACOLOGICAL   4

group, theophylline (1,3-dimethylxanthine) and theobromine
(3,7-dimethylxanthine). Both are naturally occurring substances,
theophylline commonly found in tea, and theobromine found in tea
and cocoa (Graham, 1978).

In terms of sources of caffeine for use in naturally consumed
foods and caffeine-enhanced preparations (cola and over-the-counter
medications), caffeine most commonly originates from coffee
(Coffee arabica), tea (Thea sinensis), chocolate (Theobroma cocoa),
and kola (as in the kola nut) (Cola nitida). When crystallized and
removed from the natural source, caffeine is water soluble, odorless,
and definitely bitter (Graham, 1978).

According to Curatolo and Robertson (1983), caffeine
is essentially completed absorbed (more than 99%) from the
gastrointestinal tract after oral administration. While some reports
vary peak plasma levels occur about 30 minutes to 1 hour after
ingestion (Curatolo & Robertson, 1983; Stephenson, 1977). The
half life of caffeine in the system does vary due to individual
differences, but the average half life is about 3 hours (Stephenson,
1977), although in some individuals the half life of caffeine has
been reported as high as 7.5 hours (Curatolo & Robertson, 1983).
Clearly, some individuals are more caffeine-sensitive than Others.

20

THE PHARMACOLOGICAL   5

The distribution of caffeine throughout the human system occurs rapidly and thoroughly; within minutes, caffeine enters all organs and tissues and has its effects in proportion to the amount of caffeine present (the more present, the greater the stimulatory effect) (Graham, 1978; Stephenson, 1978).

The pharmacological actions of caffeine occur on the cellular level. Caffeine's primary site of action is probably through the antagonism of adenosine receptors. A secondary site of action is the caffeine also works as a phosphodiesterase inhibitor. Phosphodiesterase is an enzyme necessary to convert cyclic AMP (cAMP) to AMP. Methylxanthines in general, and caffeine in particular, inhibit the process of enzymatic degradation allowing for the continued stimulation of cAMP at the cellular level (Robertson, Curatolo, & Robertson, 1983; Stephenson, 1977).

The rate of metabolism of caffeine has been found to be about 15% per hour. Even in high doses (e.g., 500 mg/day), there has been no demonstration of day-to-day accumulation of the drug (Stephenson, 1977). Although multiple metabolites the primary metabolite of caffeine is 1,7-dimethylxanthine. The metabolites chiefly follow a renal route for excretion (Curatolo & Richardson, 1983).

20

THE PHARMACOLOGICAL   6

On the cellular level, caffeine metabolism leads to increases in muscle lactic acid, increased oxygen consumption, and muscle twitches (Stephenson, 1977). Other larger, behavioral effects are briefly discussed elsewhere in this paper. The primary route of excretion is through the kidneys. Most of the renal metabolites are passed in the urine, but small amounts have been reported to have been excreted from saliva, semen, breast milk, and caffeine has heen found in blood from an infant's umbilical cord (Graham, 1978; Curatolo & Richardson, 1983). From 0.5% to 3.5% of caffeine will exist unchanged, mostly in the urine but small amounts will exit via the feces (Curatolo & Robertson, 1983).

The clearance of caffeine from the system can be altered by other circumstances, however. For example, caffeine clearance (elimination) slowed by alcoholic liver disease (alcoholism) and clearance is also slowed in the newborn. Caffeine clearance is accelerated with concurrent smoking (Curatolo & Robertson, 1983).

The cardiovascular effects of caffeine are mixed. While caffeine stimulates cardiac muscle which in tum leads to increased force of contraction, increased heart rate, and increased cardiac

20

output, caffeine also stimulates are portion of the brain called the medullary vagal nuclei which in turn decrease heart rate. These opposing actions may result in bradycardia, tachycardia, or no change in the consumer (Stephenson, 1977). In addition, brain blood vessels are constricted and brain blood flow is reduced. These actions may help to explain why caffeine can be effective in headache relief, and why "caffeine headaches" often appear as withdrawal symptoms in those curtailing their consumption of caffeine.

Caffeine has found to be a general stimulant in terms of metabolic effects. In other words, caffeine itself acts as a trigger for starting or accelerating the rate of general metabolism. Many weight-loss regimens have taken advantage of this phenomenon and included caffeine for its stimulation of metabolism and diuretic effects (Curatolo, Robertson, 1983).

Another major metabolic effect of caffeine is the increased release of glucose after caffeine consumption. It has been well documented that caffeine has a hyperglycemic action (Stephenson, 1977), and this helps to explain why the occasional candy bar or can of Coke acts as a pick-me-up: a quick boost of glucose available for the brain.

20

THE PHARMACOLOGICAL   8

Caffeine also affects the CNS by influencing the processes of psychomotor coordination, EEG patterns, sleep, mood, behavior and thought processes. For instance, caffeine has been found to decrease reaction time and increase vigilance in relatively straightforward laboratory tasks. Use of caffeine before going to bed can increase sleep latency (the amount of time needed to fall asleep), decrease total time asleep, and decreases subjective estimates of sleep quality (Curatolo & Robertson, 1983).

Caffeine has also been found to effect mood, behavior, and cognitive processes (hence its justification as a psychoactive drug). Caffeine users have reported increased perceptions of alertness, increased ability for short-termed behavioral activity, and relatively minor changes in cognitive processing (Curatolo and Robertson, 1983). Although effects on cognition appear to exist (hence the worldwide popularity and desire to use the drug), surprisingly little empirical evidence is available demonstrating its influence. Other than effects on vigilance, reaction time, alertness and sleep patterns, caffeine's effects on behavior have been elusive in the laboratory.

References

20

THE PHARMACOLOGICAL   9

Curatolo, P. W. & Robertson, D. (1983). The Health Consequences of Caffeine. *Annals of Internal Medicine, 98*, 641–653.

Graham, D. M. (1978). Caffeine—Its identity, dietary sources, intake and biological effects. *Nutrition Reviews, 36* (8), 97–102.

Stephenson, Phillip. E. (1977). Physiologic and psychotropic effects of caffeine on man. *Journal of the American Dietetic Association, 71*, 240–247

20

Complete Sample of an Experimental (Research) Paper

21

Samples, Anyone?

T his chapter is all about samples. It is one thing to go over the rules of APA style and format with you and translate what the *PM* means to what you need to know for your scientific writing, but you also need to see the APA rules in practice. In this chapter, we present the research paper you might have already seen in Chapter 2. Diep "Penny" Trieu of Randolph College graciously gave us permission to reprint her paper here again to point out features of APA style and format. In Chapter 2, you saw a visual *table of contents* using this same sample paper. In that chapter, we pointed out the details about APA style and format and where to find a discussion of those details in subsequent chapters. In this chapter, we include the same sample paper, but this time we spell out the rules.

We have kept each page proportional to how it would look after you printed it out; in other words, we know you are not reading this on a piece of 8½ × 11 paper, but that is the size paper *you* will print on. So the graphics in the paper included in this chapter are to scale. We purposely chose this approach so that you get a close approximation of what your final APA papers will look like, proportionally speaking.

To be honest, sometimes instructors add to the confusion of writing in APA style (for more on this, see Chapter 19). In the instructions in your syllabus, it might say "prepare a 5–7 page paper in APA format." Unfortunately, that assignment is vague. Is that five to seven pages of text? Does the page count include the title page? The references? If it is not an experimental/research paper, does

21

the instructor want an abstract? (Typically not.) So after you receive the instructions for any writing assignment, you have to translate, decipher, and interpret what the instructor really wants. What exceptions to APA style does he or she prefer? It may seem as though you are being picky with your questions, but you'd rather be picky on the front end and know exactly what is expected of you than be surprised at the back end with an unusually low grade because you didn't understand the instructor's preferences. We get that sometimes this arrangement isn't fair, but if you will be proactive and follow our advice, you can minimize those disappointing surprises.

So as you look at the formatting and read Penny paper in the pages that follow, you'll see that she had to make certain adjustments to conform to the assignment in her Research Methods class. For example, she reported nonsignificant results in her Results section; in published papers, that doesn't happen too often, but practicing data analysis and reporting techniques were part of the course goals. This assignment also required a minimum of six references and had to include a table. So aspects of the sample paper you see in this chapter may not be part of a writing assignment you must complete. The number one rule to remember is to write for your audience; in many cases, the audience for your writing is also the person with grading responsibilities.

One last thought before digging into the paper: This is a real student paper. Parts of it have been modified from the original, but this is meant to be a realistic example of student work. Is it a perfect paper? No (and Penny is OK with that). Will you find errors or mistakes in the paper? Probably. We selected this paper as an example or template but not as an exemplar of perfection. Moreover, the point is not to look for errors but to see if the author is telling a coherent and meaningful story. The goal is not to look for mistakes as if you are on a treasure hunt but to read for the scientific story. Does the story make sense, and is it compelling? Along the way of reading the scientific story, you'll also see a brief description of an APA style or format rule that you need to keep in mind when writing your own paper. Telling a coherent scientific story that communicates a meaningful message is a difficult enough task; adding the many APA–writing details is a whole different task in itself. If you'll follow the advice provided throughout this book, you'll be well on your way to knowing those many details and, in turn, being able to focus your attention on honing your scientific storytelling abilities.

21

Sample Paper

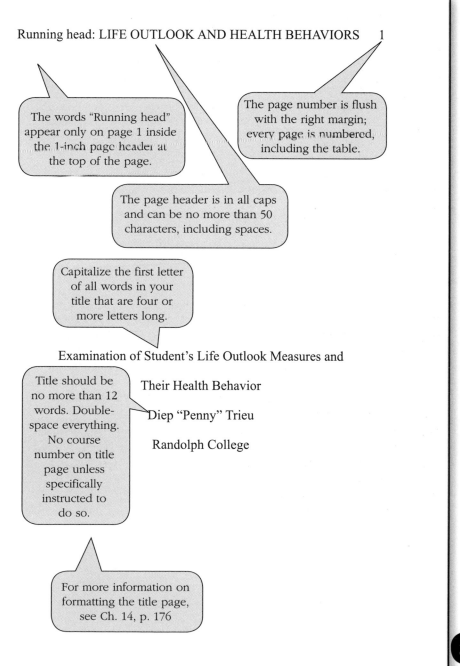

Running head: LIFE OUTLOOK AND HEALTH BEHAVIORS   1

The words "Running head" appear only on page 1 inside the 1-inch page header at the top of the page.

The page number is flush with the right margin; every page is numbered, including the table.

The page header is in all caps and can be no more than 50 characters, including spaces.

Capitalize the first letter of all words in your title that are four or more letters long.

Examination of Student's Life Outlook Measures and

Title should be no more than 12 words. Double-space everything. No course number on title page unless specifically instructed to do so.

Their Health Behavior

Diep "Penny" Trieu

Randolph College

For more information on formatting the title page, see Ch. 14, p. 176

21

LIFE OUTLOOK AND HEALTH BEHAVIORS   2

Abstract

The au| |or examined the relation\hip

c̶ ̶ ̶ ̶ ̶ ̶ ̶ ̶ ̶ ̶ ̶ ̶ ̶imism, an̶ ̶

|cer as rela|

| . Twenty-one college students

completed questionnaires measuring their internality of control,

optimism, o/ective risk, perceived risk, and healthy behaviors.

There wa̶ significant positive correlation between internal

lo̶ ̶ ̶ ̶ ̶ ̶ ̶ ̶ ̶ ̶ ̶ ̶ ̶ ̶ ̶ ̶ ̶ ̶alth behaviors. Positive

co̶ ̶ ̶ ̶ ̶ ̶ ̶ ̶ ̶ ̶ ̶ ̶ ̶th locus of control and

optimism and between perceived risks and objective risk.

Continued research on the influence of psychological states

on preventative health behaviors is warranted to understand

specific mechanisms that could help to reduce the likelihood of

disease such as skin cancer.

Keywords: health locus of control, optimism, skin cancer, skin

cancer risk

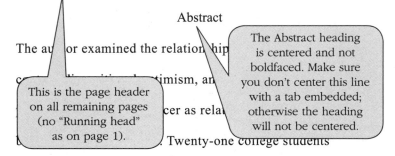

LIFE OUTLOOK AND HEALTH BEHAVIORS   3

Examination of Students' Outlook Measures

and Their Health Behaviors

Within the field of health psychology, much attention

is devoted to the degree to which our mental outlook affect

our physical one. Of interest are the various relations

among sense of control

The title from page 1 reappears at the top of page 3. The word Introduction is not used as a heading. Do not boldface the title.

behaviors. Understandably, individuals with an external

locus of control would find health behaviors of little efficacy

in affecting their health status and do not engage in such

preventions (Seeman & Seeman, 1983). Conversely, individuals

with internal senses of control may perceive their ability

to influence their health and therefore engage in the

actions. The same logic applies to optimism, as high degrees

With multiple authors mentioned inside parentheses, use an ampersand (&) between the second-to-last and last author.

of optimism encourage individuals to believe good

outcomes from cancer preventive actions and to behave

beneficially for their health (Shazia, Hailey, & Jo, 2001).

Another mediating factor is objective and perceived risk, as

a higher risk may override the low sense of control and

induce individuals to engage in preventive cancer behaviors.

Each of these factors is analyzed in relation to existing

literature below.

21

LIFE OUTLOOK AND HEALTH BEHAVIORS   4

Optimism and Health-Positive Behaviors

Shazia et al. (2001) focused their research on the link

between optim___ and_ students completed t___ Orientation Test (LOT___ Promoting Lifestyle P___ hypothetical illnesses ___

> With three to five authors, the second time (and all other times) you cite the work, use the first author's name, followed by et al., which is the Latin abbreviation for *et alia*, meaning "and others." If the reference has six or more authors, use et al. the first time a citation appears in the paper, as well as on each subsequent appearance.

Promote Health (SUPPH) questionnaire. Shazia et al. found

a positive correlation ___tween optimism score and health

behaviors. Sim___ ___ between optimism score___ ___participants

> Minimum use of abbreviations is recommended; always be sure to define the concept completely before using the abbreviation.

higher in optimism planned more health-promoting behaviors

when faced with hypothetical illnesses. The findings of this

study echo num___ ___ suggesting an encouraging rel___ ___alth-enhancing behaviors.

> Normally numbers greater than 10 are written as numerals, but when these numbers start a sentence, they are spelled out. Hyphens are needed for compound numbers.

The resea___ ___went into

more details and addressed the interactio___ ___ween dispositional

and health optimism, response to health infor___ation, health

risk-assessment, and health-related behaviors. Sixty-four

students self-reported on their dispositional optimism measured

by the LOT, health-related optimism, risk perception, and

LIFE OUTLOOK AND HEALTH BEHAVIORS 5

objective risk measured by the Brief Skin Cancer Risk

Assessment Tool (BRAT). Afterwards, they were tested

on attention to health information and recollection of the

information.

The most notable finding of the study was the significant

interactions between (a) Health-Related Optimism and Objective

Risk and (b) Dispositional Optimism and Objective Risk. In

general, people low in dispositional optimism or high in health

optimism

categ

Using an (a) and a (b) in
parentheses like this is called
seriation. Notice that you use
letters instead of numbers.

information. Within these

ional optimism pay more

attention especially when they are high in objective risk. Individuals

with high dispositional optimism paid same amount of attention

whether they had low or high risk of skin cancer. Among those low

in objective risk, low-optimism individuals paid less attention than

those high in optimism.

As for health optimism, participants high in health optimism

paid more attention when faced with high risks. Participants with

low health optimism paid the same levels of attention regardless

of their objective risk. If the participants possessed low risk,

those high in optimism paid less attention than those low in

optimism. In case of high objective risk, those high in optimism

paid more attention than those low in optimism. The researchers

21

LIFE OUTLOOK AND HEALTH BEHAVIORS   6

speculated that people with high levels of health optimism or

low dispositional optimism would be more aware of their risks

and seek out information about skin cancer accordingly (Luo &

Issacowitz, 2007).

These two studies provided strong support for the

relationship between optimism and health-enhancing behaviors.

Drawing from the two studies' methodology, I employed the LOT

in our measure of optimism and the BRAT scale in our measure

of objective risk and health behaviors. I also inquired participants

of their perceived risk of skin cancer. Due to the high degree

of causality between health behaviors and skin cancer risk, the

current study evaluated the participants' risks for skin cancer

and skin-cancer preventive behaviors.

Health Locus of Control

In examination of the correlation between optimism and

health-enhancing behaviors, the researchers of the current study

posed that a helpful component of optimism lies in the sense of

control: optimistic indi~~viduals believe in the efficacy~~ of their

actions to improve the~~i~~   is relevant to

> With only two authors, list
> both authors completely
> each time cited.

the discussion of the re~~l~~   ~~Lo~~cus of Control

to health-enhancing behavior (Seeman & Seeman, 1983). Seeman

and Seeman examined the relationships between sense of control

21

LIFE OUTLOOK AND HEALTH BEHAVIORS   7

and individuals' degrees of preventive care, health knowledge, and

physical status in a longitudinal study. One-thousand-two-hundred-

ten Los Angeles adults were interviewed every six weeks from Fall

1976 to Fall 1977 to tr_____ _eir illnesses and responses to those

illnesses. T **Avoid Plagiarism** ed participants' health beliefs

(first interv Paraphrase in your spective of cancer (last interview),
own words.

and sense-o See Ch. 5, p. 59 ween). In analyzing the results,

the experimenters also control for possibly confounding variables

such as health state and socioeconomic resources. The dependent

variables were preventive health behavior, health knowledge and

perspectives, and physical health status. There was an overall

positive relationship between higher sense of control and various

health factors, including frequency of preventive health actions,

optimism of early medical treatment for cancer, higher self-ratings

of health, fewer episodes of illnesses, and proactive responses to

illnesses. Considering this study's strong suggestion at a relationship

between locus of control and health status, the authors incorporated

this measure into our study.

The Current Study

In regard of the literature reviewed, the current study

surveyed the interrelationships among health sense of control

as measured by the Health Locus of Control (HLOC) scale,

21

LIFE OUTLOOK AND HEALTH BEHAVIORS   8

optimism measured by the LOT, self-reported risk, objective

risk and health behaviors measured together by the skin

cancer assessment tool. In this article, I referred to the score

of objective risk as t[   ]

behaviors as the BEH   her

scores on the HLOC

> In an experimental paper, the introduction ends with specific, testable hypotheses. This is followed by the Method section, with the heading centered and boldface.

reported risk, the BRAT, and the LOT would correspond to

higher score on the BEH with a linear regression.

Method

Participants

Participants ($N = 21$) were all undergraduate students at

Randolph College. The participants were of college-typical age,

app[   ]er ratio reflected the gender

rati[   ]les). The participants were

rec[   ]ass as a mandatory part of class

activities.

> For each of the subheadings in the Method section (Participants, Materials, Procedure), the subheading is boldface and flush left, and it appears on its own line.

Instruments

Life Orientation Test

The Life Orientation Test (Scheier, Carver, & Bridges,

1994) consisted of[   ]pertaining to

optimism, three ite[   ]er items. The

> Inside parentheses, a comma followed by an ampersand (&) separates the last author from the second-to-last author.

scales ranged from $0 = $ (*Strongly Disagree*) to $4 = $ (*Strongly*

LIFE OUTLOOK AND HEALTH BEHAVIORS   9

Agree). The scores on the pessimism items were reversed, with

higher score indicating more optimistic outlook.

The Brief Skin Cancer Assessment Tool

The brief skin cancer assessment tool (Glanz et al., 2003)

was used to measure objective risk (BRAT) and health behaviors

(BEH). The BRAT scale consisted of the first nine items of the

assessment tool inquiring about characteristics such as skin color,

sun sensitivity, and personal history. A high score on the BRAT

suggested a high objective risk of skin cancer. The BEH scale,

composed of seven questions, evaluated participants' tanning

frequency and protective measures

with higher score demonstrating he

> When citing multiple
> studies within parentheses,
> alphabetize the list according
> to the first author's last name.

Health Locus of Control

I used a shortened version of the HLOC scale (Wallston, Stein,

& Smith, 1994; Wallston, Wallston, & DeVellis, 1978) with six items,

with a higher score indicating a more internal sense of control. The

scale ranged from 1 = (*Strongly Disagree*) to 6 = (*Strongly Agree*).

Subjective Risk

Subjective risk was measured wit

the participants' own assessment of their

> The verbal descriptors
> for survey scale scores
> are always italicized.

The scale ran from 1 to 6, with a higher score indicating higher

perceived risks.

21

LIFE OUTLOOK AND HEALTH BEHAVIORS   10

Procedure

All the participants completed the scales during class time.
After completing the scales, they were debriefed on the meaning of
the scale and the purpose of the study.

Results

A simultaneous multiple regression analysis, with
the HLOC, BRAT, LOT, and Perceived Risk scores as the
p̲ Statistical symbols are italicized. criterion, was computed. The
regr̲ ̲on analysis was not significant (F (4, 16) = 1.410,
p = .275). When controlled for other variables, none of the
predictor produced significant correlation with BEH in this
analysis. A summary of the results of the multiple regression

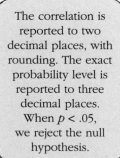

The correlation is reported to two decimal places, with rounding. The exact probability level is reported to three decimal places. When $p < .05$, we reject the null hypothesis.

The type of statistical test is indicated in italics immediately followed by the degrees of freedom in parentheses, the actual statistical test value to two decimal places, followed by the exact p value.

variables, HLO̲ ̲nd LOT produced a
̲elation (r(19) = .62, p = .002). Another
significant positive ̲rrelation existed between Perceived Risk
and BRAT (r(19) = .46, p = .018). A summary of the results of the
linear regression equation is provided in Table 2.

Discussion

Even though the results were ~~p~~ [covered by callout] support for the hypothesis, several f worth examination. First, the results literature of a positive relationship between a mo\ ernal

> Connecting the findings from the current study to past research findings is an important component of the Discussion section.

health locus of control and more preventive health behaviors. In consideration of the literature, this finding is congruent with the finding of Luo and Issacowitz (2007), where health optimism, not dispositional optimism, correlated with health behaviors. A possible explanation is that health measures, including health optimism and health locus of control, capture more intimately the participants' feelings of control and optimism towards their health. A dispositional optimism scale or a general locus of control scale measure people's general life outlooks and other factors of their lives may override the health factor. However, when health is salient, as in health scales, the scores will be more reflective of the participants' evaluations of their health status and thus correlate better with their health behaviors.

Another noteworthy finding is the significant positive correlation between participants' perceived risk and objective risk suggesting that participants' accurate awareness of their own health status, which is a reassuring finding.

21

LIFE OUTLOOK AND HEALTH BEHAVIOR   12

Finally, the strongest correlation in this study was

between the HLOC score and the LOT score. The relationship

between optimism and sense of control is intricate, as one

...ce in good

...agement for

...e their health.

...tionship

...ism scale,

...of control

> In the Discussion section, if you are going to speculate about the possible meaning of your results, it is best to be fair and label your ideas as speculation or suggestion. In fact, when reading any paragraph in a research paper like this one, if no citation is listed somewhere in the paragraph, it will be assumed that all the ideas in that paragraph belong to the paper's author. If you do not give credit where it is due, that is plagiarism, and you must avoid that.

scale, and (4) general locus of control scale. The results of such

stu... f the efficacy of each

mea... address the distinction

> Every research study has limitations, which usually appear toward the end of the Discussion section.

between ...ealth-specific scale and general scale.

The present study was also affected by several

li... ample size of 21, which

m... ation of significant results.

> Be careful to avoid misuse of words that are often confused, such as *effect* and *affect*.

Secondly, these participants were conveniently-sampled from

a health psychology class, and the awareness of certain health

psychology discussions regarding optimism and locus of control

might have reduced the objectivity of participants' completion

of the questionnaires. Lastly, I did not control for participants'

actual health status pertaining to skin cancer, which likely

21

LIFE OUTLOOK AND HEALTH BEHAVIORS   13

influenced to some extent their optimism and health locus of

control. Despite these limitations, based on the results from this

research we are more aware of the relationship between life

outlook and health behaviors, particularly with regards to the

awareness of the influence of

nt steps needed to promote

This is a great use of the first-person pronoun here. Framing the sentence this way avoids passive voice. The passive voice sentence would be, . . . "Actual health status was not controlled for . . . " The action is with the researcher, and she did the action, so why not say so?

In the closing paragraph to a research study, be sure to go beyond the limitations of the research and remind the reader of the take-home message. What void did this study fill? What is the importance or magnitude of the overall topic?

21

LIFE OUTLOOK AND HEALTH BEHAVIOR   14

References

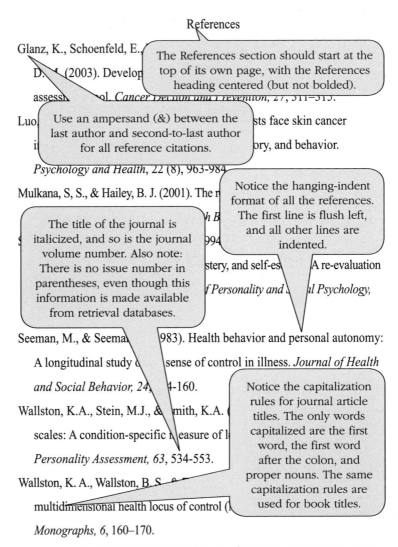

Glanz, K., Schoenfeld, E.,

> The References section should start at the top of its own page, with the References heading centered (but not bolded).

D. (2003). Develop

assesss... ...ol. *Cancer Detection and Prevention, 27,* 311–315.

Luo,

> Use an ampersand (&) between the last author and second-to-last author for all reference citations.

...sts face skin cancer

i... ...ory, and behavior.

Psychology and Health, 22 (8), 963–984.

Mulkana, S. S., & Hailey, B. J. (2001). The r...

> Notice the hanging-indent format of all the references. The first line is flush left, and all other lines are indented.

*h B...

> The title of the journal is italicized, and so is the journal volume number. Also note: There is no issue number in parentheses, even though this information is made available from retrieval databases.

994

stery, and self-es... A re-evaluation

f Personality and ... l Psychology,

Seeman, M., & Seema... ...983). Health behavior and personal autonomy:

A longitudinal study ... sense of control in illness. *Journal of Health*

and Social Behavior, 24, ...4–160.

> Notice the capitalization rules for journal article titles. The only words capitalized are the first word, the first word after the colon, and proper nouns. The same capitalization rules are used for book titles.

Wallston, K.A., Stein, M.J., & ...mith, K.A. ...

scales: A condition-specific ...easure of l...

Personality Assessment, 63, 534–553.

Wallston, K. A., Wallston, B. S...

multidimensional health locus of control (...

Monographs, 6, 160–170.

> **What About the Paper's Content**
> This same paper, with content feedback. See Ch. 19, pp. 191–203

21

LIFE OUTLOOK AN{ Notice that double-spacing continues on this table. Also, the table title is in italics. }   15

Table 1

Multiple Regression to Predict Risky Health Behaviors (N = 21)

Predictors	r	B	β
BRAT	−.05	.00	.01
HLOC	.50*	.41	.52
LOT	.26	−.04	−.06
Perceived Risk	−.24	−.13	−.06

Note: R = .511, R² = .261
p = .010

{ In an APA–formatted table, there are no vertical lines—only horizontal lines. }

21

LIFE OUTLOOK AND HEALTH BEHAVIORS 16

Table 2

Linear Regression Equation Pearson Correlation

	BRAT	HLOC	LOT	Perceived Risk
BEH	−.05	.51*	.26	−.24
BRAT		−.04	.16	.46*
HLOC			.62**	−.34
LOT				.17

*Note: *p < .05. **p < .01*

The information in the table note is invaluable because it provides a context for the reader to make sense of the numbers presented in the table.

21

How to Avoid the Most Common Mistakes

22

All Together Now

In Chapter 4, we provided a list of the 20 most common grammatical errors in all types of writing. We end this book with a series of questions to point out the most common writing errors students make when learning to write in APA style using APA format—although it should be noted that these are your authors' perceptions of the most common errors. Answers to the questions can be found toward the end of the chapter. Then we end this chapter with a list of common instructor pet peeves to keep in mind.

We included content throughout this chapter that refers mostly to formal experimental (research) papers, but when instructors say they want a paper prepared in APA format, we strongly suggest you check your work against the list provided in this chapter so you can avoid the common mistakes and the pet peeves. Attention to detail is often the difference between good and great. Said another way, attention to detail is often the difference between A-graded work and B-graded work. We do not mean to focus on the negative, but we want you to learn the nuances and techniques of writing in APA style, for if you can conquer this, you will have acquired skills that will serve you the remainder of your undergraduate career and beyond—and for evidence of the importance of attention to detail, see Gardner (2007).

So before you hand in any assignment that calls for APA format or APA style, we highly recommend that you consult the chapter on these common errors. We have also included this information as a checklist in an abbreviated format in

Appendix B so you can copy it and literally check each item before handing in any APA–style paper. Avoiding these common errors sends good signals to your instructors; you can follow instructions, you can do detailed work, and you know how to translate complex assignments into meaningful scientific writing. The ability to complete this task successfully is a marketable skill.

The more you practice, the better you will become and the faster you will be able to finish complex writing tasks. Here is a chance for you to see how much you remember—take our short quiz (and fight the temptation to jump right to the answers, all right?). You will see a number of options for how to write in APA style. We provide the RIGHT way, but we blend it in with some WRONG ways. Can you find what is what? For some questions, more than one answer is correct. So be sure to find ALL the correct answers to each question. Answers, explanations for the answers, and a checklist of reminders follows in Appendix B. Enjoy!!!

APA Style and Format Quiz

1.

A. It is well-known that over half of all marriages end in divorce in the United States.

B. According to the National Survey on Family Growth conducted by the U.S. Department of Health and Human Services (Goodwin, Mosher, & Chandra, 2010), about one third of first marriages ended in divorce or separation before reaching the 10th anniversary.

2.

A. While socioeconomic status is an interesting variable, I did not include it in this study.

B. Although socioeconomic status is an interesting variable, I did not include it in this study.

C. While our participants were texting, their driving abilities were significantly impaired.

3.

A. I tested participants in groups.

B. The study was conducted with groups of participants.

4.

A. I hypothesize that men will score higher then women.

B. I hypothesize that men will score higher than women.

5.

A. We measured the affect of the independent variable on the dependent variable.

B. We measured the effect of the independent variable on the dependent variable.

6.

A. In the next section of this paper, I will present the major hypotheses.

B. I present my hypotheses next.

7.

A. The present research is supported by previous literature (Schwartz & Gurung, 2012).

B. Landrum and Gurung (in press) used empirical evidence of learning to write their introduction to psychology textbook.

C. Landrum & Gurung (in press) used empirical evidence of learning to write their introduction to psychology textbook.

D. The present research is supported by previous literature (Schwartz and Gurung, 2012).

8.

A. The study was complete; participants were free to ask questions.

B. The study was complete; then questions.

9.

A. We considered many publishers, e.g., McGraw-Hill, Cengage, and Worth.

B. We considered many publishers (e.g., McGraw-Hill, Cengage, and Worth).

10.

A. We asked participants to complete the task and return the booklets at the front of the room.

B. We asked them to complete the task and return their booklets over there.

11.

A. I asked participants to complete the task and return the booklets at the front of the room.

B. He or she was asked to complete the task and return his or her booklet at the front of the room.

22

12.

A. Our findings confirm the hypothesis that class attendance positively correlates with exam performance.

B. My findings confirm the hypothesis that class attendance positively correlates with exam performance.

C. We need to better understand how our children learn in school.

D. I believe educators need a better understanding of how children learn in school.

13.

A. The participants were not allowed to take more than 50 min to complete the survey.

B. The participants weren't allowed to take more than 50 min to complete the survey.

14.

A. The spacing of a paper varies by section.

B. All sections of a paper other than the tables and reference are double-spaced.

C. The entire APA paper should be double-spaced.

15.

A. The age of participants was higher than expected (M = 26.43, SD = 5.44).

B. The age of participants was higher than expected (M = 26.43, SD = 5.44).

16.

A. Aram and Aviram (2009) suggest that frequency of storybook reading relates to a child's language ability.

B. Aram and Aviram (2009) suggested that frequency of storybook reading relates to a child's language ability.

17.

A. Landrum and McCarthy (2012) identify the ethical challenges faced in the classroom today.

B. In their book *Teaching Ethically*, Eric Landrum and Maureen McCarthy (2012) identify the ethical challenges faced in the classroom today.

18.

A. Participants completed the task in 45 min.

B. Introductory psychology students chose from two different textbooks available at the bookstore.

C. Participants completed the task in forty-five min.

D. Introductory psychology students chose from 2 different textbooks available at the bookstore.

19.

A. First citation: Schwartz, Landrum, and Gurung (2013) wrote a student-friendly guide to APA style and format. **Second citation:** In their book on APA style and format, Schwartz et al. (2013) included a sample paper for practicing proofreading.

B. First citation: Schwartz, Landrum, and Gurung (2013) wrote a student-friendly guide to APA style and format. **Second citation:** In their book on APA style and format, Schwartz, Landrum, and Gurung (2013) included a sample paper for practicing proofreading.

20.

A. Taylor, Klein, Lewis, Gruenwald, Gurung, and Updegraff (2000) proposed a new theory of stress called the tend-and-befriend theory.

B. Taylor et al. (2000) proposed a new theory of stress called the tend-and-befriend theory.

21.

A. In preparation for this experiment, a plethora of studies were reviewed.

B. In preparation for this experiment, I reviewed many studies.

22.

A. My data support the conclusion that taller people tend to weigh more than shorter people.

B. My data prove that taller people weigh more than shorter people.

23.

A. There was a negative correlation between average number of cigarettes smoked and life span, meaning that cigarette smoking causes an earlier death.

B. There was a negative correlation between average number of cigarettes smoked and life span, meaning results indicated that those who smoked many cigarettes were also those who lived shorter lives.

22

24.

A. In references, all significant words and proper nouns in book and journal titles are capitalized.

B. In references, all significant words and proper nouns in book and journal titles are capitalized and only the first word plus proper nouns in book titles are capitalized.

C. In references, all significant words and proper nouns in book titles are capitalized and only the first word plus proper nouns in journal titles are capitalized.

D. In references, all words are capitalized in book and journal titles.

25.

A. Only use doi numbers for references after 2010.

B. If you do not have a doi number, use an ISBN number.

C. If you used your school database or PsycINFO, a doi number is not needed.

D. Include doi numbers for references whenever possible.

26.

Identify the correct reference format:

A. Gurung, R. A. R. (2015). Three investigations of the utility of textbook teaching supplements. *Psychology of Learning and Teaching, 1,* 48–59. doi:10.1177/1475725714565288

B. Gurung, R. A. R. (2015). Three investigations of the utility of textbook teaching supplements. *Psychology of Learning and Teaching, 1,* 48–59. doi:10.1177/1475725714565288

APA Style and Format Quiz: ANSWERS

1. B. In an APA–style paper, cite a reference to support a claim about a belief or behavior. If you are going to offer your personal opinion, make sure the source/attribution is clearly identified. To some extent, most instructors assume that anything in the Introduction or Discussion section that does not have a citation is, by default, your personal opinion. If it is your personal opinion, consider using the phrase "In my opinion" in the text of your paper. If it is not your opinion but you did not cite the source, you are plagiarizing.

2. B and C. Use *while* to indicate the passage of time; otherwise, use *although* or *whereas* (see Chapter 4).

3. A. Avoid passive voice; strive to write in the active voice, using first-person pronouns (see Chapter 3).

4. B. Avoid common word confusions, such as *than* versus *then* and *effect* versus *affect* (see Chapter 4).

5. B. Avoid common word confusions, such as *than* versus *then* and *effect* versus *affect* (see Chapter 4).

6. B. When using APA style, avoid being too colloquial (i.e., informal). Avoid sentences such as, "In the next section of this paper, I'm going to talk about . . ." Writing in APA style is not like having a conversation.

7. A and B. When citing references in the text, inside parentheses use an ampersand (&) for multiple authors; outside parentheses, use *and* for multiple authors (see Chapter 8).

8. A. Use a semicolon to separate two clauses that could both stand on their own as complete sentences.

9. B. Make sure all Latin abbreviations are spelled correctly. The following Latin abbreviations should be used only in parentheses: cf., e.g., etc., i.e., viz., vs. (i.e., see Chapter 18 for more details).

10. A. Minimize the use of third-person pronouns—*they, their, them*; complete each thought, even if it means being a bit redundant in the sentence. (See Chapter 3 for more information.)

11. A. Change singular antecedents to plural whenever possible so you can use plural pronouns instead of *he or she, he/she, him or her*, or *him/her.*

12. B and D. If you are the only author of a paper, do not refer to *we* or *our*; because you are the only author, refer to *I* or *my* (see Chapter 3 for more on this). Also, APA style uses *we* and *our* to refer only to the authors of a manuscript, not to people in general.

13. A. Do not use contractions in APA format.

14. C. See Chapter 16 for details about changing the spacing using the *Paragraph* window in Word. Take off the automatic extra space after paragraphs (a Word default).

15. B. Be sure to italicize all statistical symbols and abbreviations (see Chapter 18).

22

16. B. In an Introduction section, when writing about studies previously conducted, refer to the studies in past tense because they were conducted in the past. Note: When writing a proposal for research that you will conduct, write about your proposed research in the future tense because you have not yet completed the work.

17. A. In an Introduction section, when writing about studies previously conducted, if you decide to include the authors' names within the text, be sure to avoid using their first names and the title of the work. Although, we must add here that we do not recommend starting off many sentences in your paper with the researchers' names.

18. A and B. Be sure to follow the rules for spelling out numbers and using numerals throughout your APA–style paper (see Chapter 13 for more details).

19. A. When citing a paper with three to five authors, include all authors' names in the first citation and use only the first author's name followed by et al. in all subsequent citations.

20. B. When citing a study with six or more authors in the text of a paper, use only the first author's name followed by et al.—even on the first citation—with no comma before et al. (See Chapter 8 for more details.)

21. B. Do not use sophisticated vocabulary to show off your knowledge. Aim for parsimony; communicate complex ideas in the simplest language possible (see Chapter 3). (In other words, try not to embed SAT– or GRE–type words in your writing unless the word truly fits the context.)

22. A. Be careful with the verb *prove;* we don't prove anything in science. You can avoid this issue by discussing whether your findings support your hypothesis or refute your hypothesis rather than proving or disproving it.

23. B. Draw appropriate conclusions; correlational data do not allow for cause-and-effect conclusions.

24. B. Capitalization of words of titles in the reference list is not the same as how you title your paper.

25. D. Digital Object Identification (doi) numbers are key components of references and should be included when available.

26. B. Use your Word ruler settings to make all references have a hanging indent.

Be Aware of Professors' Pet Peeves

We all have pet peeves, or certain things that perhaps annoy us more than they annoy others. After reading many student papers written by those first learning how to write in APA style, instructors often generate a list of common writing mistakes that they find particularly annoying. Though pet peeves are by nature idiosyncratic and through discussions with many colleagues who are grading papers, we have identified some common items on that list of pet peeves concerning APA style. It is worth your while to learn what those pet peeves are so you can avoid them.

These are not necessarily in the *PM,* but they are examples of what to avoid to strengthen your paper when writing APA–style papers.

- Stating that "research was done." Instead, discuss *conducting* research. Steaks are *done*; studies are *conducted.*

  Incorrect: Researchers did this study to test three hypotheses.

  Correct: Researchers conducted this study to test three hypotheses.

- Writing that "the research reported" rather than "the researchers reported." Remember to connect behaviors to humans and not to things. Studies do not report; people or researchers do.

  Incorrect: This study reported that cramming does not aid in long-term retention.

  Correct: The researchers reported that cramming does not aid in long-term retention.

- Resorting to lists rather than writing the information in paragraph form. Use lists selectively and sparsely; too many lists can appear as an attempt to avoid "real" writing. See Chapter 17 for rules about seriation (the presentation of lists).

- Using too many direct quotations. Minimize your use of direct quotations, especially long ones. Use a direct quotation only when the author has stated something so perfectly that you cannot adequately paraphrase it. Accurate paraphrasing—taking someone else's ideas and translating them into your own words—is a valuable academic skill; practice that skill. If you truly want to make sure you understand something, try to teach that idea to someone else (such as your grandmother or grandfather).

Even if your instructor does not require that every assignment be prepared in APA format, the checklist in Appendix B will help you avoid common errors; we provide numerous "redirects" that send you to the chapter that contains the

22

information you need to fix the errors. In addition to using our checklist of the common mistakes we have come across when reading student papers, you might also find helpful the checklist Rewey and Valesquez (2009) developed for a journal submission. Their checklist is comprehensive and covers APA style for formatting and typing in general, as well as rules for different sections of a manuscript. Again, keep in mind that the Rewey and Valesquez checklist focuses on journal submissions and is not necessarily relevant for a paper assignment. As we mentioned earlier in this book, be sure to review the instructions for the specific writing assignment on which you are working.

The good news is that writing in APA style and format becomes easier with practice. Of course, anything feels easier once you have learned the key elements and had a chance to practice. We hope that this book has gone a long way in reducing your fears about APA style. We can also wager that a close reading of this book will do wonders for your writing, how you learn about science, and even the way you think about science. Your three authors had a stimulating time writing this book. We tried to make it fun. We hope you have fun, too.

Appendix A

Error List for Chapter 20

L isted below are the errors we can find for the sample paper included in Chapter 20. If you find any additional errors, send an e-mail to any of the authors. We welcome your e-mails.

Title page

1. A running head is needed on the first page with the words "Running head" included.

2. The title of the paper should not be in bold.

3. The course name, number, and date should be deleted and replaced with the author's affiliation (college or university).

Abstract

1. The abstract should be double-spaced and the margins should be in APA format.

2. The abstract should not be indented.

3. This is not a conversation, so it is awkward to start with "This paper is about." It would be better to start something like "The focus of this work concerns caffeine…"

4. For the second sentence, a paper cannot talk. It would be better to start something like "I studied the pharmacological effects…"

5. The hypothesis and brief statement on how it was tested should be included.

6. Be sure to proofread; in the last sentence, it should be "known" and not "know."

7. The abstract is missing a Keywords entry at the conclusion of the abstract paragraph.

4. The running head on pages 3 through 7 of the paper needs to be left justified with the page number right justified.

5. Change "it ts" to "it is." Add a comma after Anacin.

6. The abbreviation for milligrams should be mg.

7. Alphabetize the citations in the parentheses at the end of paragraph 2.

8. At the end of the second paragraph, there should be a period (it should appear after the closing parenthesis, not before the opening parenthesis).

9. Delete the extra space between the second and third paragraphs.

10. Change the word *which* to *that* in the first sentence of the third paragraph.

Page 4

11. Change the first comma in the first complete sentence to a semicolon. Add the word *is* between *theophylline* and *commonly* and also between *theobromine* and *found*.

12. Technical terms should be italicized (e.g., coffee Arabica, Theobroma cocoa). Change the parentheses between *kola nut* and *Cola nitida* to a semicolon.

13. Change the word *completed* to *completely*. Change *while* to *although*. Add a comma after *vary*.

14. The units of time should be abbreviated (min, hr) in several places.

15. Change *half life* to *half-life* in all instances.

16. Remove the hyphen from *caffeine-sensitive*.

17. The word *Others* should not be capitalized.

Page 5

18. The semicolon should be a period after the word *thoroughly*, and the word *within* should then be capitalized.

19. The year for the Stephenson citation should be 1977.

20. Delete the extra space between the first two paragraphs.

21. Indent the second paragraph.

22. The third sentence of the second paragraph includes awkward wording (" . . . is the caffeine also works . . .").

23. Delete the extra Robertson and the comma before the ampersand in the citation at the end of the second paragraph.

24. In the third paragraph, *hour* should be abbreviated.

25. This sentence is incomplete: "Although multiple metabolites . . ."

26. In the citation at the end of the third paragraph, Richardson should be Robertson.

Page 6

27. In the first paragraph, remove the passive voice by rewriting the sentence about renal metabolites in the section starting with "have been reported to have been." Add the word *and* before *breast milk,* and change the word *been* to *been.*

28. Alphabetize the citations within parentheses. Again, change Richardson to Robertson.

29. Add a comma after *urine* in the last sentence of the first paragraph.

30. The second paragraph is justified; make the right margin ragged by left justifying the paragraph.

31. Create one sentence from the first two sentences of the third paragraph by changing the period after *mixed* to a colon.

32. Change the word *While* to *Although,* capitalized as the first word of a complete thought after a colon.

33. Add a comma after *muscle,* before *which.* Change *tum* to *turn.* Change "*are*" to "*one.*"

Page 7

34. Add a comma after *nuclei,* before *which.*

35. Delete the comma after *relief,* before *and why.*

36. Delete the indent for the block quote, and place the period after the block quote, followed by the authors and page (p.) of the quote inside the parentheses.

37. Delete the comma after the first author's name and add an ampersand to the citation at the end of the block quote.

Page 8

38. Delete the indent for the block quote. Place the period after the block quote, followed by the authors and page (p.) of the quote inside the parentheses.

39. Change *effect* to *affect* in the first sentence of the paragraph.

40. Use an ampersand instead of the word *and* in the citation included in the first paragraph.

41. Avoid using text within parentheses. Insert a comma after *alertness* in the last sentence.

42. Move the heading "References" to the next page.

Page 9

43. Use hanging indents for each reference.

44. For references with two authors, add a comma after the initials of the first author, before the ampersand.

45. For a journal article, capitalize only the first word of the title, the first word after a colon, and proper nouns.

46. For the second (Graham) reference, delete the issue number in parentheses.

47. Include only first initials, not full first and middle names.

48. The last reference should end with a period.

Appendix B

APA Style and Format Checklist

____ Cite a reference to support any claim about a belief or behavior.

____ Use *while* to indicate the passage of time; otherwise, use *although* or *whereas*.

____ Avoid passive voice; strive to write in the active voice, using first-person pronouns.

____ Avoid common word confusions, such as *than* versus *then* and *effect* versus *affect*.

____ Avoid being too colloquial or too informal. Writing in APA style is not like having a conversation.

____ When citing references in text, inside parentheses, use an ampersand (&) for multiple authors; outside parentheses, use *and* for multiple authors.

____ Use a semicolon to separate two clauses that could both stand on their own as complete sentences.

____ Make sure all Latin abbreviations are spelled correctly.

____ Use the following Latin abbreviations only within parentheses: cf., e.g., etc., i.e., viz., vs.

____ Minimize the use of third-person pronouns—*they, their, them*.

____ Avoid the use of *he or she, he/she, him or her,* and *him/her*.

____ If you are the only author of a paper, do not use *we* or *our,* because you are the only author, instead use *I* or *my*.

____ Do not use contractions.

____ Be sure your paper is double-spaced throughout. (You can change the spacing using the *Paragraph* window in Word.)

____ Be sure to italicize all statistical symbols and abbreviations.

____ In an Introduction section, when writing about studies previously conducted, refer to the studies in past tense because they were conducted in the past. Note: When writing a proposal for research that you will conduct, write about your proposed research in the future tense because you have not yet completed the work.

____ Be sure to follow the rules for spelling out numbers and using numerals throughout your paper.

____ When citing a study with three to five authors, include all authors' names for the first citation, and use only the first author's name followed by *et al.* for all subsequent citations.

____ When citing a study with six or more authors, use only the first author's name followed by *et al.*—even on the first citation—with no comma before *et al.*

____ Do not use sophisticated vocabulary to show off. Aim for parsimony; communicate complex ideas in the simplest language possible.

____ Be careful with the verb *prove*; we don't prove anything in science. You can avoid this issue by discussing whether your findings support or refute your hypothesis.

____ Draw appropriate conclusions; correlation data do not allow for cause-and-effect conclusions.

____ Do not state that "research was done." Instead, discuss conducting research.

____ Write that "the researchers reported" rather than "the research reported." Remember to connect behaviors to humans, not to things.

____ Use lists selectively and sparsely; too many lists can appear as an attempt to avoid writing.

____ Minimize your use of direct quotes, especially long direct quotes.

References

About.com. (n.d.). *Correcting errors in subject-verb agreement.* Retrieved from http://grammar.about.com/od/correctingerrors/a/ASagreement.htm

American Psychological Association APA. (2010a). *Publication manual of the American Psychological Association* (6th ed.). Washington, DC: Author.

American Psychological Association APA. (2010b). *Supplemental material: Writing clearly and concisely.* Retrieved from http://www.apastyle.com/manual/supplement/index.aspx

Bem, D. J. (1987). Writing the empirical journal article. In M. P. Zanna & J. M. Darley (Eds.), *The compleat academic: A practical guide for the beginning social scientist* (pp. 171–202). Mahwah, NJ: Erlbaum.

BioMedical Editor. (2009). *Writing tips: Active voice and passive voice.* Retrieved from http://www.biomedicaleditor.com/active-voice.html

Bloom, H. S., & Lipsey, M. W. (2004). *Some food for thought about effect size.* Retrieved from http://courses.washington.edu/socw580/readings/Bloom-2004-FoodforThought.pdf

Blue, T. (2000). *It is never could of!* Retrieved from http://grammartips.homestead.com/couldof.html

Brewer, B. W., Scherzer, C. B., Van Raalte, J. L., Petitpas, A. J., & Andersen, M. B. (2001). The elements of (APA) style: A survey of journal editors. *American Psychologist, 56,* 266–267.

Clark, B. (n.d.). *Five grammatical errors that make you look dumb.* Retrieved from http://www.copyblogger.com/5-common-mistakes-that-make-you-look-dumb/

Cohen, J. (1988). *Statistical power analysis for the behavioral sciences.* San Diego, CA: Academic Press.

DailyWritingTips.com. (n.d.). *Passive vs. active voice.* Retrieved from http://www.dailywritingtips.com/passive-vs-active-voice/

Driscoll, D. L. (2009a). *Appropriate pronoun usage.* Retrieved from http://owl.english.purdue.edu/owl/resource/608/06/

Driscoll, D. L. (2009b). *Stereotypes and biased language.* Retrieved from http://owl.english.purdue.edu/owl/resource/608/05/

Dunn, D. S. (2011). *A short guide to writing about psychology* (3rd ed.). Boston, MA: Longman/Pearson.

Edelstein, N., Krantz, T., Polaire, M., Sarde, A., & Sweeney, M. (Producers), & Lynch, D. (Director). (2001). *Mulholland Drive* [Motion picture]. United States: Universal Pictures.

EzineArticles.com. (2009a). *Five tips for subject verb agreement.* Retrieved from http://ezinearticles.com/?Five-Tips-For-Subject-Verb-Agreement&id=1107048

EzineArticles.com. (2009b). *Technical writing: A short summary of basic grammar rules in English*. Retrieved from http://ezinearticles.com/?Technical-Writing---A-Short-Summary-of-Basic-Grammar-Rules-In-English&id=1922954

Field, A. (2014). *Discovering statistics using SPSS* (3rd ed.). Thousand Oaks, CA: Sage.

Gaertner-Johnston, L. (2006). Business writing: "That" or "Which"? Retrieved from http://www.businesswritingblog.com/business_writing/2006/01/that_or_which.html

Gardner, P. (2007). *Moving up or moving out of the company? Factors that influence the promoting or firing of new college hires* (Research Brief 1-2007). East Lansing: Michigan State University Collegiate Employment Research Institute. Retrieved from http://ceri.msu.edu/publications/pdf/brief1-07.pdf

Gilbert, J. (2006). *10 flagrant grammar mistakes that make you look stupid*. Retrieved from http://www.techrepublic.com/article/10-flagrant-grammar-mistakes-that-make-you-look-stupid/6075621

Goodwin, P. Y., Mosher, W. D., & Chandra, A. (2010). Marriage and cohabitation in the United States: A statistical portrait based on cycle 6 (2002) of the National Survey of Family Growth (DHHS Pub. No. PHS 2010-1980). *Vital and Health Statistics, 23*(28). Washington, DC: Government Printing Office.

Gottschalk, K., & Hjortshoj, K. (2004). *The elements of teaching writing: A resource for instructors in all disciplines*. Boston, MA: Bedford/St. Martin's Press.

Gurung, R. A. R. (2009, August). Reaping the fruits of SoTL's labor: Using pedagogical research well. In R. A. R. Gurung (Chair), *Advancing pedagogical research (SoTL) in psychology: Models and incentives*. Symposium presented at the 117th Annual Meeting of the American Psychological Association, Toronto, Canada.

Gurung, R. A. R., & Chrouser, C. (2007). Dissecting objectification: Do sexism, athleticism, and provocativeness matter? *Sex Roles, 57,* 91–99.

Gurung, R. A. R., & Johnson, V. (2013). *Do the rich and famous get objectified?* Manuscript under review.

Gurung, R. A. R., Morack, S., & Bloch, H. (2005, June). *Skin sells (and hurts): Objectification and the Miss America 2004 Pageant*. Poster presented at the annual meeting of the American Psychological Society, Los Angeles, CA.

Gurung, R. A. R., & Schwartz, B. M. (2009). *Optimizing teaching and learning: Pedagogical research in practice*. Malden, MA: Blackwell.

Gurung, R. A. R., Weidert, J., & Jeske, A. S. (2010). A closer look at how students study (and if it matters). *Journal of the Scholarship of Teaching and Learning, 10,* 28–33.

Gurung, R. A. R., & Wilson-Doenges, G. (2010). Engaging students in psychology: Building on first-year programs and seminars. In D. S. Dunn, B. C. Beins, M. A. McCarthy, & G. W. Hill IV (Eds.), *Best practices for beginnings and endings in the psychology major* (pp. 93–106). New York, NY: Oxford University Press.

Harris, R. A. (2011). *Using sources effectively: Strengthening your writing and avoiding plagiarism* (3rd ed.). Glendale, CA: Pyrczak Publishing.

Hegarty, P., Watson, N., Fletcher, L., & McQueen, G. (2010). When gentlemen are first and ladies are last: Effects of gender stereotypes on the order of romantic partners' names. *British Journal of Social Psychology, 11.*

Instructions in regard to preparation of manuscript. (1929). *Psychological Bulletin, 26,* 57–63.

James, W. (1950). *The principles of psychology*. Mineola, NY: Dover. (Original work published 1890)

Johnson, V., & Gurung, R. A. R. (2010). *Diffusing objectification: The role of competence*. Manuscript under review.

Kesler, J. T. (2010). *Problematic Internet use and the effect on academic performance.* Unpublished manuscript, Boise State University, Boise, ID.

Kessler, L., & McDonald, D. (2008). *When words collide: A media writer's guide to grammar and style* (7th ed.). Boston, MA: Wadsworth.

Knight, K. L., & Ingersoll, C. D. (1996). Optimizing scholarly communication: 30 tips for writing clearly. *Journal of Athletic Training, 31,* 209–213.

Krieger, S. (2005). *Microsoft Office document designer: Your easy-to-use toolkit and complete how-to source for professional-quality documents.* Redmond, WA: Microsoft Press.

Landrum, R. E. (2012). *Undergraduate writing in psychology: Learning to tell the scientific story* (rev. ed.). Washington, DC: American Psychological Association.

Lorde, A. (1984). Poetry is not a luxury. *Sister outsider.* Berkeley, CA: Crossing Press.

Maddox, M., & Scocco, D. (2009). *Basic English grammar.* Retrieved from http://www.dailywritingtips.com/

Merriam-Webster's collegiate dictionary (11th ed.). (2005). Springfield, MA: Merriam-Webster.

Modern Language Association (MLA). (2009). *MLA handbook for writers of research papers* (7th ed.). Retrieved from http://www.mla.org/store/CID24/PID363

Nicol, A. A. M., & Pexman, P. M. (2010). *Presenting your findings: A practical guide for creating tables.* Washington, DC: American Psychological Association.

Nolan, C., & Thomas, E. (Producers), & Nolan, C. (Director). (2010). *Inception* [Motion picture]. United States: Warner Bros. Pictures.

O'Conner, P. T. (1996). *Woe is I: The grammarphobe's guide to better English in plain English.* New York, NY: Riverhead Books.

O'Conner, P. T. (1999). *Words fail me: What everyone who writes should know about writing.* New York, NY: Harcourt Brace.

O'Neil, D. (2006). *Ethnicity and race: Overview.* Retrieved from http://anthro.palomar.edu/ethnicity/ethnic_1.htm

PlainLanguage.gov. (n.d.). *Writing tip: Use active, not passive sentences.* Retrieved from http://www.plainlanguage.gov/howto/quickreference/dash/dashactive.cfm

Prestwich, A., Perugini, M., & Hurling, R. (2010). Can implementation intentions and text messages promote brisk walking? A randomized trial. *Health Psychology, 29,* 40–49. doi:10.1037/a0016993

Pyrczak, F. (2008). *Evaluating research in academic journals: A practical guide to realistic evaluation* (4th ed.). Glendale, CA: Pyrczak Publishing.

Rewey, K. L., & Valesquez, T. L. (2009). Presubmission checklist for the *Publication Manual of the American Psychological Association* (6th ed.). *Psi Chi Journal of Undergraduate Research, 14,* 133–136.

Schwartz, B. M., & Gurung, R. A. R. (Eds.). (2012). *Evidence-based teaching for higher education.* Washington, DC: American Psychological Association.

Schwartz, B. M., Tatum, H. E., & Hageman, M. C. (2013). College students' perceptions of and responses to cheating at traditional, modified, and non-honor system institutions. *Ethics & Behavior, 23,* 463–476.

Sic. (2003). *Merriam-Webster's 11th new collegiate dictionary.* Springfield, MA: Merriam-Webster.

Strunk, W., Jr., & White, E. B. (1979). *The elements of style* (3rd ed.). New York, NY: Macmillan.

Todd, J., & Todd, S. (Producers), & Nolan, C. (Director). (2000). *Memento* [Motion picture]. Universal City, CA: Summit Entertainment.

Truss, L. (2003). *Eats, shoots & leaves: The zero tolerance approach to punctuation.* New York, NY: Gotham Books/Penguin.

Ulrich, B. (2005). Eliminating biased language: A goal for everyone. *Nephrology Nursing Journal, 32,* 9.

U.S. Census Bureau. (2008). *Racial and ethnic classifications used in Census 2000 and beyond.* Retrieved from http://www.census.gov/propulation/socdemo/race/racefactcb .html

VandenBos, G. R. (Ed.). (2007). *APA dictionary of psychology.* Washington, DC: American Psychological Association.

Vipond, D. (1993). *Writing and psychology: Understanding writing and its teaching from the perspective of composition studies.* Westport, CT: Praeger.

Wagner, J., Lawrick, E., Angeli, E., Moore, K., Anderson, M., & Soderlund, L. (2009). *APA stylistics: Avoiding bias.* Retrieved from http://owl.english.purdue.edu/owl/ resource/560/14/

Webster's third new international dictionary of the English language unabridged. (2002). Springfield, MA: Merriam-Webster.

Wilson, J. H., Stadler, J. R., Schwartz, B. M., & Goff, D. M. (2009). Touching your students: The impact of a handshake on the first day of class. *Journal of the Scholarship of Teaching and Learning, 9,* 108–117. Retrieved from http://www.eric.ed.gov/PDFS/ EJ854882.pdf

Index

MLA Handbook, 6, 7
Modern Humanities Research
    Association (MHRA) style, 6
Modern Language Association
    (MLA), 6
Moore, K., 68
Morack, S., 193

n.d., 109, 162
Newspaper style, 6
Notes, 30, 192, 222
Nouns, 45
Numbers, 21, 23, 165
    abbreviations and, 167, 172–173
    Abstract section and, 167
    approximations and, 168
    back-to-back numbers and, 170
    commas and, 172
    common phrases and, 170
    conversion of measurement
        and, 172
    decimal places and, 23, 171
    decimal points and, 171
    equals sign, spacing around,
        23, 127
    exceptions to rules and,
        168, 169 (table), 170, 172
    fractions and, 169–170
    graphs and, 168
    guidelines for, 165, 166 (table),
        167, 169 (table)
    headings and, 168–169
    hyphens and, 169–170
    leading zero, use of, 23, 172
    lowercase letters and, 172, 173
    mathematical functions and, 167
    measurement terms, written
        forms of, 173
    Method section and, 170
    metric units and, 172, 173
    numbered series and, 168
    numeral-word combinations
        and, 170
    numerals, use of, 167–168
    ordinal numbers and, 165
    p values and, 171
    physical measurements and, 172
    plural forms of, 172, 173

Procedure subsection and, 168
Results section and, 167, 169–170
Roman numerals and, 171
sentence openings and, 168
separate-word treatment of, 23
seriation and, 168
standard measurement conversions
    and, 172
symbols, spacing around,
    23, 127, 172
titles and, 168–169
units of measurement and,
    167, 172–173
word-numeral combinations
    and, 170
words, use of, 168–170
See also Statistical findings

Object of sentence, 44
Objectivity, 3, 4–5, 33
Occupations terminology,
    66–67, 67 (table)
O'Conner, P. T., 43
Online journal articles, 27

p values, 171, 190
Page break rules, 26, 207, 211–212
Page order, 13
Paragraph spacing, 18, 177, 179
Paraphrasing, 19, 56, 57, 58,
    59–60, 61
    See also Plagiarism; Quotations
Participants/subjects in research,
    21, 117–119
    See also Biased language;
        Method section
Parts of sentences, 44
    clauses and, 44, 50
    object, 44
    phrases and, 44
    predicate, 44
    subject, 44
    See also Grammar rules; Sentences
Parts of speech, 45
    adjectives, 45
    adverbs, 46–47
    articles, 46
    conjunctions, 47